PRAISE FOR *PATCHWORK SOMEONE*

'*Patchwork Someone*, an unabashedly honest memoir, is both a coming-of-age chronicle and narrative portrait of an expatriate Hong Kong and third-culture world. Jacinta Read's revelatory self-examination does not pull punches. For this Eurasian, rebellious, free-spirited youth—she never quite fit into the privileged, confusingly unmoored and cosmopolitan world of her family and upbringing—her parents' liberal parenting style sent her on a "bumpy ride" of dislocation, wracking her with self-doubt. Her subsequent search for stability through religion and art, and her battle with bipolar disorder contribute to a journey marked by perpetual uncertainty. This is a courageous book by an indomitable spirit who creates her own path for living with uncertainty. A book for both the young (and not-so-young) who must come to terms with who they are, both inside and out.'

— **Xu Xi,** *Habit of a Foreign Sky, Insignificance: Hong Kong Stories*

'A powerful and funny tale of growing up in Hong Kong, told with charming frankness. Read takes a moment of personal crisis and uses it to spin a tale of life, love in its many forms, and growing up with that sense many of us share, that we are not "normal".'

— **Justin Hill,** *Sunday Times, Washington Post, The Times Book of the Year*

‘*Patchwork Someone* is a fascinating and intimate account of family, faith and love: of struggling to find balance, overcoming obstacles and ultimately, making peace with the unknown.’

— **Sarah Vallance,** *Prognosis: A Memoir of My Brain*

‘It is rare for a book from the heart and spirit of a disciple of Christ to tell it like it is, and so penetrate the reader’s being like an arrow striking the bull’s eye. Jacinta’s vivid, passionate and painful memoir is such a book. It will challenge you, tenderise you and also console you, because you too have dark places. But most of all it will fill you with new hope and courage. Enjoy this wonderful book, and let it speak freedom to you.’

— **Anita Cleverly**, *Deep Night, Bright Morning*; pastor, St. Aldates Church, Oxford 2002-2020

PATCHWORK SOMEONE

A MEMOIR

Jacinta Read

yellow heron press
www.yellowheronpress.com

This is a work of creative nonfiction. The scenes, events and dialogue represented in the text have been written to the best of the author's memory, with the aim of artful storytelling that best captures the essence of truth as the author perceived it at the time of writing. Some of the names or other identifiers of characters or places have been changed.

Trigger/Content Warning: This book contains references to mental illness, self-harm, suicidal ideation, eating disorders, substance abuse, blood, natural disaster, cancer, and death. Reader discretion is advised.

Published by Yellow Heron Press, United States

ISBN 978-1-8381909-3-4

Cover design: Pamela Golafshar

Interior design: Pamela Golafshar

First paperback edition.

In loving memory of my dad.

And also to Tom, Mum and my family.

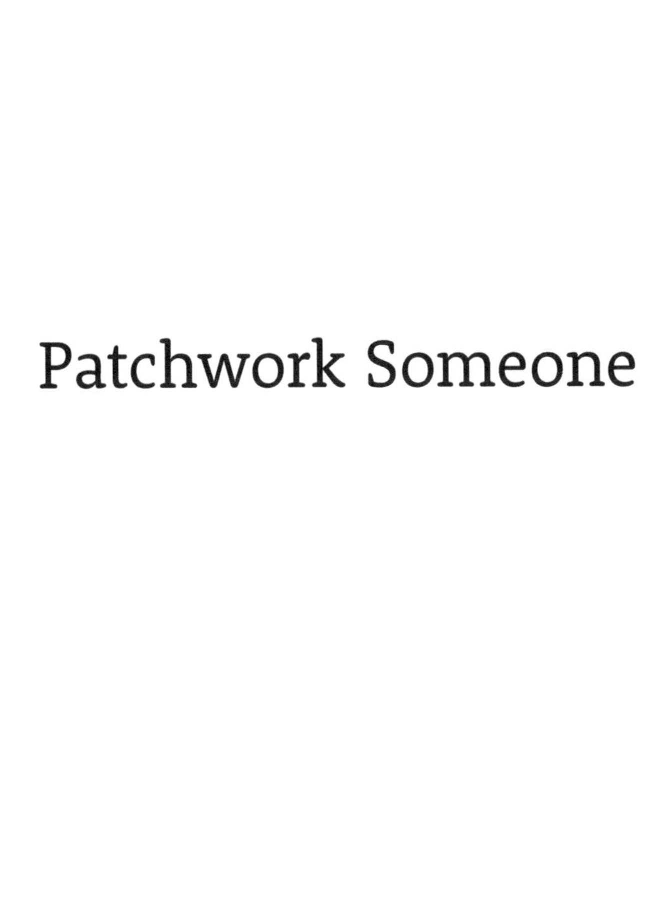

Patchwork Someone

Based on a true story.

1

2005

'ATTEMPTED SUICIDE.' NOT the words I would have chosen, but there you go. I had finally landed myself in hospital and, once you've done that, your opinion doesn't really matter anymore, anyway.

I stared up at the white ceiling over the green-tiled walls and pretended I was in the sky looking down. Hot tears ran off my face and, as one pooled in my ear, the silence gave way to a buzzing sound, which crescendoed, then cleared. I could hear the sound of sobbing. I listened, and after a minute I realised that it was me making it. Here I was, lying disjointed on a table, sobbing like a guilty child awaiting a scolding.

'Sad?'

Someone else was here. I could feel her touch on my shoulder. It was kind. She was not here to judge. She was here to fix me in the only way she was qualified. She was sewing up my wrist.

'Yes, I'm sad ...' and, as I answered, I re-entered my body. All hope that it had all been a bad dream disappeared. I made an awkward attempt at a joke. 'I'm missing my favourite TV show.'

She didn't laugh. There was a matter-of-factness about her. A nurse needs that to do her job. This is what I told myself.

'I'm finished now. Someone will come and get you in a few minutes.'

. . .

I lay, with no choice but to begin the process of trying to figure out how this had happened. I began by reviewing the events of the past hour. I had stormed away from an argument. I was jealous. I slammed the study door and locked myself in. I took a blade to my own arm. I screamed as I pressed down hard and pulled, fast. Two red drops turned into a sizeable puddle on the floor before I had even drawn a breath.

It was a mistake. It was a very bad idea. No, not an idea, because that would suggest forethought. This had been an impulse. A reflex. Definitely not premeditated. It was a mistake. I wanted it undone, but there is no way to undo a haemorrhage alone. I had gone too far.

Tom was pounding on the study door and, for the briefest moment, I worried what he would make of me, standing in a puddle of my own blood. I looked at the door handle and knew I needed to unlock it before I fainted—there was a lot of blood, and my head was starting to fuzz. He pushed past my feeble attempt to open the door just a crack. His eyes trailed the mess on the floor.

'Let me see it.' He used his serious voice. I was the naughty child. My right hand clutched my left wrist and hugged it to my chest, hoping elevation might slow the gush.

'Show me!'

I wanted to hide it, but my limbs obeyed the command. Both of my arms lowered to show Tom the full extent of the damage. I shut my eyes and turned my head away. Tom didn't speak. He went to fetch a towel from the room opposite. He came back, prised my hands apart, and wrapped the towel tightly around the wound. Then, he steered me out of the room, out of the flat, and into a taxi that seemed to have been waiting, ready for the day I finally cracked.

The nurse admitting me to the emergency room asked me if I wanted to die. I said no. The answer was no. Later, I would tell a friend that I had lied to the nurse. I must have lied: why would someone who does not want to die take a knife to her own arm? Why would someone who loved life want to die? There was only one other option as far as I could see: I wanted to live, and I wanted to bleed. There are only two types of people who want that: crazy people who know no better, or wicked, manipulative people.

I did not want to allow for the possibility that I was insane—or worse yet, that I was capable of throwing a temper tantrum of such magnitude. These were the very theories I'd spent my short lifetime dreading. But neither was I prepared to admit I wanted to die. That wasn't who I wanted to be. I had worked so very hard to assume a new identity. Serious Christians like me were supposed to be all about good things, good news, abundant life.

. . .

Life, God dammit. Who did I think I was?

Just a few short days ago I was standing in front of a room full of teenagers, parading myself as a role model, speaking words of encouragement and hope. As a volunteer youth leader, this is what I had done every week for years, and for the years preceding those I was watching my leaders. It was my youth group, the place where any of the many lost and searching teenagers of Hong Kong could come on their quest for acceptance, a sense of belonging—or, at the very least, something to do on the weekend. It was what we had done as kids, and now it was our job to make sure the legacy continued.

I had given the talk a couple of weeks ago. It was a Bible-based sermon on self-acceptance. I'd asked the kids to close their eyes and raise a hand if they felt they truly liked themselves. A few hands went up; most stayed down. I can't remember what the point of the survey was, but I remember clearly what I said after telling everyone to open their eyes again.

'Personally, I love my life!'

I probably then rattled off a list of why life was good and how I had come to realise I was fearfully and wonderfully made. I was a full-on, faith-filled, life-loving Christian. I was happily married. I was more serious than ever about pursuing an active relationship with my God. I had cross-checked everything against the Bible.

And now I was in hospital.

At last a warden came, handed me a letter and ushered me out to the main waiting area to find Tom.

. . .

Tom. He didn't deserve this. He stood waiting, shoulders hunched with his hands in his pockets, the dark features of his face softer than usual. Tom had always been someone who commanded respect. He rarely said anything stupid and I had never seen him lose an argument. If he wasn't sure he was going to win it, he just wouldn't engage. Once, he told me that his verbal and mental strength had sprouted about the same time that his younger brother outgrew him in height. I had seen guys much taller shrink away from confrontations with Tom. He was someone who knew where his strengths lay, and he rarely stepped outside of his bounds. He was the antidote to me. He was Mr Right.

The uneasy look on his face afforded me a glimpse into the gravity of what I had done. He was not going to tell me off; he knew I couldn't take it, and he probably didn't have the strength, anyway. The very fact he was standing there meant he was not giving up. I wouldn't have blamed him if he did. I wanted to. But there he was. He said nothing, took my arm to inspect the dressing, then wrapped his arm around my waist to lead me out to the taxi stand.

The sliding doors parted, and the noise and cool humidity of winter enveloped us. Hong Kong is a loud and crowded city in constant motion, but an eerie stillness localised outside the Ruttonjee Hospital that day. Four taxis idled at the rank in an otherwise empty driveway. An old man was taking his birdcage for a walk and paused to have a good look at us. The whole world seemed to want to know what our next move was going to be.

Tom's brown eyes were slightly glazed, but his voice was calm and steady.

'We have to tell someone,' he said. 'We can't keep this to ourselves this time.'

2

AT SOME POINT under the age of seven, I cottoned-on to the fact that there was something wrong with me. Something bad. The bad feeling was a permanent fixture on the underside of my skin, an irritation I could not reach. Even as a very young child, I knew all too well where the wild things were. At least one of them was living inside me—it had always been there, steadily growing, and threatening to take over. My very body was an obstacle and it wanted out. Every once in a while, it surfaced, shrieking past the point of no return faster than I could see it happening.

A little girl cannot physically explode when internal pressures get too much. All she can do is try to find a way to let some of the pressure out before it overcomes her completely. This is what I did. I'd grit my teeth, scream and cry, and when that didn't work, I'd bang my head repeatedly against the nearest wall before collapsing, spent, into a deep and thoroughly restful sleep.

From as far back as I can remember, these fits took place every few weeks. After I would wake, I was able to continue with life with no further mention of the episode from anyone who had been present—usually my mother. Actually, only ever my mother. There was nothing for her to say that she hadn't already said—I needed to calm down ... I was behaving very badly ... I was having a temper tantrum ... I had the devil in me ... I was a misunderstood angel ... I had used her as a punching bag (and that was fine) ... I needed a smack on my bottom ... I was very clever and would be loved unconditionally. Nothing worked.

I'd get up and go about my young life in blissful ignorance until the next time the underneath of my skin began to itch and the beast inside stirred again. And he always did. He was strong and looking for a fight. He'd show up and shove me into the background with a single swipe. I did not fight back. I learnt to escape inside myself. I could flee down the inside of my own leg and hide in my big toe until it was all over. The beast was long gone by the time I returned to myself, and selective amnesia was the coping mechanism that lasted me between visits.

With minimal investigation I concluded that other children did not lash out the way I did. My big brother never did; he was, and still is, the calmest person in my world. And, while my parents often engaged in fiery disagreements ('It's much healthier than bottling feelings up, darling'), I could see that they were in control of themselves. No, I was on my own when it came to these episodes. I was different, unusual, not like everyone else. I was *not normal*. With that, *normal* naturally became the thing I wanted most in life, the exotic thing most excruciatingly beyond my reach.

. . .

I **LIKED TO BLAME** all sorts of things on Sansan Ching. There was nothing conventional about her and, for the best part of my life, this had been the big problem. All I ever wanted was a normal mother and she was consistent only in her refusal to comply. Her name means 'number three' in Chinese because she was the third born of five children. In her later childhood years she had been educated in Australia and California, graduating from Berkeley at the height of the hippie era. She returned to Hong Kong, ready to stick it to the man. She challenged the government on matters of education and worked as an assistant to one of her uncles, who was the chairman of the urban council, a local mayor-like government role.

From old photographs, I could see that she had always been a very beautiful woman. She used to wear large, glamorous hairpieces, big clip-on earrings, and huge rings on her fingers that could pull focus in any conversation. She outlined her Chinese eyes with black or bright blue eyeliner, and applied lipstick to her lips, then to her cheeks via the outer edge of her palms, rubbing them together and then onto her face for rouge. She was always open-minded and otherworldly and, on the scene in Hong Kong at the time, considered to be quite a catch. The man who won her heart would have to have been very special.

My dad was an actual genius. He was born in Newport, Wales, and came from a working-class family. He was the eldest of five and from a young age he worked to contribute to the family. Academic pursuits were not a priority in his home, but after he taught himself to read, he discovered there was great joy and consolation to be found in using his mind. He won scholarships to three of England's top universities and, after graduating from Oxford, he took a teaching job in Kenya, and then went to Hong Kong in the late sixties to become a lecturer at the Hong Kong University. He was in the university's senior common room the first time he saw my mother on the television. She was the youngest candidate in the urban council elections. She was giving a campaign speech, and she was very beautiful.

'Who is that?' he had asked his colleague.

'Don't even think about it, Tony. That is Sansan Ching, and she is Clive Robert's girl.'

'Not for long.' His first marriage had ended, and my father had seen all he needed that day on the TV screen. 'Mark my words, I am going to marry her.'

And a year later, he did.

Mum says she was unfazed, delighted even, by the fact that he was divorced and already had three children. They were now living in England with their mother; however, whenever they visited their dad in Hong Kong, Mum says loved them like they were her own. She could always find creative ways to occupy any of the stepchildren, or numerous nieces or nephews who were put in her charge. Many an innocent child spent hours sitting on the balcony, staring at a potted plant because they had been told (on questionable authority) that, if they sat still enough and looked hard enough, a little elf would come out from behind the pot to play.

Dad had a penchant for giving pet names to significant people and things. He himself was known as Hob, after J.R.R. Tolkien's *The Hobbit*. He renamed Mum Goss, short for gossamer, because she was gracefully ethereal—and also short for 'gossip', because she talks a lot. Mum was quick to subscribe to the nicknaming. Two years into their marriage, my brother was born and was given the name

Justinian Caradoc Renald Ching Sweeting. Hob called him Tinnie or Justini; Goss called him Big Man, Jing Do (his Chinese name), Nam Tsai (Cantonese for 'male') or Justinino (when she was pretending to speak in Spanish). I call him Jus.

Two years after he was born, I arrived. Jacinta Louise Rhiannon Ching Sweeting. Dad called me Beepo before I even left the hospital. This was because Jus was playing with his toy car at the time and he greeted me with 'Beep beep'. Mum still calls me Lou Lou, Loulie, Nui (Cantonese for 'girl'), Rhian, or Jacatina (fake Spanish), while Jus calls me Cinta.

The 'Three Js' was the collective term for my half-siblings. There was a fifteen-year age gap from eldest to youngest in our family, and although we never all lived in the same country, I loved being the youngest of five children. Being around any combination of the Three Js was better than Christmas for me. Our visits happened both in Hong Kong and in the UK. The Js were old enough to take Jus and I out, unsupervised, but young enough to be an inordinate amount of fun. We were often given our parents blessing to skip school and go to the beach or to Ocean Park. They showered us with time and attention, and equipped us with all of the best skills for childhood: gymnastics, skateboarding, football, conkers, banana sandwiches, playing the guitar, art.

As a young child I had no concept of how long each visit would last, they simply came in and out of my life like a happy dream, joyous and completely thrilling. However, the older we all got, the less frequently we were all together. The university had given us the largest flat in order to accommodate all of Dad's five children, but as most of them did not live there full time, and Jus was more independent then me, I often found myself alone in it.

. . .

When we were little, Jus and I usually snuggled down to sleep in our parents' bed at night.

'Why can't they sleep in their own beds?' our exasperated dad asked, knowing he was to spend the night with at least one elbow in his ribs, and a foot or two in his face.

'They need to feel close to us,' Mum said, 'and I've been at work all day and hardly seen them, and I just can't bear the thought of a kidnapper climbing over the balcony in the middle of the night. I won't be able to get any sleep if they aren't here with me.'

Justin and I waited patiently, tucked under the covers, for this nightly exchange to wrap up so we could all move on to story time. When Dad read to us, it was usually classic children's literature by J.R.R. Tolkien, C.S. Lewis or Roald Dahl. I relished his perfectly gentle Welsh lilt and let it meld into dreams of lions and chocolate rivers.

When it was Mum's turn to put us to bed, she often seized the opportunity to educate us on the risks of the real world and our need for training in personal safety.

'No, Mum, we won't talk to any strangers,' we promised her, huddled together under the duvet like Hansel and Gretel.

'But what if?' she'd press on, signalling seriousness by lowering the tone of her voice and pulling down her eyebrows. 'What if a nice old man offers you candy?' She squinted her eyes, slowly turned her head, and settled her gaze on me. Then, with a sinister smile, she'd drop her voice an entire octave. 'What if he says to Lou Lou,

"Hello there, little girl, give me your hand and I will give you a very special treat…"?'

By the time she got to the word 'treat', my mother—supposed life source of comfort and nurture—had morphed into something else entirely. I sat frozen, eyes squeezed shut to avoid having to look at the figure of a dirty old man I knew Mum had just contorted herself into, praying Jus would take over the role playing.

'Please don't do the voices, Mum,' was all he could squeak.

She smiled, a little proud of herself, realising that the power of her performance had frightened us, then shook the old man away. She was our mother again.

'You do remember what happened to Mummy's old college friend, don't you?' She continued, now in a more conversational tone, friendly even. 'She was a beautiful ballerina, just like little Loulie wants to be when she grows up.' She changed tactics again and hooked my trust anew as her graceful arms floated up into a balletic fifth position. 'She was so, so pretty, but, one day, she did something very stupid indeed. She decided she wanted to see the world, so she packed her bags, and headed for the highway—that's what they call motorways in America.'

Justin and I had heard this story many times, but Mum was spellbinding, and we were drawn in. 'She did something many people in America do: she stuck out her arm like this and held up one thumb.' Mum sat facing us, and for this section of the story she smiled innocently and tilted her head sweetly to one side. 'This tells the cars driving past that you want a ride—it's called hitchhiking. She was going to hitchhike all the way across the country. But you know what?'

We did know what, but for some reason we shook our heads. In a flash, the sweet voice disappeared, and Mum's eyes were evil again, squinting, with pupils darting back and forth from Justin, to me, and back again.

'She didn't make it very far at all. She got into the car of a very bad man, a man who had the devil in him, and not long afterwards, she was found in the woods with her head chopped off. Now, never you forget to stay clear of strangers and never, ever even think about hitchhiking! Goodnight, my darlings.'

I often fell asleep fearing it might actually be Mum who had the devil in her and worrying about how on earth I was supposed to control my thoughts enough to not even *think* about hitchhiking.

. . .

When given the chance, Jus and I asked Mum to 'take us flying' instead. She opened the bedroom window and we all flew out into the warm night sky. We flew over Victoria Harbour and into the Kowloon Hills, where our spirits whirled and played on the grass and explored the cave that we discovered the last time we were actually there. Sometimes, Mum flew us all the way to our summer home in Oxford, but we usually fell asleep before we got there.

Even as a young child, I had little choice but to wonder about the world of the unseen. As far as I was aware, most other children were not flown out the window by their mums. I had a couple of friends who couldn't play on Sundays because they had to go to church, and I envied them. Church sounded like a club we weren't members of. I assumed my parents had no stance at all, what with being so open-minded about everything, so I decided to do some investigating.

'What religion are we?' I asked Dad in the car one day.

'Well, I am an Anglican,' he replied, 'and right now your mother is in a Buddhist phase. But we would like you and Justini to make up your own minds about what you believe in.'

A couple of days later, I thought I'd made up my mind. 'Dad, is there a name for someone who doesn't have any religion?'

'Yes, there are atheists and then there are agnostics.'

I could tell he was about to kick into academic mode and launch into a lengthy exposition, so I cut him off. 'Okay then, I am an atheist.'

'No, no, Beeps, don't say you're an atheist.' He wouldn't entertain my statement for a moment.

'Why not?'

'I wouldn't want you to close yourself off to all possibilities of a God, especially at such a young age. There are lots of wonderful religions to explore. Why don't you give yourself some more time?'

. . .

'I'm a witch,' said Mum, when I asked her.

'What does that mean?' I asked, wide-eyed and hoping for the start of an adventure.

'It means whatever you think it means,' she replied. 'But you will discover more as you go along. For now, you are just a little Itch, that's a witch in training. You haven't earned your W yet.' She was very matter-of-fact about it all. 'There is nothing average about us, Little Loulie. We are superwomen, not like normal people at all.'

I was never sure how seriously to take Mum when she said things like this. But a huge part of me hoped that what she was saying was true, and that the correct line of questioning might just get us to the point where she would reveal that she had a flying broomstick hidden away for the day I earned my W.

Mum did go through a Buddhist phase; she went through several different phases. For a time we were vegetarian, and enjoyed the illustrated story about Prince Siddhartha's discovery of suffering and a subsequent journey to enlightenment. We explored the I Ching; we discussed reincarnation; she trained my memory and my third eye.

'There's no need to be exclusive about anything,' she said. 'There are many paths, my darling. They all lead to heaven, if that's where you think you want to go.'

But this lackadaisical, haphazard view on life bothered me something awful.

'What? How can ALL different paths take you to the same place?' I asked. 'What if you walk backwards? Are you saying some people don't want to go to heaven?'

'Darling,' she began—and when she began like this, I knew we weren't going to get anywhere. 'You cannot be black and white about these things. You cannot say this is right or this is wrong, or this is clean and this is unclean. Everything is clean.'

'What about vomit?' I had her now. 'You said never to touch vomit! What about poo? What about if a dead bird has been lying in the gutter for a week and then a sick dog wees on it?' I was desperate for a solid answer, but she had a way of defusing tension by laughing at me.

The only time I saw Mum get serious about these issues was when she railed against close-mindedness, either mine or someone else's.

'Don't be so rigid,' she said. 'That's not who we are. It's usually just Christians who think that theirs is the only way. God must get so tired of it. You've got to keep your mind open.'

3

IT WAS VERY common for both parents to work and for a live-in maid/nanny, also known as an *amah*, to be the primary carer for children of any age in Hong Kong. Today, the correct term is 'domestic helper'. One Saturday afternoon, our *amah* Josie came to my room to take me to my ballet lesson, and she found me already dressed in leotard and tights, each of my legs bound tightly like roasting meat. I was four and fed up with wearing soft ballet shoes held on with elastics. Those were for babies. I had placed red polyurethane string stirrups under the heels of my ballet shoes, crisscrossed them up my calves and secured them at the front of both knees in quadruple knots.

I did not ask for Josie's thoughts on my appearance, and she knew better than to reason with me. The ballet teacher was amused but got nothing more than a shoulder shrug after shooting a quizzical look at Josie. When the teacher questioned me, I informed her, straight faced, that Mum had taken me to a real ballet shop and bought me these real ballet ribbons, and that they were the same as those worn by real ballerinas. Later when Mum arrived to collect me from class, she corroborated my story, also straight faced.

You can do anything you set your mind to was more than a family motto—it was an expectation, a dare, a minimum standard held in common amongst those on the Chinese side of my family, each of whom danced to their own song.

The ballet lessons took place in the Union Church hall next to my grandparents' home, and after class Mum brought me next door. Every Saturday night was spent with various combinations of the extended family, which consisted of mixed marriages including Swiss, Canadian, Australian, Malaysian, American and Welsh. Por Por, my maternal grandmother, was the head of the family, and expected us all to show up for the weekly meal. This was sometimes at an aunty's house, and sometimes at a classic Hong Kong restaurant like the American Peking Restaurant in Wanchai, or the place in a basement in Central, where they pulled fresh noodles and gave out golden hammers with which to hit the mud chicken.

However, most of the time we were summoned to my grandparents' home at Kennedy Terrace in Hong Kong Island's Mid-levels. Wherever we gathered, stories were told and retold about how someone helped lead the Allied forces through the sewers under the Great Wall during battle; how someone else was one of the Empress Dowager's scholars; how Por Por was a third generation descendant of Rice Christians, peasants who were given free food in exchange for giving their souls to the Lord; and how someone really ought to write down all the stories before they were lost from our collective memory forever.

My grandparents' flat was quite a famous place. Taxi drivers could get people there with only 'The Eye Doctor' given as the destination. When the building's intercom system was out of order, and it often was, the guard posted downstairs would let me in. His little metal desk had a glass top under which he displayed various newspaper clippings, on top of which he kept his radio and a Chinese mug with a stainless-steel lid. Every child within his reach had her cheeks pinched.

The flat was part home, part antique medical clinic, because Gung Gung, my maternal grandfather, was a renowned ophthalmologist. He was the first one to bring contact lenses to Hong Kong. The flat was an enigma and a never-ending opportunity for exploration. It beckoned me and then spat me out again like a malfunctioning cartoon washing machine. Our family's headquarters was both a major setting and a living metaphor for the chaos of my early life.

'Jacinta, go and say hello to Gung Gung and ask him to show you a box of glass eyes.'

'Yes, you can ride the tricycle on the balcony, but go through the bedroom door so you don't disturb the acupuncture patients.'

'I think there is a violin that would fit you in the cupboard behind the hot pots.'

The place was custom fitted for its own purposes, but its purposes were just not typical.

Por Por, the family matriarch—or Louise Ching, being her English name—was a highly sociable lady. She was in the habit of picking up strangers to invite to her dinner parties. The extended family would be summoned by imperial command of their Empress, but the random guests tended to come willingly, either for a free meal or just to catch a glimpse of the home of a character like my Por Por.

Dr Renald Ching, my Gung Gung, was originally from Canton. Por Por was from Peking. They were amongst the early waves of Chinese students sent to the West to get an education. They met and married while studying in Chicago. Por Por had set her mind on finding herself a husband—specifically a tall, Chinese medical student who could play the violin—and that was exactly what she did. Gung Gung was a mad scientist. Medical professionals now came from all over the world to investigate the unorthodox methods he used to cure over one hundred supposedly incurable cases, acupuncture being one of them. Besides medicine, he fed his curious mind with other seemingly random interests such as worm farming, sparrow training, and cubic zirconia.

The Ching home was rarely empty. When it wasn't filled with patients and staff, the extended family were there—some combination of Por Por and Gung Gung's five married children and seventeen resulting grandchildren. Anyone with a pulse was welcome at the Ching flat. Actually, a pulse was not compulsory—there were two human skulls Gung Gung kept for medical purposes. Mum informed me that they had actually belonged to Gung Gung's sister, Aunty Merritt, whom had died young.

'Is that why she died? Did Aunty Merritt have two heads?' I never got a straight answer, because Mum burst into laughter and then repeated my question to the nearest grown-up.

. . .

MUM FOUND ME hilarious. She often laughed, delighted at the naivety of my questions. Questions like, 'Can you make me a nice packed lunch to take to school one day?'

I envied my classmates, watching as they ate the lunches their mothers had lovingly packed for them at home that morning.

I suppose some of the lunch bags had been packed by maids, but clearly there was a conscientious mother giving out instructions somewhere in the picture.

I grew up with packed lunch envy. There was the odd occasion of Nutella on white bread, followed sporadically by Vegemite on white bread. No indication was ever given as to which day would be which—an unfortunate game of Russian roulette for a hungry kid. I never had anything as thoroughly thought through as a brown paper bag containing chicken mayo with alfalfa between two slices of multigrain goodness, and apple slices or carrot sticks for break. This was just the way that some mothers were wired. Not mine. The mother of my year seven classmate, Emma, froze a bottle of orange squash every night before school, so that her daughter could enjoy an icy cold drink in its varying stages of defrosting throughout the hot school day. I hated Emma and her stupid frosty drink.

There was a yearning inside of me for Mum to be different—no, 'different' is the wrong word, she was already too different. There was a huge void inside me that longed for Mum to be *less* different. I needed her to make sense in the wider context of all mothers.

'What's your mum's job?' was the question I struggled most to answer. I knew a complete answer could never be a simple one, so I took to giving different partial answers each time I was asked:

'She runs a double-decker bus full of toys.'

'She has an organic farm.'

'She used to be a figure skater.'

'She teaches piano.'

'She hassles the government about stuff.'

'She sells skincare products.'

'She designs schools and playgrounds.'

'I'm off to Fight Crime!' or 'I'm going to Save the Children!' she would say as she left for committee meetings of the various charities she worked with.

I couldn't appreciate Mum's quirks. I couldn't explain her to my friends, and I struggled to tell her how I felt. All I could come out with was that on top of wishing she were normal, I wished she would bake me cookies, like my friends' mums did for them.

'Don't compare yourself to others,' she said. She simply was not a normal mother, she explained. She simply was not the kind who could stay home and bake me cookies. And she was right.

. . .

Mum often took me by surprise—either in being very upset over something I didn't think warranted it, or by not being at all upset by something I was angling for a reaction over. I was rarely sure of what would make her laugh, and was never prepared to see her cry.

She laughed in hysterics, almost crashing the car when, at the age of fourteen, I decided to show her my tattoos.

'You are so funny!' she said. 'I cannot wait to tell your daddy how creative you are!' This comment related to the string of flowers inked onto the inside of my lower lip.

'You are such a clever girl!' she said years earlier, on the occasion of my taking a pair of scissors to the brown velvet curtains in the dining room. Standing wrapped within them, I was a medieval maiden in a dress made perfect by hand-snipped armholes.

She rarely cried, but there were three occasions when she did that struck me to the core, rearranging parts of my very being. The first two instances happened when I was young, while the third would not happen until about twenty years later.

The first was during a family holiday in Paris. I couldn't have been much more than five years old. We had just bought two fresh, hot baguettes from a bakery and were making our way back to the hotel via the metro. Dad and Jus were walking ahead, too fast, the way all men seem to insist on doing, and I skipped along beside Mum several paces behind them. We passed a beggar woman, sitting on the ground nursing a baby. By her side was another child, grubby and slightly smaller than me. The child saw us, jumped up and ran to us, and tugged on Mum's arm, pleading in French. Mum gently pushed her off and hurried me through the turnstile of the metro station. It wasn't until we sat down on the train that I realised there were tears flooding down her face.

'That could have been you ....' she said.

The second time she cried was a few years later, on the morning of 4th June 1989. News had been released of the massacre of student protesters in Beijing's Tiananmen Square.

'What's wrong?' I asked when I found my parents in the kitchen, both with red eyes.

'Something very bad has happened to some innocent young people, my lovely,' Dad said.

'They're just children!' Mum wailed. 'Babies! Somebody's babies!'

There had been a student protest and the Chinese government had managed things very badly. The Chinese students were about the same age as my beloved half-siblings and I worried that they were somehow involved. At ten years old, I could not grasp the full significance of what had happened in China that night. I saw people in Hong Kong wearing black armbands and, later that day, a school bus full of international students shouting 'Democracy!' passed me on the street.

I wondered if any of us really knew what was going on. It was my parents' solemnity as they discussed the events that troubled me the most. If they didn't have the answers, then there was little hope. There was something out there in the big world that could make them feel fear and sadness they couldn't hide from me. The days of my carefree childhood were suddenly numbered.

In an attempt to make a rough sketch of the road that lay ahead of me in life, I set about gathering information from various sources, asking anyone who gave me a chance, 'What's going to happen to Hong Kong?'

'It's safe for now, Cinta, try not to worry,' Jus said. 'But right after you finish your A Levels, the whole place is going back to China.'

China kills young people with tanks.

'My dad says we're getting out of here before the handover,' said a friend at school.

'You'll be better off than most Hong Kong people because you have a British passport,' said one of my Chinese uncles.

There was no point in worrying. Change, for better or worse, was the only thing I could bank on. As a child, my world was like the animated snowman—a wonderful thing to enjoy whilst I could. Knowing it would eventually melt away meant I had the upper hand. I could be hit by a bus before next Tuesday, anyway. The best thing I could do was get on with life while there was time.

. . .

Mum set very few rules, instead leaning more towards scare tactics.

'I wouldn't go up into the hill if I were you, in case the big bad wolf wants to kidnap you. Or a troll is hiding under a bridge to follow you home!'

The hill, naturally then, was my main haunt. Whenever possible, I would ask my quiet friend Sophie, from up on Po Shan Road, to join me for some form of outdoor adventure. Sophie was half Japanese and half Pakistani. I wondered if the grownups frowned upon our friendship, on account of my bad influence, but I had too much fun with her to let it bother me. We both loved animals. We adored wild ones, as well as the hamsters, guinea pigs, turtles and birds in the private menageries we each had at home. We climbed trees and travelled exclusively up and down the storm drains all over our neighbourhood. We leaped off the roof of the garages below my flat. We caught tadpoles in the university pond and rang people's doorbells and ran away.

In the early years of primary school, I dropped my egg in an egg and spoon race and Sophie, who was lightning fast and would definitely have won, stopped and waited for me to pick it up again. A year or so later, a boy from an older year announced that he was going to catch, and then kiss me in the playground. This was the most horrifying threat I had ever received, and I proceeded to spend the rest of my playtimes hiding in the girls' toilets, thoroughly ashamed at having been singled out in such a way. When Sophie finally found me, she stayed with me. She was a perfect childhood best friend, who I would later drift apart from, for no reason other than being placed in different classes at school.

Another friend I spent time with after school was Amanda, who came from a wealthy Indonesian family. Amanda and I could spend hours 'playing musical', which involved communicating only through song. However, our fun was interrupted by her hour of after-school private tutoring. I would be left to my own devices in Amanda's bedroom as she and her little brother studied at the dining table.

Amanda was a Catholic and had a small bottle of holy water on her shelf. I wondered if her special little bottle was something along the lines of the one Aslan gave to Lucy.

'If someone was hurt or sick, could you put this on them and heal them?' I asked Amanda one day.

'I don't know, but please be careful with it,' she said. 'It is blessed water, it is *holy* water.' She didn't seem to want to take the conversation any further, and I interpreted her nonchalance as condescension. She was holier than me, and we both knew it.

I wanted a bottle of holy water. So, I took hers. I stole it. I stole lots of things from her room. I helped myself to absolutely anything that took my fancy. The pilfering went on for a couple of playdates and escalated quickly to grand theft. I found a beautiful flowergirl dress hanging in Amanda's closet and I wanted it. The fabric, draped over layer upon layer of fine tulle netting, crunched when I touched it. I stuffed it into my school bag and waited happily for Mum to collect me.

'Look at the size of your school bag!' Mum said, tutting as I got into the car. Amanda and her mum had come downstairs to see us off. 'This is one of the issues my organisation is pressing the Board of

Education on,' she said to Amanda's mum. 'Children, even the very youngest ones, are made to carry such heavy bags full of textbooks—it's really no good for their physical development, let alone their love of learning!'

There was a large cupboard with a water heater in my bedroom. It was my treasure trove. In it, I hung the flowergirl dress and the several other outfits I had taken, and on one of the shelves I displayed the bottle of holy water and other trinkets. I was admiring my loot when there came a knock at the bedroom door.

'Loulie, I need to talk to you,' said Mum. 'It's serious. I have just had a phone call from Amanda's mummy ....'

'Just a minute, Mum! I'm just doing something. I will let you in, in just a minute!' I ran to my pencil case and pulled out a felt tip marker. I ducked into my treasure trove and put pen to taffeta. The plan was to write my cousin's initials on all the clothes and pass the loot off as legitimate hand-me-downs.

I wrote 'A.C.' for Amy Ching. *Oh wait, Amy isn't a Ching, she's a CHOU!* I was panicking. I scribbled out the A.C. and then realised I hadn't needed to, so I wrote it again. And, just to make sure, I also wrote 'Amy' again after the scribble and the A.C.

Mum's face fell as she saw my attempted act of fraud. She left the room and got back on the phone. The next day, she came to me and said that she'd had the dress cleaned and taken all of the things back, and also bought Amanda another very expensive dress to say how sorry we were. There was nothing more to be said. Or if there was, neither of us knew what it was.

I retreated to my bedroom, sat on the floor and hugged my knees. I looked at my empty treasure trove. There, again, was the heavy sense that I'd been doomed from the start. I hadn't lost my good standing: I'd always been bad. My character was bad and here was yet another incident of proof. This time, I had taken my misbehaviour outside the family. I wanted to peel myself off like an old snakeskin, but there was no way to undo what I'd done. I didn't know how long it would take for the immediate damage to wear off.

I was summoned to my parents' room to apologise to Dad.

'You know I still love you, Beepo,' he said, 'but I just don't understand. Can you tell me why you did it?'

'I don't know why,' I said, very honestly.

'Is it because you feel like we don't give you enough things?'

'No. I don't know why. I just liked her things.'

Nothing more was ever said about my crime. I laid low at school and avoided Amanda until the end of the year, ever thankful that, over the summer holidays, our memories would automatically be erased, etch-a-sketch style. Each school year brought with it a clean slate on which to begin again. Amanda seemed as embarrassed about the whole episode as I was and acted like she never knew me. For most of my free time, then, I played alone.

4

SECONDARY SCHOOL WAS where most of us would lose our innocence. Before the school year started, Dad mentioned that I needed to be mindful of the legacy my eldest brother had left at Island School, one that I'd be safest not to brag about in front of some of the longer-serving teaching staff. My brother had dressed a dummy up in the school uniform and thrown it off the roof of block five, right past the staffroom windows. He had been suspended for this particular prank, as well as for other acts of mischief he'd been found guilty of in his time. These stories only elevated my big brother to new levels of cool in my estimation; I banked them as proof that rebellion ran in my blood. I was also delighted to find that his fame was already legendary with several of my new schoolmates.

The school's history was punctuated with a few dramatic events, stories of which each student would need to integrate into their own lives somehow. When my sister was in sixth form, the Braemar Hill Murders happened. Two of her schoolmates, Nicola Myers and Kenneth McBride, had gone up into the hills behind their buildings and were brutally murdered by a group of young triads. The shockwaves of this horrific crime would be felt for generations to come. The Chinese mafia and the expat community were two completely separate worlds that very rarely collided.

When I was in second form, a boy named Michael Bill was washed away down a storm drain during a typhoon. His body was never found but what happened to him changed Hong Kong forever. It was not uncommon for children to venture into the hills or to play in storm drains when I was young. New safety measures were put in place and a rainstorm warning colour system of yellow, amber, red or black was established in an effort to prevent further loss of life.

These two terrible stories formed just a part of our collective experience in those years. They were exceptional, but close enough to home to be very important. We assimilated these stories and others like them, sometimes on a subconscious level, sometimes holding them respectfully in our hearts, and then had no choice but to proceed with growing up.

. . .

On a more mundane level, secondary school was where we became aware of our appearance, social standing and general status in life. By some strange phenomenon, it turned out that the houses in my school not only provided a way to rank us in athletic ability, but they were also a bizarrely accurate measure of popularity and, therefore, potential for teenage happiness.

The boys and girls in the purple, blue and red houses—Einstein, Nansen and Fleming—were generally more confident, better-looking and popular (with a couple of exceptions, of course). The orange, green and yellow houses—Da Vinci, Rutherford and Wilberforce—mostly contained the nerdier, less popular kids. I was in Wilberforce.

By the end of the first term of first form, everyone pretty much understood how this worked. Boys and girls from Einstein, Nansen and Fleming mixed freely, and 'went out' with each other with an efficiency that suggested someone somewhere had organised a roster. The non-exceptional girls and boys from the earthier-toned houses were left to accept their lot and get on with their studies and less interesting lives.

Island School had about 1,200 students, representatives from every nook and cranny of the globe. I don't remember being interested in anyone's nationality at the age of twelve—we all spoke English and that's all the really mattered. We were given a mandatory Cantonese lesson for only one hour a week, and only in our first form.

That poor Chinese teacher. Class upon class took up the goal of making her cry as frequently as possible. One day, a class collectively agreed to walk into the room backwards, dressed in school uniforms turned inside out, and saying everything in opposites. Students would often buck their teeth and speak in a Chinglish accent for the duration of the class, before poor Ms Chiu would realise it was a personal attack. Another favourite joke was to sneeze with an exaggerated 'ahh chooooo' when addressing her. No one took that lesson seriously, and as far as I know, nobody addressed the blatant racism.

It felt like we were all foreigners growing up in Hong Kong, slightly detached and observing through our Third-Culture eyes. There was 'them' and there was 'us', with several sub-layers of 'thems' and 'uses' in between, with several mixed kids like me, straddling more than one category. Maybe we knew that we were an endangered species. The British Hong Kong in which we were growing up would not last much longer at all, as 1997 was just around the corner. But still no one knew what that meant. We let our parents worry about it. We had growing up to do.

At one point there was a grand total of five Toms in my year group. My Tom—the one I would eventually marry—was in Fleming. He was sporty and busy working his way through the dating roster. We did not interact during our Island School days—as I said, I was in Wilberforce. We would have been star-crossed lovers, to say the least. We hardly noticed each other. Contact was not to happen for several more years, not until we had individually learnt to transcend the status quo. We now refer to it as 'Island School Bitchiness', but back then it was the compass that guided us between what was and was not socially acceptable.

A new school is like a fresh start. Like so many other tweens, I approached high school carrying with me questions that only my peers had the power to answer—raw questions of self: *Am I acceptable? Or am I really as bad/stupid/ugly as I have always feared?* Those concerns would be eased for only the fortunate few.

Secondary school took no prisoners. You were either hot or you were not. I was not. I accepted this quickly and reverted to plan B: stop caring. According to teen law, the only redeeming feature for a loser is brains. An unpopular kid who didn't even get good grades might as well not bother. That was me. I was in Wilberforce, and a below-average student. While I had several wonderful friends throughout every stage of life, I tended to hold myself slightly apart, never quite feeling like a deserving match for any of them. From where I was sitting, my classmates all seemed to understand what was happening in our lessons, while I rarely did. I just couldn't keep up. There are rules to the game of thriving (or surviving) at school, and the one thing I felt sure of was that I did not know what they were. I loved my own company, and when it came time to interact with others, whether teacher or peer, I felt stupid in every way.

Dad insisted I was intelligent. 'Listen to me, Beeps,' he said, 'I know what I'm talking about.'

But I knew better. I was average in height and build in my class. With olive skin, dark eyes and long, frizzy, brown hair, I never once thought myself beautiful, despite what my doting parents said. Beautiful girls had blonde hair and blue eyes, like the dolls I collected. I was not beautiful. I accepted that, as well as the fact that I was academically and socially challenged. I didn't try to change anything at all. In the first few years of secondary school, my main interests were ballet and animals. My heroes were Margot Fonteyn, Jane Goodall, Diane Fossey (and Sigourney Weaver by association).

After school, I volunteered at the zoo, a feature of Island School that, though no one at the time noticed, was quite a quirk. The zoo was home to an eclectic group of animals. There was one neurotic naked cockatoo who, legend had it, having been locked in a dark closet by an irresponsible owner, had plucked out his own feathers in despair. I didn't care for the ducks or the reptiles, but the grumpy goat did offer some entertainment. I swept the floors and cleaned out rabbit hutches and hamster cages, wishing the school monkey was friendlier, longing to be given a chance to be his trainer. Special volunteers were allowed to sign out a rodent or some terrapins for the weekend, but I already had plenty of my own pets at home. The zoo was shut down shortly after my secondary education began, but the steps at the back entrance near where it had been would remain known as The Zoo Steps for generations to come.

Walking down these steps one afternoon, an American-Japanese girl called Miko asked if I wanted to join her at Time Out, the bimonthly Friday night school disco. I asked her what it was.

'You don't know? It's a dance. You like dancing, don't you? You should come!'

I did go. I wore my ballet slippers.

'Are you wearing your ballet shoes?' Miko asked when we met at the front entrance, smiling and incredulous.

'No,' I said, appalled by the mere suggestion, moving into the shadows to prevent her from getting a better look at my feet.

. . .

When I got home that night, there was no time to re-evaluate my wardrobe choices—an exciting opportunity was about to be offered to me.

'Would you like to go to Australia to represent us at Jessie's wedding?' Mum asked. 'Daddy and I aren't able to get away from work, but it might be nice for you to go, if you'd like to.'

This was a no-brainer. I had spent every summer of my childhood in England, watching *Neighbours*, sometimes twice a day. I had the accent down pat and dreamt about visiting Ramsey Street. Since no one else in my immediate family could go, I was sent to Perth, Western Australia, with Por Por at the age of 12, to be an overgrown flower girl at my cousin's wedding. This would be my first trip away from home and from the rest of my family.

I liked all of my Chinese cousins very much. These ones had been regular playmates until they emigrated to Australia, where their parents set up a church. They wrote me little letters, and always signed off with 'Jesus loves you'. I never understood how this was something that they could possibly know, or what had given them the impression I would care, but I appreciated it, nonetheless.

I left my unexceptional Wilberforce life behind for two weeks, not realising that I was to spend the entire time immersed in a bizarre Asian-Christian parallel world.

Everything familiar was left behind, and everything in Perth was 'Bless you' for this and 'Praise the Lord' for that, all in Malaysian or Singaporean accents. The houses looked like what I had seen on TV, but there ended the similarities. I was as alone and as defenceless as a sheep separated from her flock, and there was a herding dog on a serious mission. In the midst of wedding preparations, I was cornered by a sister of the bride, and asked to repeat the Sinner's Prayer. It was a setup. It suddenly became clear that my family knew well enough to not get caught in this trap, but not one of them had had the common decency to warn me. I knew resistance was futile. My best course of action was to do as I was told, say thank you, and then get the hell out of there. And I did.

'I'm sorry for everything I have ever done wrong, Jesus ....' I acknowledged my sinful nature. 'Please come and be my Lord.'

'And Saviour!' prompted my cousin.

'Yes, sorry ... Lord and Saviour.' But I must have done this a little too readily.

'Oh, this is wonderful, Jacinta-Lou! You are doing very well. Now, we don't normally do this until you have been a Christian for at least one week, but since you are so enthusiastic, I am going to go ahead with the next step. Baptism in the Holy Spirit!'

I listened, caught like roadkill waiting to happen. I do not remember the explanation I was given about what baptism in the Holy Spirit was, because it was what came next that demanded all of my attention.

My cousin looked me in the eye and said, 'The ability to pray in tongues is a sign that you have received the Holy Spirit's baptism.' And so, I was to do it. 'Now!'

'Do I have to close my eyes?' I tried to stall.

'It doesn't matter.'

'Can you do it at the same time as me, so I know what to do?'

'Fine, but you should be louder, so I can hear that you are actually doing it,' she said.

'Okay ....' I began. 'On three. One, two, three ... Shamma shamma shamma lamma lamma lamma dinnggaaaladooonnggaa la. Amen.'

'Praise the Lord.'

The headlights dimmed and I fled to my room with some 'follow-up literature' in hand. I thought for sure that my lame stab at praying in tongues would not fly, but somehow it had.

And that was that. Breaking news was released to the extended family that I had received Jesus and was praying in tongues. I was very embarrassed and a little bit annoyed, because I hadn't reckoned on this information being broadcast around the world. I hoped that my parents—and, most importantly, Jus—wouldn't find out how easily I had succumbed. No such luck.

'So, the joy of the Lord is in you now? Maybe it will push the devil out of you!' said Mum on my return home.

'Well, I don't think it's fair,' said Dad. 'How do we know she wasn't bullied into it?' He was annoyed, worried that I hadn't been given any choice in the matter—which, to be fair, was a legitimate concern.

Jus made no comment.

Try as I did to get back into my pre-Perth groove, if I could call it that, something had changed, something that I was not able to put a finger on. There was this feeling that I had reached the end of a road and needed to figure out my next move. I wanted to keep the whole Jesus episode under wraps; however, despite my best efforts, this was not possible.

'Look how much she smiles now,' my parents remarked to one another, whilst I tried to mind my own business. In my family I was famous for not smiling. 'It must be the joy of the Lord.'

Someone from the Perth crowd had decided to post me a substantial parcel. Its arrival drew plenty of attention from my family.

'Who is sending you packages?' Dad asked, with a glint in his eye. I inspected the ends of my hair, trying to hide my mortification.

'Looks like our girl has an admirer!' Mum was always ready to jump right into a 'tease Jacinta' session.

'What is it?' Jus asked, casually.

I took the dreaded thing to my bedroom and opened it. Alone behind closed doors, I was free to roll my eyes and make a gagging noise at the discovery that the package contained a huge, hard-backed illustrated-in-colour *Bible for Teens*. A short note accompanied the book. 'You have been on my heart. May God's love fill your life. I will be praying for you. Jesus loves you!'

Good grief.

The 'joy of the Lord' feeling followed me around like I could only imagine an annoying little sister would. It kept popping out to flash cute smiles, in spite of my efforts to shove it behind my back.

. . .

JUS WAS BECOMING increasingly cool in my eyes and I was developing a strong obsession with the idea of gaining his approval. The Perth experience had set me back a long way in these efforts. It was the first time we had been separated by both distance and significant experience, and I had genuine fears that the damage done was irreparable. I took great pains in becoming the sort of little sister I thought he would accept.

'Can you just leave me alone?' He always seemed irritated by my endeavours.

I snuck into his room every chance I got, borrowed and recorded as many of his British indie music CDs onto cassette tapes as I had time to. I thought that shared music preferences might do the trick but forgot that trespassing and pilfering would not. As his departure for university loomed, I finally acknowledged that the pedestal I had placed him on was so far out of my reach that I might as well stop trying.

The *Bible for Teens* called to me from the bottom of my closet every time I was alone in my room. I had to admit I liked the pictures of the Bible characters; Dad had raised me to love books, so I decided this was okay. I was a little bit scared of the Bible. It was not something I was familiar with. I was under the impression that it was a sin to put a Bible on the floor and I wondered if illustrators had to be specially ordained to draw images of Jesus.

At the front of my *Bible for Teens* there was an owner's profile page. It was decorated with lightning bolts and other 80s fashion shapes in fluorescent colours. It wanted to know my likes and dislikes, my dreams for the future, and who in my life I was grateful for. The fill-in-the-blank questions reminded me of the personality quizzes in *Teen Magazine*, and I liked those, so I decided it would be okay to fill them out. No one needed to know.

As I wrote onto the semi-gloss page with a blue ballpoint pen, I learnt things about myself: I liked Australia, my brother and my dog. I disliked being crazy, and my dream for the future was to be married to someone who would always love me. Finally, I pushed the book to the back of a bookshelf and managed to forget about it.

I didn't even need to explain the Bible's whereabouts to Amy, another of my Chinese cousins, when she came to stay with us the following winter. Amy, the youngest of my Australian-Chinese cousins, was also a Christian, and she had come to Hong Kong to visit a Christian ministry called St Stephen's Society. I had no idea what this was but was soon to find out.

'Come on, Jacint,' she said at the end of her first week. 'You should come and let me show you why I'm here.'

I went with her. As the second youngest of my large Chinese extended family, I jumped whenever this particular relative gave me the time of day. She was the ringleader of the younger half of the Chinese cousins.

. . .

Hang Fook Camp was the premises being used by St Stephen's Society. They had previously operated within the boundaries of what was once the lawless Walled City, the most notorious and densely populated place in Hong Kong. For years, it had been a place governed by neither China nor Britain; there had been an administrative blip and, as a result, no one could lay claim to it. It became overrun with the most depraved level of Hong Kong society, gang warfare, drug trade, brothels, and extreme poverty—things that a child like me knew nothing about.

The Walled City no longer stood—the government had finally torn it all down and moved St Stephens Society to Hang Fook Camp—we walked across a dusty and barren-looking pitch before coming to what looked like a huddle of marquees. Inside the tents, a church service was already underway. The congregation consisted of a mix of Chinese and foreign faces, all singing loudly in Cantonese. We slipped into the empty end of a row, just as someone went forward to pray. It was a Caucasian woman, and she prayed into a battered old microphone in Cantonese. I was baffled. I had never seen a white person utter more than an instruction to a taxi driver in Chinese. This woman, Jackie Pullinger, went on for what seemed like an hour straight.

It was hot that day, and all I wanted to know was when it would end so we could go home again. I couldn't understand what the woman was saying, and was not comfortable with the idea that a white person spoke better Chinese than I did. Maybe I should have listened to Mum when she said I'd regret it if I didn't speak Cantonese more. I took a mental note to find a way to decline if Amy asked me to come again.

'She's a really big deal, Jacint,' Amy tried to convince me on the bus ride home. 'She's like the Mother Teresa of Hong Kong. She's been here for decades, and has helped thousands of drug addicts withdraw, painlessly, just by praying for them in tongues!'

My cousin's words were lost on me. The church service had gone on too long, and I was not entirely sure who Mother Teresa was.

. . .

AMY HAD A couple of other motives for coming to Hong Kong. The first was to see Brian Adams in concert. Mum had bought tickets for us, and dropped us off at the venue, where we met up with a couple of my friends from school. We enjoyed a night fully loaded with unbeatable melodies, Canadian vocals beyond compare, crowds, sweat, power ballads—and all on a school night. I came home feeling liberated and wild. I still hadn't had my first boyfriend at the late age of fourteen, but that night I was no longer just a loser who liked monkeys and had a secret Bible in her cupboard. I had been to my first rock concert.

Amy's second motive for coming to Hong Kong was to get a tattoo. She didn't like the idea of doing this alone, so she invited me to tag along. Our shared Brian Adams experience had repaired any damage done by the long, hot church service, and my sense of compliance had returned intact.

'You're a good artist, Jacint,' Amy said. 'How about you draw a daisy and we'll both get the same thing?'

'Okay.'

I did love to draw, but attention to detail was never my strength.

I drew a white flower with a yellow middle. The petals were not rounded, but pointed, like a hippie's sun. No matter. Amy went first, smiling at me reassuringly, pleading for me not to chicken out. Was she kidding? I had been to my first rock concert and was now in the circle of trust with an adored older cousin. Then it was my turn. The sharpness of the needle was not a problem, even though its vibrations were very loud, and far stronger than I'd reckoned on. I was brave and, before I had time to settle into the sensations, it was over. I smiled back at Amy as Ricky wiped it with a cotton ball dabbed in rubbing alcohol, then stuck a folded Kleenex onto me with surgical tape. Amy and I would both walk away from Ricky and Pinky's in Wanchai with my original artwork, inked forevermore upon our respective left breasts.

. . .

Amy's visit soon came to an end. I was fourteen and, dressed in my winter uniform, I climbed the stairs to the top of Island School's block five, and prepared myself for another unexceptional term. To my chagrin, Josh, the exception to the Wilberforce rule—the cool guy of the class, if not year, if not the entire school—was standing at our classroom door. Josh was one of those larger-than-life boys who looked several years older than he really was. He was unreasonably confident, to the point of dating girls in older years, bantering with teachers and generally wielding the power to decide the fate of anyone's social standing with either a nod of approval or a public serving of humble pie.

He stood at the door of our classroom, holding it open with

one arm, body leaning against the doorframe, inviting me to duck and enter under his arm. My head would be forced to hang low, acknowledging my place in this world.

'Wait! Is that a tattoo?' He had seen straight through the thin white cotton of my uniform shirt.

I didn't know whether or not to lie. I hadn't planned on telling anyone about the tattoo. I was stuck at the door, dumbfounded, unable to spit out an answer.

'It's cool,' he said. 'I won't tell. That's amazing. Did it hurt?'

I don't think I answered him. I had seen too many fall prey to this precocious student in the great game of high school life. I had watched too much banter turn bad, and had long since concluded that the best way to avoid ridicule was to stay under the radar.

Word got out at school that I had a tattoo. This was probably where things began to change—not for the better or the worse really, just different. Or maybe things changed because word also got out that I was a Christian.

My classmate, Jang, invited me to her Korean youth group. I went, and once again found myself an anomaly amidst a group of genuinely lovely, but different, people who sang happy songs to Jesus. I smiled, and then left as soon as I could. Hurrying down the stairs of the walk-up building in Wanchai, I caught up with another youth group escapee. Mary went to South Island School and we soon discovered that we had in fact been classmates in our early primary school years.

'You getting out of here too?' Mary smiled. She had thick, perfectly straight hair parted in the middle, and thick black eyeliner covering the entirety of her Korean eyelids.

'Yah, um, no offence ....'

'None taken. Where you heading? I'm getting a cab to the south side if you want a lift? Come to the Cubby, even—I mean, if you don't have to be anywhere ....'

'Okay,' I said, despite the fact home was westward. 'What's the Cubby?'

'Oh, you know, like an old abandoned building below Parkview, where we hang out—you should come. What's that you have around your neck?'

It was a thin leather necklace with a large seed from an Amazonian rainforest. I had bought it at a Christmas craft fair, but was undecided about whether it was cool or not. Mary seemed to like it. We chatted happily as the taxi wound up Stubbs Road and finally arrived at our destination.

We squeezed through a gap in the chain-link fence and made our way past some trees on a dirt path. The path led to a clearing in front of a dilapidated brick bungalow with a Chinese tiled roof. Twenty or so teenagers I had never seen before were dotted around the place. Some were smoking, others were holding cans or bottles of alcohol. Mary led me over to some girls and introduced me to her friend, Tina.

'Tina, I'm going to go meet Danny,' Mary said, and then turned to me. 'Enjoy!' And she left.

I couldn't believe I had been left in the midst of a group of strangers. I would need to wait a few minutes before I could excuse myself. I didn't want to look uncomfortable.

'Oh God,' Tina said, 'she's done it again. She's always ditching like that.' She turned to me and smiled sympathetically. 'What did you say your name was?'

I stood and chatted awkwardly for a few minutes, trying to act casual and take it all in. There was a battery-operated boom box blasting grunge music; there were kids in plaid shirts and Doc Marten boots; a couple emerged from the darkness of the trees holding hands.

'Want a smoke?' asked a guy called Mike, as he approached. He had long, greasy hair.

'Go on then,' answered Tina, helping herself to three. She placed one in her own mouth, passed one to her friend Mandy, and then held the last one out to me. 'Want one?'

'Thanks.' I took it. I knew how to smoke. I had smoked an entire pack years ago, with my friend Claire. It had been one summer in Oxford, in the shed behind the old house across the street. Claire was two years older than me—I was aged ten at the time. She had stolen the pack from her dad's carton, and the two of us had a great old time with it. I lit the filter of the first one I'd tried to light. Claire had laughed at me as I spat out the toxic taste of melted chemicals, and then she insisted on being the only one allowed to light up from that point on.

Back in Hong Kong, Mum was an occasional smoker. Just to prove I could do it right, I had stolen a cigarette or two of hers to practise lighting when no one was around. So now I was ready. I knew what to do. Looking very carefully at the Marlborough Light in my hand, I raised it confidently to my lips and leant in toward the Zippo lighter that Mike was holding up.

5

FROM THAT POINT on, Friday nights were for Repulse Bay Beach—occasionally on the sand, sometimes purchasing cigarettes and alcohol from 7-Eleven, but most usually inside Son of a Beach, the tiny bar that took no issue with serving minors. The bar was raided sporadically by combinations of the police and furious parents, but these raids did little to hamper our fun; they probably intensified it.

I loved being out at night. I knew that, sooner or later, it would be time for me to find a boyfriend, but I had no idea how to go about it. Before I had time to address the challenge, I was presented with a much simpler proposition.

'Want to smoke a joint?' Tina asked, a couple of weeks in.

'Okay.' I didn't see why not. I followed her onto the sand and we walked several yards onto the darkened beach. A group of about five others were sitting in a circle in a solemn, almost reverent state. Toby finished rolling the thing, and Mike tossed him the Zippo. I didn't like the distinct herby smell, but I stayed put and waited for my turn to smoke. As we sat, Nick rolled onto his back and lay facing the sky. I looked over at Tina.

'What's wrong with him?'

'He's had something stronger,' she said.

'Like what?' I wanted to know.

'He shot up.' Tina gestured to her forearm.

'Oh ....' I was intrigued. 'Do you do that?'

'No,' she answered. 'I don't do the heavy stuff.'

'Yah.'

Tina had clearly thought this through. I hadn't, and decided I needed to have a think about whether or not I wanted to try something stronger at some point. Maybe the joint would be enough for now. It was time to find out. I drew in, filled my lungs, held it for a moment, and exhaled slowly. I waited to feel its effects, and then they came, heavy, thick and slow. My body relaxed and sunk into the sand just an inch or two. My cheeks and my scalp felt a little heavier than usual, and that was about it. The physical experience was something I could take or leave, but the closeness I felt in the group was something I would hold on to for as long as I could.

I took a taxi home and snuck in as quietly as possible. I changed my top, sprayed myself with deodorant, swished some mouthwash and spat it into the rubbish bin in my room before going into my parents' bedroom to tell Mum I was safely home. I got on with the rest of the weekend and was ready to go back to school on Monday, no longer really worrying about my social status.

. . .

'YOU KNOW THEY don't even sterilise their needles at Ricky and Pinky's, don't you?' My accuser had taken her shot from behind me in the corridor outside the assembly hall.

Kate was one year above me in school, and not someone I'd ever had anything to do with. I didn't know why she even cared, but it turned out she did care enough to pay special notice anytime I did something she felt was significant. In me she had found an easy target and took it upon herself to give me her opinion whenever the mood struck.

'You could have AIDS, you know.'

I didn't answer her. This was not an exercise in self-control; it was because I didn't have a reply. I hadn't even thought about the sterilising of needles. I ignored Kate and went on my way, wondering what it would feel like to have AIDS, and whether I should ask someone. I decided to do nothing and hope for the best.

'So, you're a druggie now, are you?' Kate sneered as she passed me in the corridor a week later.

'Do you think you're cool or something?' she wanted to know, after the weekend Tina and I had put a streak of purple in our hair.

'That is the most disgusting thing in the world. I hope it gets infected,' she declared, on hearing the news that I had pierced my own bellybutton with a safety pin.

I had failed to stay off the radar and my weekend activities had bought me no popularity at my own school. Now I was the freak. The cool kids at Island School, having just learnt the fresh art of sarcasm, dealt it out in thick lashings:

'I heard she got a tattoo on the inside of her mouth.'

'Oh my God, that's so cool ... NOT!'

'And what's with the black eyeliner? Is she trying to be a goth or something?'

'Is she trying to be Satanic or something?'

'Oooh, she's so alternative ... NOT!'

It never occurred to me to wonder where these people were getting their information from. Nor did it occur to me to defend myself—I was not confrontational. For the most part, they had their facts right—all except for the devil worshipping. All I really cared about was that my new South Island friends didn't discover how lowly I was in my own school and disown me. I figured it would probably happen at some stage; and so, until then, I would make the most of having a life, maybe even try to get a boyfriend out of it. I continued to go to the beach every weekend, and to smoke or drink whatever was handed to me.

. . .

AFTER TURNING 15, I went on a second solo visit to Perth. I had been invited to go to a church camp. I had no idea what it would entail, but I wanted to spend some more time with Amy. After the tattoo and the Brian Adams concert we had shared in Hong Kong, I bestowed on her the title of Favourite Cousin. I trusted her judgement and went to the camp with her because she told me I should.

The hosting church was contemporary in style, meeting in a rented lecture hall at the nearby University of Western Australia—not a cross or stained-glass window in sight. The congregation consisted mostly of university students from Singapore and Malaysia, none of whom I could find anything in common with. It was the mid-nineties and the scene was meant to be grunge rock, plaid shirts and Doc Marten boots. The Christians in Perth were completely friendly and appeared to have no edginess whatsoever. All I could see were goofy grins fixed permanently on their faces as they went about their good works.

'Praise the Lord, hallelujah,' was a typical response to my hello. Or, 'You are my sister in Christ.'

The only redeeming feature in the church was the music. There was a band that included an electric guitar, bass, keyboard and drums. Surely Jus would approve. But there was more to it than that. Something in the music was beautiful, but I kept quiet about this for fear of becoming one of them.

At the youth camp, we slept in cosy bunk beds in well-insulated cabins, and then met up in the main auditorium three times a day to sing praises and listen to a sermon. It was the season in contemporary Pentecostal Christian history known as 'The Toronto Blessing'. This involved highly demonstrative reactions to God's Holy Spirit. Some people would respond to the presence of God by shaking, shouting, falling over, or vibrating, as if they had been struck by lightning.

Although the revival in question had broken out in Canada, and I was at a tiny youth camp on the opposite side of the globe, I would not miss out on experiencing the phenomenon. A famous minister called Rodney Howard Brown had recently been in Australia, and this seemed to have set the tone henceforth for some of the local ministers.

When the camp's speaker wrapped up his talk at the first night's rally, he announced that those of us who wished to experience God's love first-hand needed to stand up, form a prayer line, and lift our hands in a position ready to accept the anointing. It had been presented less as an invitation than an order. I did as I was told, but very soon regretted it. I stood somewhere near the middle of the back line, beside Amy. As soon as the minister started to pray for the first person in the front line, all hell broke loose.

Hysterical sobbing and laughing spontaneously erupted around the room. I looked at Amy to see if she was as freaked out as I was, but she was not. Her head was bowed and without lifting it, she leant toward me and said, 'Don't worry.'

Don't worry?! I looked around the room and saw one guy jumping up and down and flapping his arms, an impression of a dodo trying to lift off.

'What is happening?'

'Different people react to the touch of God differently,' said Amy quietly. 'It's not something you can control.' Her head was still bowed.

'If it's different for everyone, why are the people standing there ready to catch each other?' I asked. 'How do they know they are going to fall backwards? Does it hurt? Why does God want to knock everyone over? What's he getting out of this?'

'Don't ask so many questions. People just get weak in the knees when God shows them how much he loves them.'

'What are you going to do?' Up until that point, Amy had been the only normal person I had at this camp, and the thought of her whooping and tearing at her hair was the last straw.

'I just get a very strong feeling of peace, and sometimes I cry a little,' she said. 'I have been slain in the Spirit before.'

She had been one of them, all along. There was nowhere for me to run. We were at a campsite in the middle of Western Australia several years before smartphones were invented. I had no means of contacting my family for help. I sat down and stared as madness unfolded around me. The people nearest me, previously so meek and mild, descended into a state of mass hysteria. I was confronted with the fact that I would be stuck there for another two days, and soon concluded that the God they were going crazy over was neither loving nor someone I wanted touching me, especially if his goal was to make me look like a freak.

However, the two days went by very slowly, and they wore me down. By the last night, the pressure to stand in the prayer line was more than I could fight. There were church leaders sweeping the back corners of the room for anyone trying to hide. I reverted to my old trick of doing whatever they wanted, just so I could get out of there as fast as I could.

Silently, I told God how much I resented the situation. The minister placed his prayer hand on my shoulder, and blew weird, minty breath in my face, demanding, 'More, Lord! More!'

Okay, God. If you are real, let's have it. Knock me over. Go on.

Nothing.

God was not going to knock me over. I had never felt so sure of anything in my whole life.

This did not stop the feeling that I needed to fall. The man was still praying for me and blowing in my face. 'More, Lord!' He wasn't going to go away until either God, or I, did something.

Okay, God. What's the problem? Am I not what you're looking for? Is it because you don't love me? Is that why you aren't knocking me over? Am I Ye of Little Faith? How about I start it off and then you catch me?

I told my knees to go weak. I 'fell'. I chose to feign a fall. I went back into the hands of the catchers, slithered onto the floor and kept my eyes closed. I wanted it to be over. I lay, hoping my fake fall had been convincing, feeling disappointed that God had not met me on the way to the floor.

Nothing. This is stupid. I hate myself. I want to go home.

Later, as I sat in the back of the van, squashed between camping bags and Christians, I closed my eyes and pretended to sleep. I asked God why he hadn't knocked me over. I got no answer. I strained my memory to recall the melodies of the worship music. God might not have knocked me down, but the music still sounded like angels singing, even in my head. I savoured the sounds and concluded that I was not good enough for God.

Soon enough, however, it was time to leave and head home to Earth, back to Hong Kong to try to pick up where I had left off.

. . .

I **WAS BEGINNING TO** like my life in Hong Kong, and made a conscious effort to forget about Christianity, until one night I was forced to pray because I found myself in a situation that I had no other way of dealing with.

My friends and I were at the Manhattan, in the foundations of the luxury apartment complex. We spent many nights there after leaving the beach. We played loud music, smoked cigarettes and drugs, burnt anything that looked flammable, and decorated the walls with amateur spray-painted images of marijuana leaves or faces smoking joints. We loved to play at being homeless outcasts of society, but in truth we all had luxury homes equipped with maids and laserdisc players to go back to in the morning. The main action of the night had died down, but crackling music continued to blare from the stereo. A couple of candles provided just enough light for me to survey the surroundings. Everyone was either fast asleep or passed out. I had little concept of the fragility of life and had taken any substance ever offered to me. However, since my return from Perth, I had found the effects of drugs disappointing. I feared there were no more highs for me to find.

I was looking for a spot to sleep, when I noticed Simon, one of the younger guys from the French school, lying on a mattress in the corner. He had shot up; he was one of the guys who always did. As I watched, I realised he was shaking. He was convulsing; his eyes were slightly opened and his eyeballs kept rolling back. There was a small amount of foam catching in the corner of his blue-tinged lips.

I watched, not knowing what else to do. He looked like he was locked in a nightmare, and then it occurred to me that he probably wanted it to stop. I went over and gave him a gentle tap, then shook him a little, but he wouldn't wake up. He groaned, as if he was trying to tell me something, and began to shake even harder.

As I knelt down beside him, my knee split open and blood began to soak into the mattress. There was broken glass on the mattress, and Simon was lying on it. I didn't try to wake anyone else; I was transfixed on the tormented face in front of me. I remembered Jackie Pullinger, and I started to pray. I leant down to Simon's ear and began to pray in tongues, just the way my cousin had taught me, loud enough so that Simon could hear me. I was aware of the strangeness of the moment. I should have felt embarrassed, but I didn't. I felt brave, I felt like I was saving his life.

As I prayed, Simon's convulsions stopped and his face became peaceful. I don't remember how long I had prayed, but I know it was quite some time. I remember getting tired and I stopped a few times, but then Simon would start shaking again, so I would start praying again. As soon as daylight broke I went home, feeling like the worst was over, hoping that Simon would have no recollection of what had happened. But he did remember. The next time I saw him, he walked straight over to me.

'Thank you,' he said. 'You were my angel last time.'

I still have a scar on my left knee from where I knelt on the broken glass that night. But more pertinent than the physical scar was the idea that I just couldn't shake off—that something very real, yet completely out of this world, had happened. The impression left on me by that experience led me to choose to go back to Perth when my time to leave Hong Kong eventually came.

We kids all took for granted the temporary nature of our circumstances. It was assumed that international kids would complete secondary school and then move on to university overseas. Most people would go to university in the home country of a parent, or wherever the parents felt the best education was to be had. Some of us would leave early for sixth form colleges, or to complete high school at home if a parent's expat job contract had ended. None of us really knew what happened on the other side of university graduation. It was too far off for our young minds to fathom. As the transient tempo of our expat culture sped towards 1997, the parties got wilder.

'I have something for you,' said Tina excitedly one night. She pulled her hand out of her pocket and held up two little white pills. 'Speed. It's crazy with dance music.'

'Okay,' I said. 'Let's go.'

We swallowed the pills with water and headed down to Son of a Beach. I danced for hours on end with energy that just kept coming. I was weightless and free, calm but on fire. Sometimes, Tina was there with me, sometimes I was with other friends, sometimes with strangers, and sometimes alone. I had finally found something I loved, something real, something that I was already looking forward to doing again—and, given the opportunity, would have wanted to do daily, for the rest of time.

I did not think to ask Tina where she had gotten the pills. Practicalities like that didn't factor when we were together. I didn't even think to ask her when we would have them again. I just waited patiently—sometimes we had them, sometimes we didn't. She and several of our other friends were due to move away from Hong Kong soon, and so we enjoyed each other's company for the time we had left.

As people's departure dates approached, things got increasingly out of control. I was sure I had experienced something supernatural the night I prayed for Simon, but I did not know what to do about it. I just kept going out, partying. I knew there was something more to experience, perhaps through the substances, perhaps not. I was gathering evidence. This chaos flew under my parents' radar—it happened to coincide with more pressing things that were happening at home.

6

BESIDES WORKING, BOTH of my parents became heavily occupied with supporting an older loved one who was unwell. I didn't see any of it happening, all I knew was that someone who had been a part of our lives was suddenly no longer around. My parents must have been doing all they could to manage the situation. Perhaps they were shielding me, or maybe they simply had no answers. The situation was delicate and complicated, not one that could easily be explained to a teenager. Not knowing what else to do, I stayed away from home as much as possible, or else hid in my own room when there was nowhere else to go.

. . .

AUNTY MICHELLE, A well-meaning Christian friend of the family, came to visit to offer moral support to my mum and to check on me. She had heard about the trips to Perth, that I had accepted Jesus into my life. She knocked on my bedroom door and asked how I was doing, and if I was in the routine of praying and reading my Bible.

'Yes,' I lied. I had wanted Jesus to stay in Perth.

'I want to talk to you about something,' she said. I started to look around my room for an escape route.

'It's those dolls you have up there. Do you know what they are?' Aunty motioned toward my collection of Ugly Troll dolls, standing in a row on the curtain rail box, mute faces smiling, multi-coloured hair standing up tall.

'Yes.' I felt relieved for a misguided moment. 'They're Trolls. We got them in Wanchai.' I couldn't see what the problem could possibly be, so I started to think my aunty was going to ask me to give them to her because either she wanted them, or she wanted to give them to charity or something. It was a very respectable collection.

Aunty Michelle went on to explain that, although the dolls were cute in appearance, they were, in fact, representative of evil spirits. They could have the power to invite bad things upon the household. They needed to be removed from my room and destroyed. She produced a plastic bag and gathered up the offending items.

'You let her take them?!' Dad was furious.

He had begrudgingly kept silent while my Australian relatives converted me to the Christian faith, but he had not supported the style in which it was done. In his commitment to letting his children find their own way, he had tried to hold a respectful distance. I interpreted his silence as a lack of interest. I thought perhaps none of it mattered very much; that, in the grand scheme, anything goes. Had he spoken up, I would have listened. I was desperate for some guidance and I was beginning to take comfort in the Christians' style. It was, for the most part, clear-cut, black and white, and that was all that was making sense to me at the time. I had also voluntarily surrendered my Guatemalan worry dolls and several secular music

CDs but did not mention those to Dad. I was no longer sure whose side I was on.

The removal of the Trolls triggered an argument between my parents. Things were already tense at home. To top it all off, Dad's mental health was suffering as well. He went through months of fallow periods followed by bouts of unbearable energy. Both states were accompanied by plenty of drink.

. . .

I HATED TO SEE him drunk. When drunk, he was not himself. Not wise, not strong, not the pillar that held my world in place. Drunk, he was a flaccid imitation of himself. Although he always remained affectionate, I could not bring myself to trust him once the smell of alcohol punctuated the air between us. I did not want to see him weak and clumsy. I did not want to be within reach, where he would inevitably reach out a hand to ruffle my hair or squeeze my knee too hard, harmless affectionate gestures that I dreaded because they only happened when he was drunk. I could not say anything to him that mattered because, the next day, once he was sober again, once the genuine article had replaced the imposter, he never remembered a thing. Sober, he was a wonderful man—so wonderful, that we all readily forgave and forgot, optimistically hoping it would be the last time we'd need to.

One day, when he was quiet and sad, but had not been drinking, he tried to answer some questions I had about mental illness by explaining that there were problems of the mind, some of which he struggled with himself, that often ran in families. What I took from the conversation was that, as a member of the family, I was next in line to go crazy. Everywhere I looked, our patterns of normal life seemed to be breaking down. Jus was packed and ready to go to university and, at the age of fourteen, I did not want to be left behind to cope with all of the changes.

'I wish I could go and live in Perth,' I said to Mum the next day. 'Like the way you lived in Australia when you were my age ....'

As a child she had brought all of her books home one day, point-blank refusing to return to her prestigious girls' school ever again. Her mother, my Por Por, responded by bringing her along on tour with the musical band formed of students from the school for the blind the family ran. After completing the tour, Mum was put on a ship that took her and her little sister to a boarding school in Melbourne.

I rarely had trouble convincing my open-minded mother to give me whatever I wanted. At the age of four, I had spotted a wedding party outside a church and declared that I simply had to be in a wedding, somebody's wedding, anybody's. Mum approached strangers outside of the registry and did not give up until somebody agreed to let me be their flower girl. They even bought me a dress.

A few years after that, I got Mum to buy me a pair of ballet pointe shoes 'to play with'. In the ballet world, pointe shoes are something to be earned through many years of consistent training. Pointe work is supposed to be introduced gradually and under strict supervision. Although I took lessons, no teacher on the planet would have agreed to this purchase.

And so, there it was in my life, a regular pattern of me making inappropriate requests, and those requests being granted me. I launched into this new appeal to leave Hong Kong full of zeal, and void of understanding of what I was really asking for.

I had asked my parents to send me away.

Dad put up a fight, but his reserves were low. In the end, he reluctantly agreed to send me away to live with the Christians in Perth. Within months, the family nest would be empty. I joined the ranks of those about to leave Hong Kong, and proceeded to party harder than I knew I could.

I still had a couple of months at Island School to complete before leaving for Perth, but I stopped paying attention in class, or handing in homework. Only idiots who wanted to get caught would smoke before school, and I was an idiot who did not want to get caught, so I would visit the 'drama studio toilets' before morning registration and chew on a small, gritty wad of hash. The effects ranged from disappointing to undetectable, but the sense of rebellion was highly satisfying. I took regular days off school, choosing to hang around shopping centres with Mary instead.

I continued to make Repulse Bay my home every Friday, Saturday and, sometimes, Sunday night, always drunk by 8pm. One evening, at a time substantially later than 8pm, I was drawn into a conversation between Matt, one of our gang, and two men I had never met before. One was a tall white guy, who looked very much like MacGyver, the American TV action-adventurer who could defuse bombs with his hands cuffed behind his back using nothing but his calm mind and a chewing gum wrapper. The other guy was a tough-looking Korean-Filipino with tattoos on his arms.

'Hey, check this out!' Matt was so excited that I felt sure the men must have been offering him some free drugs.

'You want one of these?' The Korean guy handed me a business card.

It read *Saturday Night Alive—not your average Christian youth group!*

'My parents go to church all the fucking time!' said Matt, slurring his words. 'They try and make me go with them.'

'Me too! I have to go to church sometimes, too!' I replied, words equally slurry. 'I think it's kinda cool in some uncool kind of way, you know?'

'Yah, that stuff is like, hardcore.' Now Matt was getting excited. 'People like, jumping all over the place, and demons and shit, yah?'

'Yah, I know man! And praying in tongues, too, right?'

The two men were not saying very much at this point. Matt and I had taken over. I was irritated by their lack of enthusiasm, so I addressed them.

'I'm a Christian, you know? Jesus and everything. I've seen people, like, slain in the Spirit!'

'Okay, sure thing,' said the tall, white guy. Neither of them seemed impressed by me at all, so I stuffed the card in my wallet and stumbled off.

. . .

I didn't need another youth group, anyway. I had youth groups coming out my ears—there was Agape in Perth, the Korean one Jang had taken me to, and there was Delta Chi—the group in Hong Kong my aunty had instructed me to go to. It seemed church folk had connections all over the globe, and my aunty's reach was very long when it came to my spiritual well-being. Delta Chi was full of good, wholesome American kids to whom I could not relate. No matter which lot of people I was with, I acted like I had better things to do, because I did not feel like I fit in with any of them. I felt like a bad influence.

I knew this to be the case for my new friend Ryan, from Delta Chi. He was a good boy trying to decide whether or not he wanted to be bad. It didn't suit him. He always looked very shifty as he tried to convince me he was totally comfortable smoking my cigarettes after Friday night meetings. Ryan was a year younger than me. When we first met, I remember thinking he looked a lot like a quarterback sort of character off Beverly Hills 90210. His family, originally from Texas, lived on a luxury yacht in Hong Kong while his father did missionary work in China.

Ryan and his siblings were students at the prestigious American International School. The first time we met, I was very clear with Ryan about the nature of my attendance at the youth group. I was not there by choice. As I partied and got ready to leave Hong Kong, Ryan continued to encourage me to 'get real with God'. He had started to turn down my offers of cigarettes and was now refusing to accompany me to Repulse Bay. Something about boundaries. He and my other closest friends made me mixed tapes and wrote letters with enclosed photos to take with me when I finally left Hong Kong.

And then my time finally came.

I sat alone and leant my head against the cold window as the airplane gathered speed along Kai Tak Airport's famous runway. The plane passed the point of no return and I took in a deep breath. I had really done it. I'd gone and left. All my life, I had travelled from one airport to another with my family; now, here I was, fifteen years old and alone, on my way into the sky.

I wondered if this hunk of engineering could carry me far enough away from my family to ensure I would not end up like them; if I could find some way to belong in Perth instead of in Hong Kong. I wanted a fresh start. It was best if I disappeared. Did I even want to belong in Perth? Maybe, if I tried hard enough, eventually God would knock me over. I didn't want to be like the Christians, but I didn't want to be myself, either.

I was running away, but I was heading into uncertainty. Sitting under the cold blast of the plane's air-conditioning, I pulled my blanket up over my shoulders and turned my head to quietly cry.

7

1995

I WAS FIFTEEN YEARS old and living in Perth, and the Christians were out to get me. On some level I knew I was too weak to resist, that sheer forces of loneliness would eventually overpower me. They seemed determined to love me, but I was determined not to go down without a fight. Summoning every ounce of strength I had, I put on an unfriendly and disinterested front for as long as I possibly could, but the match was fixed. I was the wayward niece of the pastors. I was probably number one on the hit list of every evangelist in the church. Everyone was praying for me, they all kept telling me so. I didn't stand a chance.

School was my only respite from the church. This was another interesting place, made up entirely of Asians who had come in search of education in an English-speaking land. Little did our parents know, and contrary to what the school brochure would have had us believe, not one of us would say 'G'day, mate' to a blonde, blue-eyed local the whole time we were there. English was my mother tongue and, being half Welsh, I was the closest thing to a white girl in the whole school. Once again, I stuck out. Much of my time in Perth was spent wondering where all the Australians were. By the time I would complete my year there, I'd have my Mandarin up to a fluent level, with just the faintest hint of a Singaporean accent.

Everything and everyone in Perth felt like a threat. They had funny accents, terrible grammar and a sense of humour I did not appreciate. To make matters worse, it seemed that the majority of them were obsessed with the eternal destiny of my soul. I didn't dare accept the offers of cigarettes from the cool crowd—my relatives had mentioned there were a couple of other church-goers in my tiny school, and I could not risk word getting back to them. Living outside of my comfort zone, I became timid and terribly afraid of being caught. Juxtaposed against the church, I had become even more acutely aware of my badness: embarrassed, ashamed even.

On one of the leaflets I had been given at the Study Abroad fair, I read that I ran the risk of being deported if I broke the law during my time as an overseas student in Australia. I had been told by various people that I was expected to be on my best behaviour. The warnings were made with such severity that I started to feel quite paranoid. The risk of being ID'ed and deported for trying to purchase cigarettes in a shop terrified me. I never had any money, anyway. The allowance sent by my parents would have been more than enough, but I didn't know how to manage it. Every time I received it, I spent it immediately on nail polish and hair dye at the nearest chemist.

I could not bring myself to buy cigarettes. The withdrawal process left me with no dignity. During the first few weeks at school, I would escape into the surrounding suburb at lunch break, searching the gutters for discarded cigarette butts. One hot and sunny day, a car slowed down beside me as I trawled the pavements, looking for something to smoke. He was trawling for something else.

'How arya?' An Australian man, probably in his forties, leant out of his car window and smiled a friendly smile. But it was the cigarette in his hand that caught my eye.

'Hello.' I smiled, knowing that he liked what he saw.

'What are you doing?' He slipped his sunglasses up, onto his head. He was much too old for me. He had wrinkles around his smiling eyes.

'I'd like a smoke, but I don't want to get carded in a shop.' I didn't have much time, lunch break was almost over, but if we could move this along quickly I could smoke a whole cigarette and deodorise before my next class.

'Is that right?' He took a drag of his cigarette and exhaled in a long, exaggerated breath. 'Too young, are you?'

'That's right.' I kept smiling, even though I was getting impatient. 'Do you want to give me one of yours?'

'How about this.' Now his eyes were sparkling. 'How about you get in and I drive you to the corner shop? I'll buy you your own pack.'

I was desperate, but I was not naïve. 'I don't think so.'

'Come on, I'll pay for them.'

He had no idea whose daughter he was dealing with. I would have passed a test as obvious as this one at the age of five.

'How about I wait here,' I said, 'you go buy me a pack and then drive back here to give it to me?'

He stopped smiling. 'Forget it. You're not even worth it.' He pulled his glasses back down and drove away.

It turned out that the inhabitants of my particular suburb tended to smoke down to the filter, so after two weeks I was forced to go cold turkey.

. . .

In the boarding house, I shared a room with two Indonesian girls called Maya and Murni. They were not related in any way, other than by their common Islamic faith. I often woke in the early hours of the morning, startled by the sight of the two of them wrapped in shawls, standing, kneeling, bowing on their carpets pointing to Mecca. No one told them to do it. They just got up every single day and did it.

Although I had not wanted to associate with the Christians, I'd unwittingly been influenced from my time with the church. One day, I found myself chatting with Maya about God and drawing her a diagram we had been taught at the youth group. The diagram depicted a cross-shaped bridge spanning the great chasm between God and man. I had little personal experience with which to pad out the story, and when I was finished Maya drew the Islamic equivalent for me. When she calmly explained that Jesus was not a bridge, but was, in fact, one of multiple prophets, I accepted that I was out of my depth. Neither of us was sure what to do after completing our respective drawings, so we agreed to leave it and head downstairs for dinner.

. . .

We were served a greasy meal of fried meat on white rice, with a token bite's worth of veg in an oily plastic box, three times a day. The school offered no physical education whatsoever, and I had quit ballet shortly before I left Hong Kong. My body was beginning to protest. I felt heavy and sluggish. I was a giant compared to most of my tiny Asian classmates, boys included. My skin was as greasy as the food I was fed, and my stomach growled loudly, regardless of what I put into it. In class, I would feel a rumble coming on and then try to fake a coughing fit to cover the highly embarrassing sounds. The embarrassment was so much that I finally went to see a doctor. She was an older Australian lady, and I'd had to navigate my way right across the strange new city to get to her clinic.

'My stomach is making really loud grumbling noises when I'm not even hungry,' I said.

She looked at me like I was a wicked schoolgirl, deliberately wasting her time.

'Well, it must be the bread,' she replied. 'I know you Asians don't eat a lot of bread where you come from. Your body isn't used to the Australian diet. It doesn't matter; a grumbling stomach won't hurt you.'

'Can you give me some medicine to clear up my skin?'

She stared at me as if I had insulted her mother.

I had come all that way and didn't want to leave empty handed. 'My doctor in Hong Kong gave me some pills once, and they worked very well.'

'Oh, really?' She was looking straight into my soul and could see I was a bad person.

'Yes, so if I could just have those again I'm sure it would help ....'

'I don't know much about Chinese medicine,' said the doctor, 'but I will tell you, from an ethical point of view, that I am loathed to hand out drugs for vanity's sake—I won't do it, unless the condition is so severe it is causing the patient significant distress. Yours is not. Unless you can tell me the exact name of whatever it was you used to take, I will not be able to help you. What were the pills called?'

'I don't know,' I said. 'They were red and yellow capsules, and I wasn't allowed to drink milk after taking them.'

'No,' she replied, 'I just can't give you anything based on this information. I suggest you eat less bread and drink less milk.'

'Thanks.' I left with nothing.

. . .

I BEGAN TO MAKE myself vomit after every meal. Maybe life had become all too much for me to swallow, or maybe I was just bored and I had seen someone do it in an episode of *Models, Inc.* Whatever the reason, I began a shamefully intimate relationship with toilet bowls everywhere I went. I was quite smart about it, though.

Human Biology was my favourite subject at school. Something about the teacher's technique fitted my learning style. Four times a week, she would stand at the front of the class with her eyeglasses suspended low on the bridge of her nose and dictate the entire lesson from a piece of paper. We, the class, would take down the dictation and then sit quietly to go over what we had written. The first thing I did when I returned to my room at the end of the day was rewrite the lesson, twice—first in a blue pen, then in black. And then, I coloured the important bits with a yellow highlighter before filing them. It was fascinating stuff: the reproductive system, the respiratory system, the lymphatic system, the digestive system ... Each system came with big long words I enjoyed spelling out and colourful diagrams to draw.

I was taught that digestive acid from the stomach could travel upwards when you vomit, causing heartburn, and that chronic vomiting could result in damage to the oesophagus. I also learnt that the tell-tale signs of people with bulimia included bad breath, rotten teeth and brittle hair and fingernails. Armed with the power of knowledge, I went to the chemist and purchased a very large bottle of thick pink liquid antacid, chewing gum, and hot oil treatment for my hair. I already had a good collection of nail polish.

Every day after I had done my homework, I settled on my bed to unlatch my little suitcase full of tiny bottles and paint my nails. The acetone fumes, like aromatherapy, helped me to forget my cares for those moments. At dinner, I downed my greasy meal as everyone commented on my nail-art skills and asked me to do their nails, too.

I never chatted for long. Experience taught me that the sooner I regurgitated my meal, the less painful the process would be. I had perfected my system. I knew exactly how much drink to have with the meal in order to achieve optimum vomit consistency. Not only did the varnish mask any discolouration of my nails, but the bitter chemical taste also helped my gag reflex along. I experimented with doing jumping jacks and then handstands against the wall before moving into the bathroom. Eventually, I developed enough muscle control to wretch efficiently and completely silently without any need of pre-vomiting acrobatics. I stuck my hand deep into my mouth and un-swallowed my food, my drink, my loneliness, my stupid decision to leave home, and all the religious propaganda I felt had been forced down my throat. Once it was flushed away, I replaced the void with a large capful of the chalky pink stuff, brushed my teeth, and went to bed.

The school and adjoining boarding house were a repurposed motel with a few temporary classrooms made out of shipping containers, albeit quite nice-looking ones. We were situated in one of several Chinatown areas in the city of Perth. Dotted about the surrounding area were Asian restaurants, parks and small businesses. The air was clean and the skies were blue.

That blue sky felt a million times bigger in Australia than it ever did in Hong Kong—I stared up at it and tried my best to believe that that same sky stretched all the way over my family back at home. I would close my eyes and bid my spirit fly. I lifted up into that quiet blueness, up over the short Australian houses, the Swan River, the dark open sea. I drew in the pungent smells as I neared Hong Kong's not-so-fragrant harbour. I wove between tall buildings, up the hill, over the university campus and then into my parents' open bedroom window. I snuggled into bed between Mum and Dad, closed my eyes and thanked the heavens that I hadn't really grown up and left home after all.

But I had. The vacant roads and empty pavements in Perth were wastefully wide and under-utilised. There was no jostling or nudging of passing foot traffic. No contact to be had whatsoever.

. . .

One block down from the school was a grassy park area. I felt awkward about the park because, during one of my first few visits to the school before the year officially kicked off, I had noticed a group of Aboriginals sitting in a large circle on the grass. They seemed so content with life, sitting there, spending their day in community and fellowship. It was everything that was missing from my life. I fancied the idea of befriending them, learning their culture, finding my place in the world with them. As a child, I had built my expectations of Australia on a questionable foundation of Crocodile Dundee, Rolf Harris and *Neighbours*. Somewhere in my heart, I think I was hoping to find an unlikely sense of belonging with this minority group. They sat on the grass like one big strong family, each deserving of their spot and all perfectly at ease with one another. I thought that, perhaps, they would be able to lead me to some koalas or teach me to bake grubs and sweet potatoes by burying them in the hot desert sand.

I confided in Amy, who was horrified by my plans to befriend the Aboriginals. She sternly explained that there was a strong chance that they were unfriendly, unemployed and very drunk.

'They won't want you intruding.'

I didn't believe her and went to the park the next day despite her warnings. As I got up close to the group, the smell of spirits hit me, just as one of the men looked up.

'What the fuck are yous looking at? Get away from here.'

So I did.

. . .

Opposite the park was an Asian supermarket where we Asian students were able to buy most of our soul foods, like instant noodles, Vitasoy in glass bottles and snacks like Calabee potato chips and White Rabbit candies: imported and sold to us at insultingly inflated prices. These Asian supermarkets all around the world smell the same: herby, artificially sweet and exotic—and, ironically, unfamiliar. Coconut candies, Hi-Chews, Haw Flakes and Vita Lemon Tea could not comfort me, though. They were powerless set against a backdrop of eucalyptus trees and pickup trucks. If I closed my eyes whilst sucking on an over-priced wah mui and tried to imagine I was in Hong Kong, my ears would let the pretence down: the local soundtrack of galahs and crows clashed with my heart's cry for pile drivers and slamming minibus doors. Those bloody birds kicked up their awful din every morning before sunrise. It was a taunt, a personal reminder that I was not at home.

During a half-term holiday, my parents and I agreed it would be best for me to stay in Perth instead of travelling home to Hong Kong. They were going to Oxford for the summer, as our family had always done; only, now that I was on the Australian school calendar, I could not join them. It shouldn't have made any difference to me where in the world they were, since anywhere still amounted to *not here*. Yet, knowing they had gone to England left me feeling more isolated than ever. My roommates and most of the other boarders went home for the week, and I sat alone with my memories of happy family summers that felt a lifetime away.

'Won't be lonely, what?' said Jacqueline, from the room next door, having overheard me telling Maya that I was planning to stay in the boarding house.

'I'll be fine,' I said, closing our door.

'Don't like to go home, is it?' said Samson, a Year 12 boy, as he pulled his suitcase past me at the main entrance later that afternoon. He was one of the last boarders to clear out for the week.

'I might go and stay with my cousins,' I lied, heading back to my room for the night.

I was left almost entirely alone in the boarding house. Everyone else went home or went to stay with their guardian. I always had the option of going back to see my relatives, who lived in a very nice house in a very nice suburb. On this occasion, however, I chose not to. Although I could not put a finger on what it was, I knew it was time to deal with something. Something just under my skin, the problem I could not identify, but knew had been there for too long. It was still very much present, rustling around just beneath the surface. If I could finally deal with it, perhaps I could feel better.

Alone with my thoughts in the boarding house, I began to hatch a plan. *Perhaps I need to be in hospital.* If people went to live in a hospital until they felt better, why shouldn't I do the same? Hospitals were where damaged people got fixed. I did not know exactly what I needed to do to secure a bed in a hospital, but I was quite sure a broken bone would at least get me through the door. Once in, they would realise I needed more attention.

The next evening, I turned on the TV for noise coverage. I piled up some textbooks and leant my left forearm against them. I took up one of my rollerblades with my right hand, raised it high, drawing it slightly behind my head. I closed my eyes and slammed it down on my left forearm.

Nothing happened. I needed to be stronger. I tried again, and again. I mustered up all the pain and hatred I could lay claim to and directed it at my left arm, pummelling with all my might. I bashed myself for two straight minutes before admitting defeat. I could not break my own arm. I was unbreakable. And trapped. I didn't even bruise.

. . .

I slid the rollerblade back under my bed, where I noticed a crumpled scrap of paper. It was the diagram I had drawn for Maya. Looking at my illustration of the gulf between man and God, I sunk further into despair. The picture meant nothing to me. The people and the land I had surrounded myself with meant nothing to me, and I meant nothing to them. My family were the only ones I felt safe with, and I had been stupid enough to leave them. I couldn't go back. They weren't there, anyway. It was night and even the noisy birds had shut up. There I was, in the silence. I had nobody. I was nothing.

I walked out of the boarding house into the middle of the grassy park. I didn't care whether the group of Aboriginals would be there or not. I didn't care if I got locked out. I didn't plan on going back. I planned on ending my life. Somehow, I would not let this go on any longer. My mind was made up.

'I'm done,' I said to no one.

No one is here, I told myself. *No one can hear me.*

No One, can you hear me?

If you can hear me, if *you are real, and* if *you are listening, then this is it. This is going to be your one and only chance with me. Either you tell me you are there, or I am going to kill myself. I am done with this.*

I looked up, belligerent.

That big black sky was too dark to be the same sky hanging over Hong Kong, or Oxford. If my parents looked up at that moment, they would not see the same blackness I saw. I stared upwards, heels dug into the grass, a face-off with the heavens. I was not going to cry.

My eyes settled on just one of the billions of stars on display that night. I'd grown up accustomed to seeing only one or two through Hong Kong's smog. The Australians were spoilt. There were billions of stars to look at here, but that night I was only going to deal with one. There it hung, smug and carefree. It was not fat, or stupid, or unable to break its own arm. It did not have my problems. All it had to do was be there, up there, as far from me as anything could possibly be. It had nothing to prove, and I hated it. It flickered more than all of the others. And then it flickered even more. It was clearly trying to tell me something. It started jumping up and down, waving frantically, and trying to hold my attention.

A second later, it unhinged itself from its place in infinity and shot across my view, fizzling spectacularly out of sight. But it wouldn't let me go. I was transfixed. It had flung itself out of the heavens, and was gone. Although I could no longer see it with my eyes, I knew exactly where it had gone. It shot straight out of the sky and into my mouth, down my damaged throat, burning as it went, and lodged itself in.

God? Was that you?

A temperate breeze softly rattled the dry eucalyptus branches, and somewhere in the night a dog barked.

Did you do that for me?

Two cars drove down the road and one large, wet teardrop formed over my right eye, and then another in the left.

Are you there?

Tears spilled down my cheeks and my heart began to throb. Everything was burning.

Have you been here all along?

The trees stood still, they held their breath, and finally I inhaled. I took in what was happening. I had taken in that fiery star. I had taken it all the way in. It was still burning in my very depths. Settling into every cell. Stilling me to the core.

8

THE SCHOOL YEAR came to a close. I went through the necessary motions to complete my work. I was unable to comprehend what had happened that night in the park, unwilling to attempt to deal with it until I was home. Mum picked me up from the airport in Hong Kong and, as we drove home, I told her, in no uncertain terms, that I would not be returning to Perth.

'I hated it, Mum.'

'Oh, my darling, why didn't you tell me sooner?' She was genuinely surprised. 'I thought you were doing very well at school.'

For the first time in my life, I had done well in my studies, and had even managed to cross some small sections of the cultural gap dividing me from my classmates. They told me they'd decided I wasn't as bad as I first looked. I had absorbed some of their ways. I learnt to spin my pen in class, and pass notes on little bits of paper folded into delicate origami shapes. Still, all I wanted to do was leave. I had packed my Year 11 life into two boxes and put them in the school's storeroom, hoping never to see them again.

'I hated it, Mum. I won't go back, no matter what.'

'Alright, my darling,' she said, only slightly miffed. 'We can talk about this later.'

The minute we got home, I rushed to my room and called Ryan. He was waiting for my call, ready to tell me all the latest developments.

'I'm going to a different youth group now! You have got to come with me.'

I allowed myself to be happy to hear his voice; I allowed myself to feel the joy of being at home. I thought it would be okay to engage in life in Hong Kong a bit, even though I didn't know how long I would be there. I told him about what had happened that night with the shooting star. I told him I knew that God was real, but that I still didn't want to be part of the church.

'I reckon Christians still suck.'

'This is a really big deal,' said Ryan. 'No, it's a really, really big deal. You got saved! Really saved! I've been praying for you. Meet me tomorrow outside McD's at Pacific Place and I'll take you to SNA. I think you'll really like it. It's cool.'

. . .

SNA, SATURDAY NIGHT Alive, was held weekly in the basement of the English-speaking Methodist church in Wanchai, just down the road from Island School, my old secondary school. Ryan walked me into the basement room, proud to be seen bringing a friend to church—a practice always encouraged by youth leaders (that is, until good young men walk in with bad young girls).

We walked in, and a couple of the youth leaders looked up. I was ready for the pending disapproval of any adult I met; they always seemed to know the truth about me. This time, however, it appeared I was welcome; and, as it happened, I was not the worst sinner in the room by a long shot. Still, Ryan was under strict instruction to leave me in the care of the girls and not to date me. Not a problem for either of us—we were just friends.

SNA meetings consisted of a set of worship songs led by someone singing into a mic and playing an acoustic guitar. Worship was followed by announcements, then a Bible-based message from one of the leaders, and then there was 'ministry time', where we would be asked to pray for one another's needs. After that there was 'hang out time', which usually involved sitting on the floor outside the British fish and chips restaurant, Harry Ramsden's, down on Queens Road East.

The youth group was founded and led by an American guy called Jym. He was that spitting image of MacGyver I had met at Repulse Bay. I breathed a sigh of relief when I realised he did not remember me from a little over a year before. He earned instant credibility with all the teens on account of his previous job: Jym was the former drummer of City Beat, a *gweilo* rock band who sang in perfect Cantonese.

The youth leader in charge of the music was the Korean-Filipino guy from the beach, an ex-triad member called Carlos, who also did not remember me. He had a huge tattoo of a topless woman on his arm. The question he was often asked by the precocious teenagers was why he didn't have a shirt tattooed onto her after he became a Christian.

'God accepts me just the way I am,' was his standard response.

Carlos had a singing voice that cried, melting our hearts and giving even the most image-conscious teenager permission to sob like a repentant sinner. Wads of wet tissue paper lined the wooden parquet floor at SNA when Carlos led worship. Something in the music touched the Something in our souls that no words could ever reach.

'I didn't do so well in school,' said Carlos, when the singing was done, and it was time for us to 'listen up'. 'But one thing I know for sure, is that I've tried things my own way. I lived what I thought was the tough life, the hardcore life—drugs, sex, rock and roll and all that. I tried everything, but none of it brought me anything but trouble. None of it did a single good thing in my life. You know what I did with the Bible someone gave me in prison? I smoked it. That was who I was. But then I tried Jesus. I found out that Jesus' love is the most radical thing out there, and that surrendering myself at the foot of his cross was the most radical thing I could ever do with my life, man.'

I sat, crossed-legged on the floor, stunned and in awe of what I was hearing, as if for the first time. *You can be into Jesus and still be cool.*

Daughin was another of the leaders on the SNA team. He had been a helper at St. Stephens, Jackie Pullinger's drug rehabilitation ministry, where Carlos had been a 'brother', the same one that Amy had volunteered at all those years ago. Daughin was an American-Chinese Eurasian. His parents had been drug dealers and were responsible for giving him a Hindu name on a whim.

'Spell it,' he demanded, after I told him my name was Jacinta.

'Well, how do you spell *your* name?' I tried to act unfazed.

'It's D-A-U-G-H-I-N. You say it *dog-in*. Welcome to SNA; go hang out with the girls.'

Daughin had an in-your-face style. There was no hiding from

him. He was direct and saw no reason ever to soften his gospel-fuelled blows of truth. No subject was out of bounds with Daughin: not sex, pornography, masturbation, addiction, stealing, cheating, jealousy, or insecurity. He kept no secrets from us, and demanded we return the favour.

His approach was strangely effective with my peers and me. Daughin was engaged to Priscilla, a Swedish beauty. Priscilla was a missionary kid who had grown up in Pakistan. She came to Hong Kong after graduation to smuggle the good news into China wearing a long skirt with deep, Bible-width pockets sewn into the lining. She stood tall and slim, with huge blue eyes and blonde hair down past her waist. She was beautiful and friendly, and brave enough to love a character as complicated as Daughin. All this made her the ultimate role model, capturing the attention of every teenaged girl in the youth group. We all wanted to be like her.

Two other new friends at SNA were Nic and Ben, Chinese-Malaysian brothers who had graduated from the French school and were now home for the holidays. They were at university in Melbourne and knew the plight of an overseas student all too well. They played in a band called Punkture and were friends with someone whose dad owned a record label. Ben was a skater with pants bigger and slung lower than the laws of physics could explain. Nic was the same, only with an old-skool punk mohawk to boot.

I fell in love with all of them instantly. The kids who made up SNA were a motley crew. The group was a like a Benetton poster, or a UN meeting of the teenaged social tribes: punk rock skater kids, nerds, drama geeks, dropouts, homeschooled randoms and athletes. Within these genres were representatives from the French, English,

American, and German international schools, and even a few from local schools.

The kids who found themselves at home in SNA were often the ones who struggled to fit in at their schools. Little effort was needed to maintain harmony within the youth group. The leaders kept us busy dealing with the deepest issues of our souls, teaching us about God and community, hosting visits from the 'brothers' from St Stephen's, or serving the poor in Hong Kong. We went overseas on mission trips to places like Manila's Smokey Mountain to serve the homeless scavengers who lived on the decomposing rubbish heaps, or Thailand to perform evangelistic dramas and maybe even minister to lady-boys.

I am pretty sure that a few of us weren't genuinely interested in God, but stuck around just for the camaraderie of it all. We were all misfits living on the melting icecap that was colonial Hong Kong, and because of this there was a strangely tangible sense that we were living in our glory days. This sentiment was heightened for the likes of those of us who were only home in Hong Kong for the holidays. Our days were literally numbered and, once gone, we knew we'd have nothing but memories to see us through the year.

. . .

That first day, when I showed up in the basement of the English-speaking Methodist church, I was confronted with my past. There, apprenticing under Carlos in the art of worship leading, was Tom Read from Island School. I don't remember ever saying more than three words to him during our time at school because we ran in such different crowds. He was popular. I was not. He was the captain of the volleyball team. I was the weird girl with tattoos. But here, at SNA, with the playing field levelled, we took the chance to reacquaint.

'Jacinta Sweeting…' He spoke the official Hong Kong international-kid accent that is no accent, and all accents, depending on whoever you were talking to. When two international kids speak to each other, the tone straddles the line between question and statement, ending each phrase with an upward emphasis.

'You are the last person I would expect to see here.'

He had a point.

Tom came from a Christian home, and had been in Hong Kong since he was six. He was blessed with British parents who did not force their way when it came to faith. He had nothing to rebel against. He had done his share of partying and dating, but he told me he was tired of the school scene; it was superficial. He had begun to turn down invitations from the cool crowd, and he was already on the receiving end of the stigma that is part and parcel for an openly Christian teenager.

Island School was a bitchy scene. Tall Poppy Syndrome did not discriminate between gender or social tribe. Anyone who dared step outside the boundaries set by the Lead Bitches was fair game. I had never succeeded in high school politics, but Tom had. He had done pretty well, but his conscious decision to step away from the school crowd did not make sense to most people. The Island School Skaters caught wind of the fact that Tom and some of the SNA guys had electric guitars and skateboards. The SNA guys were mockingly dubbed *The Brotherhood of Righteous Skaters*. They all actually loved this, and took it as evidence that they were making some sort of impact. We all embraced the title with glee, even going so far as to have silver dog tags engraved and T-shirts printed with BORS across the front.

. . .

AUSTRALIAN SUMMER COULDN'T last forever. The start of my final year of high school loomed in the distance, and I realised my whirlwind romance with SNA was nearly at an end. I could not bear the thought of returning to Perth. Fortunately, Mum had been very cooperative, agreeing to a compromise: Melbourne.

She had studied at Melbourne Ladies College and had fond memories of her time there. She kept in touch with her school friends, and knew one of them would make an excellent guardian for me if she could get me a place in the school. MLC was full that year, but another friend put us in touch with Melbourne Girls' Grammar School, an equally prestigious, traditional Anglican school. Plans were made, money was paid and soon it was time to pack my life back into a suitcase—only, this time I went joyfully, knowing a substantial slice of SNA—Ben and Nic—would be there to meet me when I arrived in Melbourne.

Before I could connect with my SNA friends, I had to settle into my new boarding school. MGGS could not have been more unlike Beaufort College. After leaving my things in my room, I was given a tour of the boarding house and a chance to meet some of the boarders.

'This is Webby, Pru, Chez, Mon, Ceels and Al,' said Suzie, the head boarder, as she showed me around.

'G'day, Jaceentah,' said every girl I met, friendly and easygoing.

Many of the borders were country girls whose families lived very far away.

'And this, is the Breville,' said Suzie. She was showing me a kitchen appliance that looked like a flat waffle iron sitting next to some bread, cheese and Vegemite. 'You can have one of these any time you are hungry, and later we'll teach you how to do the Tim Tam Toke.'

. . .

Chapel is a common feature of Anglican school life. We had mid-week chapel at school, and us boarders also had to attend weekend chapel. I liked chapel, even though it was not cool like SNA; there were no baggy jeans or electric guitars. It was church, but church with a bit of dignity, without anyone being on my case. We just sang songs, listened to some Bible readings and went on our way. I was amazed as I watched the blonde schoolgirls belt out the hymns, and assumed this meant that they were as passionate about Jesus as the SNAers were.

'Nah, we just always sing like this, Juzzy,' Al explained. 'It doesn't mean anything.'

'Oh,' I said. 'Can you please not call me Juzzy?'

The vice-head had told the school Chaplin that I was serious about my faith and, as a result, I was invited to speak in chapel on two occasions. I remember preparing and delivering a five-minute message about why we should all pray.

'Nice speech,' said my schoolmates as they left the room.

I watched as they walked out, and became acutely aware of

yet another cultural chasm threatening to swallow me whole if I attempted to cross it with anything less than my best effort. I did not have the strength. I was mere months away from the end of year 12, but it was time for another move.

Perhaps I could go to dance school, I thought. Ballet was something I had always loved. Hong Kong didn't have what I would call a ballet boarding school—something I wasn't entirely sure existed anywhere in the world, but must have read about in a children's book at some point. It sounded heavenly—a school where work meant dancing. You danced and ate healthy food, and then slept deeply to rest your weary muscles so you could do it all again the next day.

I had passed an academy of performing arts on my way into Melbourne's city centre by tram, and later found the telephone number in the yellow pages. I made a secret trip to the phone box outside the school to avoid having to tell anyone what I was hoping to do. I phoned the academy and said I was interested in being a dancer.

As soon as the words left my lips, waves of self-consciousness and inadequacy broke over me. The woman on the other end of the line was saying helpful things, like how wonderful that I had called, and she would need me to come in to get some more information, but I was no longer listening. All I could hear was the shameful lapping of that tide: *Stupid idiot, what the hell are you doing?* I hung up the phone and pretended the incident had never happened.

. . .

Living in the boarding house limited my access to Nic and Ben, so after a quick phone call to Mum, then another to the principal, I was permitted to move into my own one-bedroom flat, two tram rides away from school, two blocks away from Melbourne Uni, and one block from my SNA brothers. Mum sent money for furniture, which I bought, and soon after had to sell again due my lack of budgeting skills.

With only four months left of school to complete, I lived in an empty apartment with only a desk at which to do my homework, a pillow and two duvets: one to sleep on top of, one underneath. I quickly learnt the cheapest foods to eat: every morning I had porridge oats cooked in water with a sprinkling of sugar. I had no fridge for storing milk. For lunch, I ate a Breville toasted sandwich from the Year 12 common room, and on the way home I bought the smallest possible amount of bak choi from Victoria Market to eat with white rice and oyster sauce for dinner. Mum insisted we speak on the phone every single day. At the age of sixteen, she trusted me enough to live alone in another country, but not enough to make it through the day without speaking to her.

'I have some exciting news,' she said one day. 'I'm coming to visit you!'

'Oh ... great, Mum ....' I hadn't expected this. I didn't have so much as a spare cup for her to drink from.

I decided the best plan of action would be to wait until I met her at the airport before explaining what the sleeping arrangements would be.

'You mean, you don't have any furniture at all?' She was delighted and intrigued.

‘Well, I have a desk.’

‘I was wondering why you sounded a bit strange when I told you I was coming. This week will be fun. We can pretend we are camping in the woods! What a clever little thing you are! Just wait until your father hears about this! A clever little Itch indeed.’

Here was something I had needed to discuss with her. ‘Mum, I want you to stop saying we are witches.’

‘But we *are* witches. I am a witch and you are a little Itch.’ She seemed almost offended that I had even questioned this fact.

‘It was funny, or cute, when I was a kid, I guess,’ I said. ‘But I’m not a kid anymore, and I want you to stop saying it.’

‘Oh darling, what are you getting in a knot over this for? You should be very grateful for being an Itch—it’s not something people just get to choose, you know. You were born with it. It means you are special.’

‘Mum, I’m serious. I’m a Christian now and I don’t want you to say we are witches. In fact, I want you to say you are not a witch. I want you to say you made it all up. You don’t cast spells on people. You don’t practise the dark arts. You aren’t evil. Do you know how freaked out my church leaders got when I told them my mother is a witch? There’s nothing good about being special; it’s dumb. I want us to be normal!’ I was getting upset and I could see she was holding back a fit of giggles.

She took in a breath and tried to compose herself. ‘Now listen, Lou Lou. There’s more to being a witch than magic potions and spells. That’s the stuff of children’s books. I’m not saying I wear a pointy black hat and have a wart on my nose!’ She took a moment to let out a laugh, and then tried to look serious again and went on. ‘But we are very powerful, my darling, and we do have magic. There's just so much more to this world than you could even imagine, more than those Christians know about ... I know this because I am a Christian, too, among other things ... There are many paths, my baby.'

'Oh, you're a Christian, are you?!' Now I was mad. More than anything in the world, I wanted her to be a Christian, for her to be one of the normal ladies at church who brought food to potlucks and carried a fat Bible in a handmade quilted Bible cover with handles. And I wanted to feel the assurance that she would be going to heaven when she died. I had believed that, if I could just trick her into saying the magic words of the Sinner's Prayer, then it would be a done deal. But even though she had willingly obliged all of my church-related demands, her behaviour and her refusal to renounce all other spiritual affiliations were a big problem. I looked at her. I looked at the women I saw in church, and back again, and just knew I did not have a match.

'Mum, you can't be a Christian and also be a witch! You have to say you aren't a witch!' I couldn't believe the words that were coming out of my mouth. I couldn't believe this was a real conversation.

'You need to be more open-minded, Jacinta Louise,' said Mum. 'If it makes you feel any better, I will say I am a Christian witch—I'm a white witch who has a friend in Jesus, alright? Are you happy with that? Is that good enough for you? You Christians are all so narrow-minded, but Mummy will say what you want because I love you. So? Are you happy now?'

I was not the slightest bit happy now, but I knew that once she started talking about open-mindedness, all hope of a meaningful discussion was lost. I didn't actually want a meaningful discussion.

I just wanted my mother to renounce witchcraft.

. . .

We spent the week sleeping together between my two duvets, snuggled in just like when I was a child. She picked me up after school and took me to the cafés I had spent the year resenting—I never had any money, so I never let myself even look into their windows. She took me right in and bought me an expensive sandwich with a side of chips every day of her stay. That week of being with Mum was like the coming true of a dream I hadn't allowed myself to dream during my two years of homesickness. But the dream week ended and Mum left. It didn't occur to me to ask her for some more money. I was so ashamed of the fact I had failed to manage things myself, too proud to explore the possibility of coming home, and too close to the end of the year for it to be worthwhile, anyway. It hadn't occurred to her that I needed anything but a week's worth of sandwiches and a good pep talk. As I said goodbye, I took in a deep breath. I needed it. I would not allow myself to really exhale again until the school year was over.

I saw Ben after school almost every day of the week, doing my very best to hide my poverty. We went skateboarding or just wandered around the city, talking about our love for Hong Kong and how much we missed SNA. We doodled and drew designs for an imaginary skate brand into a lined notebook we called the Tag Book, which we occasionally posted to Tom for his contributions.

I felt cooler just having met Nic and Ben; they were two surrogate brothers unaware of the void they filled in my heart. Knowing we were spending the year in Melbourne together was strength enough for me to make it through another year away from home. I loved everything SNA had added to my life, yet it all felt too good to be true and I knew that it would just be a matter of time before I screwed it all up.

I still wanted to smoke. Part of me still wanted to party, but I didn't know the right sort of people in Melbourne. I went to the petrol station near my flat and bought myself a pack of cigarettes. After I said goodbye to Ben for the day, and had made sure he was well on his way home, I crouched in the corner of my balcony and smoked.

Serious Christians didn't smoke. I knew this. Ben and Nic were totally straight-edge—drug-free in every way. I was sure I would be struck off their list of approved people the second they found me out. But I just could not stop. I was living a double life and hating it. It was cool to have been a smoker, or drug addict, or worse, but it was not cool to continue to mess with the dark side once you'd made your stand. I had made my stand, but somehow, I still wanted to smoke. I didn't want them to know I had not had a miraculous conversion—the sort that should have left me totally devoid of the desire to do any wrong. So, I hid. I hid and I smoked, and I brushed my teeth and sprayed air freshener, and I continued to do this for some time.

Nic was heavily involved in his university, and often off doing cool stuff like being the DJ on the punk rock hour of campus radio. Ben and Nic were connected with the members of a famous Christian death metal band called Mortification—and, with them, were involved in a small Bible study, called Metal Kingdom. I was invited to go along from time to time. We took the train from Flinders Street Station to a suburb called Yarraville, and met in a converted garage, which was also Phil, the drummer's, bedroom.

I was a sixteen-year-old schoolgirl from Hong Kong, amongst a group of metal/punk/bogan men, each a perfect gentleman, each another big brother for me. There, I felt more at home than I ever had in Perth or my Anglican boarding school. We read the Nicene Creed together and often prayed for Steve, Mortification's lead singer, whom I never met. He was battling cancer and needed much prayer.

Mortification, therefore, was on hold. Phil, Ben, Nic and a punk called Craig formed a new band: a straight-edge hardcore band called Callous, and I was the self-appointed number one fan, despite the fact that I was too young to get into any of their shows.

During the school week, I listened to mix tapes that Ryan and Tom had made in Hong Kong and sent to me via snail mail. Tom and I had become pen pals. His letters were fast becoming a weekly highlight for which I would rush home from school. I couldn't wait to get back to Hong Kong, to get back to SNA and to spend more time with Tom. Melbourne was more fun than Perth had been, but I still felt very much like an unwelcome intruder. This was not helped by the political climate at the time. Australia was home to a rapidly increasing number of immigrants from all around Asia, and some Australians were not happy about it. Pauline Hanson, a politician speaking out against immigration, was gaining popularity, and to me it felt like everyone was on her side.

'Are you Chinese?' A hobo on Swanston Street squinted to get a better look at me after I put a coin in his hand.

I didn't respond.

'You are! I don't want your money—GO HOME!' He threw the coin back at me.

I'd gladly go home right now if I could, don't you worry about that.

Finally, my dream of finishing school came true and I found myself back in Hong Kong again.

9

DUE TO OUR different school systems, I graduated half a year before Tom. I returned to Hong Kong just as he was completing his A levels. We remained close friends for a couple of months after I got home. At the age of seventeen, neither of us knew what to do with a relationship like the one we had established by post. We hung out in groups with our SNA friends, and then rushed home to talk for hours on the telephone. We were under the ever-watchful eye of Daughin, who, at that point, was living with Tom's family.

Tom was an avid music fan and, like many of the other boys at SNA, was doing his best to keep up with what was happening in the Christian music world—this was in Hong Kong in 1996, a time before MySpace, YouTube or iTunes, before email and the internet had even become a mainstay in the average household.

Tom had a crumpled-up copy of a product catalogue from an alternative Christian record label called Tooth & Nail. He made a long-distance phone call to place an order for a couple of CDs and T-shirts that would take over a month to arrive in the post. When they were finally delivered, he rushed to my house to give me a girl-sized band shirt of MxPx, the pop punk band that was our current favourite. Their album was called 'Teenage Politics', and their lyrics—*legalistic people suck / legalism makes me sick / I wonder what makes them tick*—became a running theme in many of our late-night phone conversations.

We both loved God, but did not want to slot ourselves into conservative Evangelical Christian culture. We thought faith should be more than external appearances. But, more than anything, we wanted to make sure we were both on the same wavelength. Alternative band shirts were not easy to come by in Hong Kong in the 1990s. This had to be love. A year earlier, Tom had travelled all the way to America with his friend, Andrew, to attend a Christian music festival called Cornerstone. He had found a new scene that excited him much more than being in the popular crowd at Island School, and he was doing all he could to keep up with it. We talked often about the possibility of going to the Cornerstone festival together. His parents agreed to send him again as a reward for completing secondary school, so I decided to get a job at a coffee shop—partly to save up the money for my ticket, but mostly to fill the time as I waited for my best friend to graduate.

When I mentioned to Tom that I had liked the idea of being a backing singer, he arranged straight away for me to join the SNA worship team. I did not know the first thing about singing harmonies, so I mouthed my way through worship sets week after week. The music was always so loud, that I figured it made no difference to anyone—and it didn't, until the day we were presented with a guest speaker who had The Gift of Prophesy.

SNA meetings were facilitated by SNA leaders for the most part, but every so often a visitor was invited to preach. We rarely knew anything about who they were, but this one guy, called Prophet Bob was an American man in his fifties, and introduced as someone who was not going to preach, but instead would speak prophesies over the group as we worshipped. This was something Daughin and Carlos had prepared us for. They told us it was good for Christians to try to use the gifts God had given them to encourage the church. However, as the church, it would be our job to test everything that anyone ever said to us against what was written in the Bible, that cults start because people believe false prophesies and fail to test what people say.

So, we, the worship team, stood up at the front and made music. During quieter instrumental moments, the Prophet would say things like, 'The Lord is pleased with your worship!' or, 'God is looking for a generation of youth to lift up holy hands and make a difference in this world!'

Albeit a little weird, and a lot showy, the guy seemed harmless enough. He was not pushing people, like the minister back in Perth had done, and he wasn't telling anyone that they were going to burn in hell. But then, to my horror, he started turning to individuals and saying personal things directly to them.

'God knows your heart is broken for the lost,' he said to one person. 'He has a special calling on your life! Work that only you can do!' And to another, 'God knows your weakness. He sees you when you fall, each and every time, and he wants you to know that he shall be your strength!'

By now, I was feeling a combination of terror and jealousy. I did not want him to say anything to me in front of my friends, but I also desperately wanted to know if God had anything to say to me in front of my friends. Since I was up at the front in the worship team, though, I figured it was unlikely he would.

'God is your true father,' he declared over a girl in the back corner, who was blubbing into both of her hands, snot dripping through. 'Where your earthly father has failed you, your heavenly father will never fail. He loves you with an everlasting love, and he will never leave you nor forsake you!'

Fair enough, I thought, *there's nothing wrong with that. I don't think I'm in a cult. He's not saying anything wrong. We'll go away and test everything later.*

I closed my eyes and tried to focus on the music and my lip-syncing, and I was almost lost in a moment when I sensed someone in front of me. I opened my eyes just in time to see the Prophet, eyes locked on target, taking the final three steps needed to get into my personal space.

'You!' he boomed, and pointed at my heart. For a fraction of a second, I was sure he was pointing at the microphone I was fake-singing into, and feared he was about to blow my cover, but I was wrong.

'God says, "You are a dancer!"'

With no idea how to respond to this statement, I held eye contact because my mother taught me that eye contact equals strength. If I closed my eyes and assumed the pray-for-me position, he was bound to pray for me, so I held my eye contact. And, to my relief, he moved on to the next person.

'What do you make of your prophesy?' asked my friend, Madeleine, as we sat outside Harry Ramsden's after SNA had finished.

'I don't know,' I said. 'I guess he was right in that I used to take ballet, but it's a bit random, don't you think?'

'You'll need to pray about it,' she said. This was both the correct answer to any question, and the quickest way out of a conversation that wasn't going anywhere anyway. All I wanted was to belong with this new group of Christian friends, not to be singled out, and not to be called away.

. . .

It was February, and I came home from work one day to find a hand-delivered letter from Tom in my mailbox saying he missed writing me letters, but reiterating how pleased he was that I was now home. We were both aware that Valentine's Day was approaching, and I was feeling threatened by the obvious interest another friend was showing in Tom. The ball was in my court. I stole a bottle of port from my parents' collection, downed half of it, said a prayer, picked up the phone and dialled his number.

We talked as usual, both knowing someone needed to say something. We were both terrified of getting it wrong. Neither of us wanted to make a move that could potentially destroy our friendship. Tom was the best friend I had ever known. After the first hour or so of chit-chat, I guzzled some more port.

'Tom ... I need to say something ....'

'Yes?'

There was an uncomfortable and awkwardly long silence.

'... I think, I could, maybe, like you ...?'

Pause.

I quietly gulped down more port.

Tom finally spoke up. 'Well ... I know I like you. Let's hang out, just you and me.'

'Okay. Deal. Yup. Got to go. Bye.'

. . .

WE HAD OUR first date at Dan Ryan's, Hong Kong's family restaurant most loved by our generation. It was Valentine's Day, 1997. After eating our potato skins, cups of chilli and World's Smallest Sundaes, we walked around Hong Kong Park, holding hands. After our first kiss at the top of the stairs by the butterfly house, it was official: we were boyfriend and girlfriend.

We walked about in a giddy dream for a month or so, hanging out with the crowd from SNA, then ending the night alone, sitting on a bench behind a pillar on HKU's campus—our favourite rendezvous—a five-minute walk from my house, and ten minutes from his. We drank coffee from the vending machine around the corner and looked over the university's fish pond, talking about music, church, fashion, tattoos, school, friends, and our dreams for the future. We wanted to live creative lives, to be in Hong Kong and to put our faith first, happily ever after.

Yet, at the end of our first month of dating, we began to quarrel. I wanted more time alone with my new boyfriend, but Tom said I was losing my sociable side, the part of me he loved the most. We fought and made up often, all the while continuing toward our goal of travelling together to the music festival in the US. We had six months before a serious decision had to be made. We had both approached our relationship having previously come to the conclusion that dating was pointless unless there was even a remote possibility it would end in marriage. I was due to start my university studies in Melbourne, and Tom would be studying in England—this, according to his parents, was non-negotiable.

'We could make it through three years long distance,' said I, optimistic and naïve.

Tom nipped this idea in the bud. I called for a discussion with my parents and, less than thirty minutes later, was granted their blessing to begin the process of applying to universities in England. I had not visited England in three long years. My experience in Australia had voided me of all desire for adventure. I did not want to have to meet another group of friends. I did not want to explore my way around another new city. I did not want to start all over again. The only way to minimise the hassle attached to another international move was to study in Oxford. At least there I had some family history and, therefore, some tiny right to exist.

. . .

It was 1997, and the handover date was fast approaching. Britain was going to give Hong Kong back to China. Some deal had been made by people we never knew, and the consequences of this deal would ripple through our futures in ways no one could predict. We had been a British colony for over 150 years and, speculation about communism and revolution aside, nobody really knew what was going to happen once we were handed back. All I knew was that I wanted to go to the Unity Rave, a huge dance party that was happening in the lead up. I wanted Tom to come, too. I secretly hoped I could find some speed and that Tom would want to try some with me.

Most of my old friends, the non-church-going ones, had left Hong Kong by this point, but when Mary or Tina were back on visits, I felt a tension between my old and new identities. I loved my old friends and wanted to spend time with them, but when I was with them, we tended to get into the exact things the youth group existed to prevent us from getting into: drinking, smoking, partying, being interested in anything beyond church life. My two social groups seemed incompatible and I dealt with this by switching loyalties depending on who I was with. But Evangelical Christian culture has a tendency to set itself against anything 'other', and to demand your All-with-a-capital-A. In hindsight I think it very unreasonable, but at the time I was desperate to belong somewhere, and to be assured I had made the right choice. The church offered me this, so I labelled my old friends and activities 'bad' and began a very ungracious process of forgetting them.

Tom was the one person who understood this tension and did not seem to judge me for it. We went to the rave together. We danced, we drank, we did not take any drugs, and then we came home. Tom was going to sleep on a mattress on my bedroom floor. Halfway through the night, I joined him on the mattress. We loved each other, as much as teenagers knew how. My parents would not have cared if we were having sex, since they were open-minded to the point of asking me to consider experimenting more before settling down with one boy.

At the forefront of our minds that night, however, was the gnawing knowledge that even just sleeping on the same mattress together was enough to warrant what the SNA leaders affectionately termed a 'butt kicking'. Not that anyone had laid down the law in so many words, exactly. Our church was a hodgepodge of Christian styles, with members from all over the world representing various denominations and traditions.

It was not one of those churches you hear about, rigid and in the express business of turning out holy rollers. It was cutting-edge experimental, contemporary in musical style and liberal in its welcome of oddballs and moody teenagers with tattoos. At our church the odd profanity was issued from the pulpit, all in the name of adding a bit of oomph to the preacher's point. I was in no way part of a typical religious institution. The level of overt Thou shalt not ... was negligible.

At the youth group, when it came to sex, any appeal regarding what we should, or should not be doing with, or to, our bodies was made on a personal level, peer to peer. It was an appeal to our better nature and understanding of God's best plan for life on Earth, a plan that involved a few guidelines that were ultimately put there for our own benefit, motivated by the love of a father for his children.

'I have no right to tell you what to do,' Joe Leader, or Visiting Speaker, would say, 'but I can tell you my own story ....' These stories always went one of two ways. It was either, 'I tried things my way, and regret it, so now want to spare you learning the hard way,' or, 'It was really hard, but by God's grace I managed to do things God's way, and I'm so glad that I did.'

A friend reported back to me on a visit the youth group had had from a visiting speaker during term time, while I was in Australia.

'She had all us girls in the little room, and the boys went to some other place. She cracked two eggs into a glass bowl and mixed them up, and said that's what happens to two souls when you have sex.

Try to separate them again if you can.'

This was probably why we struggled. No one ever held a gun to us, assigned us chastity belts, or so much as tapped us over the head with a Bible. The facts were simply presented, and we readily accepted the logic of not sleeping around. Scrambled eggs were not sexy. But, for two teenagers in love, the reality of this was not easy at all, so we fought not only our carnal desires, but with them a permanently engorged sense of guilt.

It was the leaders' ongoing job to steer us all in the direction of purity.

'The Bible says sex is a gift from God, to be enjoyed within marriage,' said one. 'If you choose impatience, don't be surprised if there's heartache. It's not because God's punishing you—he's said not to do it because he wants to spare you the pain that is the natural consequence of offering yourself to anyone who isn't committed to you. But, if you choose to wait, you get to experience sex as the Creator intended it.'

Thus, wedding night sex, in the minds of many of us teens, was built up to become an epoch-making experience, unfathomable and beyond the realm of our immature understanding of pleasure; to be striven for, and earned, only by the pure of heart. A popular book at the time had encouraged many of the kids at SNA to 'kiss dating goodbye'. However, those of us like Tom and me, who were already dating, made a gesture of our devotion to God and his plans by agreeing to be kept accountable by the leaders. Daughin and Priscilla spent extra time and energy on us, coaching us through tiffs and asking us starkly direct questions at regular intervals. More often than not, an aforementioned butt-kicking was needed: they'd guide us through a time of confession, repentance and re-dedication for the minor slips that happened, also at regular intervals.

'Why didn't you tell them to mind their own business?' someone would ask me, two decades down the road.

It was a question I had never even considered. Accountability and full disclosure were the culture of a club I was set on belonging to. The other members were good fun value in teenage terms, but the club itself came with rules, a strong sense of yes and no, right and wrong, and I now suspect that this was what I kept going back for more of.

I fancied my boyfriend, but I had also begun to fancy the idea of one day being a leader, holding a microphone at the front of a room full of young girls, kicking my own share of butts, talking with thinly veiled pride about how I overcame my flesh and earned my pure white wedding dress. Maybe even cracking a couple of eggs into a bowl of my own. As far as sexual purity went, the pros outweighed the cons, so I kept my pants on. Anyway, from what my more experienced friends had told me, it just wasn't worth it.

. . .

ON 1 JULY 1997, we gathered in Tom's living room with friends to watch the handover ceremony on TV. Tom's house was a common gathering place for the BORS. His parents welcomed the entire youth group into their homely home.

His father, Tony, a tall and quiet Englishman with white hair chuckled, never grumbled if he came home and found over a dozen teenagers in his living room. He had had a long career as an engineer, but would eventually go into ministry. Drusilla, Tom's mother, managed the household with great care. She had what was known in Christian circles as The Gift of Hospitality. Whenever we kids arrived at the Read household, a spread of chips, dips, crudités, fun-sized chocolate bars, fizzy drinks and disposable napkins appeared within seconds. I watched in wonder as the whole thing unfolded, hoping, like a Dickensian orphan, that I would be invited to the table.

I desperately wanted in on Tom's family. They looked like my idea of what a family was meant to be: proper, stable, normal. But I was not a suitable match, having neither the confidence nor training in how to interact with a family like the Reads. I had no idea what they thought of me, or even if they thought of me at all: did they know I was madly and jealously in love with Tom, or was I just one of his many SNA friends in their eyes?

We all sat together on the living room floor that day. Our schoolmate, Alice, cried as she stood on deck of the *HMY Britannia* with her father (Hong Kong's last governor, Chris Patten) and Prince Charles, as they waved goodbye and set sail. I was glad to see her go. There was one less girl I had to worry about losing Tom to.

Later that night, our parents dropped us off at Kai Tak Airport, and Tom and I boarded our flight to Chicago. The heavens had opened and thunderous rains pummelled the plane. We held hands during take-off and did not let go. The seatbelt sign stayed on for over an hour as our plane flew through the black rainstorm and between blinding bolts of lightning. We leant into each other and prayed for the plane to carry us safely through the storm, so that, together, we could partake in the most rocking music festival of our young lives.

. . .

I HAD A SERVING of American-flavoured cultural shock when I went for my first shower at the festival campsite. I was confronted by a communal arrangement and the most gargantuan naked bodies I had ever had the misfortune to lay eyes on. I tried to look away, but, in each direction I turned, I was met by a bigger set of boobs. For the first time in my life, I felt tiny. How I wished Mary or Amy had been with me there to marvel at this landscape of mountainous nakedness—but I was alone in the female shower room and too terrified to stand my ground.

I retreated quickly and resolved to go for as long as I could without washing. In the end, I resorted to showering during the main stage shows when the shower room was empty.

I was the only girl in our group of friends and Tom wanted some space. He and the guys would go off to see their favourite bands and leave me behind. I sulked for one day and then decided not to let it ruin my time. I had worked hard to earn the money to travel all the way to Cornerstone, and I was determined to enjoy myself. The boys went to see bands like Plankeye, Starflyer 59 and Fold Zandura, while I took in Out of Eden solo, and then the highlight of my trip, Joy Electric. I sheepishly entered the dark dance tent, cried silently and told God how rejected and alone I always felt. I appreciated the darkness of the tent and decided to stay a while longer. I conjured an imaginary friend called God who turned and asked me if I cared to have this dance. I accepted his offer and we danced the rest of the night away in blissful defiance.

The festival was a gathering for alternative Christians in the middle of a field in the countryside of Illinois, but I felt like a small-town girl going to the big city for the first time. The assortment of people was a feast for the eyes. It was alternative church to the extreme. For an insider, it made perfect sense. What could be more alternative/hardcore/rock and roll than saying no to sex and drugs, and living instead for Jesus? The most extreme even threw in a vegan diet for good measure.

It was all about swimming against the flow, a saying of *up yours* to the devil, and *yes* and *amen* to the Lord. Punk rockers—old skool (tight jeans) and new (baggy)—joined with goths, metalheads, rappers, big band brass players, nerds and nobodies, to make music all to the glory of our God. It was like SNA but on a much bigger, much cooler scale. Post-cool maybe. At this point, it all got quite confusing.

I wore a T-shirt, bought from Mong Kok market, with an ironic glittery red Chinese communist star and '1 July 1997' printed on it.

'What's so special about the date?' asked an American guy with a shaved head and shaved eyebrows, as we lined up for a drink.

'It's the date Hong Kong stopped being a British colony and was handed back to China. It was a really big deal.'

'Oh, okay. Yah, right on.'

10

WHEN I FINALLY got to university in England, I found that Hong Kong wasn't much of a topic for conversation there, either. I had secured a university place in Melbourne, Australia, but Tom was going to England, so I had adjusted my plans. Oxford was a second home and the natural choice. Dad was delighted about my interest in returning to the British system, and told me that Oxford's polytechnic had recently upgraded its status to a full university, and he helped me with my application.

It had been several years since my last visit to England. I had been away from my family, studying in Australia and unable to take part in the yearly summer trips that had been such an important part of my childhood. Oxford was where my parents had got married and where they bought their first house together, and where I had now returned. Dad had loved his time in the university town. Every summer of our childhood, Jus and I would breathe in the crisp English air and then fall asleep in the back of the rental car on the drive from Heathrow to our England home. Mum and Dad would wake us after we had driven down through Headington, rounded St Clement's, entered Iffley Road and were finally approaching our house.

Something awesome had happened at the site, many years ago. Roger Bannister had run a mile, raised a figurative middle finger at all his naysayers, secured his place in world history, and delighted every onlooker, all in less than four minutes. The track is still there today, beside a rugby pitch, part of Oxford University's sports grounds, right beside our family home. The dreaming spires rise above the tree line in the distance. You feel dignified just looking at them.

Sometimes I would go to the window when a rugby match was in play and pretend to appreciate rugby: a little girl attempting to muzzle in on her dad and brothers' bonding time. The Three Js were part of the package of being in England. The floodlights and the sound of the spectators graced the place with energy for a night or two each week during the season.

You had to go up to the top floor in order to see over the spectator stands—our tiny little garden used to spill onto the back of the stands, until they erected the fence. They needed a way to stop us children helping ourselves to some extra space to kick a ball. I loved to find knots in the wooden fence and push them through, creating perfect little peepholes. I wanted to keep the knots—but the problem was, you had to push to get them out of their planks, and that left them on the wrong side of the fence that had been put there to stop the likes of me from trespassing. I imagined mountainous piles of them back there, along with a few of the apple cores I had chucked over the years, and some cigarette butts.

Unfortunately, the back of the stands provided nothing of interest to peep at. One day, I spooked myself at the thought of someone else's eye peeping back at me, trying to 'kiss eyes' through the hole. I spooked myself so badly that I never peeped through again.

The front and back views from our house were landscape representations of town and gown, respectively. The front looked onto Iffley Road, nearing the front end—close to the incense and fried chicken smells of Cowley Road. Outside The Fir Tree, the pub across the street, a drunken man once told me to go back to China. I went straight home and cried.

When looking out of the back window, I used to love to watch the groundsman cut the grass on his huge ride-on lawn mower, the kind that looked like a little tractor. His grandchildren used to visit on Sundays and they were allowed to run on the grass.

The old lady at No. 6 did not like us at all.

'Gypsies,' she had said to No. 4.

Mum said it was because the lady had never seen anyone string up laundry across the garden and over the balcony the way we did. Neither did the old lady like the way I squeezed through the front iron fence to get to the shop across the street, instead of walking all the way around it. She did not like that I played with the Pakistani children, whose parents owned the shop. Mum said we were all God's children, so I could play with anyone I wanted to; but we were also Chinese, so we had to be polite and respectful to our elders, 'no matter what'.

'Old biddy,' Dad said.

Our summer holidays were spent driving through the countryside and visiting our Welsh relatives. In Oxford, we often went walking through the Christchurch meadows early in the morning, ending up at the covered market, where Dad would allow us each a packet of sweets, or rejuvenation tablets, as he called them.

Every day involved an hour of summer homeschool, where we were forced to work our way through Maths and English workbooks that had been purchased at Blackwell's on the Broad. Jus and I writhed in our seats at the dining table in deep and earnest protest, begrudgingly making pencil marks on our books until the hour finally came to an end and we could go outside to play, or down to the living room to watch some British television. We savoured the clever commercial slogans and chat show catchphrases, storing them up to keep us going for the year back in Hong Kong. This was the annual rhythm of our childhood. This is what had come to an end now.

. . .

I had just made my third major move in three years, and consequently mastered the skill of shutting down my heart. I didn't consciously think of it in such dramatic terms, though; I considered it more a case of holding my breath for a year, or three. A simple biding of time. Deep breath, head down, jump through the hoops, then get the hell back to Hong Kong.

In truth, however, this couldn't be done without deactivating significant chunks of emotion. And this is what I willed. I split myself up and put some of me, Actual Me, on ice, to be thawed after graduation, and set the rest, Going Through the Motions Me, the task of showing up at class, seeing my boyfriend at the weekends, and generally just staying occupied. What I could not have known is that there are only so many times this intentional split can be made. Like the riddle about a goat, a fox and a cabbage who need to get to the opposite riverbank in a two-seater boat, or like the warning against pulling an ugly face in case the wind blows and it sticks. I had already split myself one too many times, and had done so quite a while back without even realising it.

Specific memories of childhood summers in Oxford re-emerged during my time at university. I caught a glimpse of myself, a little girl, walking with her dad in the crisp, chilled air on an early misty morning. I held hands with the phantasm of Mum, and whispered to her in our secret language—Cantonese—on the way to Tesco. I gratefully allowed my sisters, Juliette and Janine, to tuck my dress into my undies so that they could teach me to do cartwheels on the lawn. I took in the different aromas in the covered market and remembered the time my parents went to Prague and left me in Jus's care for three days. Jus, only two years older, forbade me from leaving the house, but allowed himself one trip into town each day for a pizza slice from the covered market. I felt the momentary panic triggered by the unmistakable sound of the rubbish truck outside our house—had the correct bins been put out? Every wooden pub bench, damp and smelling of beer and salt and vinegar crisps, brought back the thrill and horror of watching my brother trap wasps in an upturned pint glass, soon to be filled with second-hand cigarette smoke.

Resurfacing from a place inside where they had been buried, these memories caused me to stop and wonder. Where had they been? Why had I buried them? The past was rumbling in a shallow grave. My past, all of it—my family, our home, our city, the chaos and the happiness, all bundled together. That was all that I had. Those were the many parts of the sum that was me, my very self, whether I liked it or not. It seemed I had not liked it.

I had joined a religious club that caused me to take pride in devaluing my past. Over the years, I had systematically rejected those parts. I had boarded the plane to Perth and kissed my old life goodbye. On take-off, I had assumed that Hong Kong would slip away, like landslide mud. And it did. While the city was still technically there, the bulk of my Hong Kong, the one I grew up in, was gone. Life as I knew it was hell-bent on changing.

I'd wanted to stop it but had failed. So, on principle, anything I could not have I simply willed myself to stop wanting. I shut down sections of my heart. I cut off those longing feelings at the source and bludgeoned the very thought of the past, all of it. And then I tried to cover it up like nothing had happened.

Janine had picked me up from the airport, taken me out for lunch, and then delivered me into my new life at university, and my big brother would coach me through a three-year degree in Fine Art. Tom was going to study in London, and I had time on my hands in Oxford. I decided to enrol in some dance classes. I had always loved to dance and had missed it terribly. I drove myself to a dance shop in a little village and bought a black camisole leotard, an elastic belt, pink tights, soft shoes, hair nets and bobby pins—the Royal Academy of Dance regulation.

I brought it all home and climbed up to the loft to retrieve Mum's sewing kit. The kit and her sewing machine had been put away at the end of summer, a few years ago, after she sewed us both several new outfits from Simplicity patterns. We had shopped for fabric in the haberdashery department at Debenhams, and at home I sat behind her chair, playing on the floor, hypnotised by the thunderous cry of the machine as she worked all day and late into the nights. She had even made a soft toy rabbit for me. Oxford was the only place I saw her do anything remotely like homemaking, and this was the most domestic thing she'd ever done.

There they sat, the Singer and the sewing box, on a beam in the loft, right where they had been left. To put something down, and for it to still be right there years later, was certainly an idea to marvel at. I had the urge to explain myself to the items in the loft, to say that I had grown up, had been to Australia, joined the church, got a boyfriend, and had only just now made it back to our house—only now, I was here alone.

I took the sewing kit and my new ballet slippers to the dining table. Folding a satin heel into the sole, I marked the corners gently with a pencil, then set the shoes aside. I retrieved a disposable lighter from the kitchen drawer and brought it to the table. I unrolled the length of pink ribbon that came with the shoes and folded it in half, twice, then used scissors to cut it into quarters. I lit the cigarette lighter and brought each end of each portion of ribbon to the flame, just long enough to watch the freshly cut edges melt in surrender to the heat. Once through the fire, those ribbons would not fray.

Taking a shoe in hand, I pressed the end of a ribbon to the pencil mark and held it there with my thumb. I tied a knot and proceeded to sew the ribbons on, each stitch somehow pulling parts of me back together. When I was finished, I lifted the shoes to inspect my work. Imperfect, but good enough. I was ready to attend my first ballet lesson in five years.

. . .

The dancers one finds in a class like mine are adult-sized, or thereabouts. These dancers know, on some level at least, that they are not bound for stardom. Lucky young dancers with professional performance potential are identified and steered into appropriate channels long before they get to this size. Larger, older dancers stick with the highly demanding art of dance training, either for practical reasons like staying fit, completing the grades or gaining a teaching qualification—or for other, highly impractical reasons, but these are more difficult to convey.

There is a solemn, almost monastic ambience in a room full of amateur dancers, dedicated to training, despite lacking the promise of the tangible reward of a moment on a proper stage. There's sadness in it; perhaps we are in denial about our lack of prospects, and hold out hope that the teacher might still notice us. Or perhaps we live in completely self-effacing devotion to the art form. It would take years of grappling before I would be able to consider that, maybe, the amateur's motivation to dance is not so pathetic, or sacrificial, or pure, or noble. Maybe it's the opposite, an antithesis. Maybe we just have to do it. Maybe people like me insist on dancing because it hurts so much every time we stop.

In class I stood up straight, pulled skyward by the invisible string tied to the end of my tailbone, threaded through my spine and out the crown of my head. Remembering that a ballerina must never appear to strain, I rested two hands lightly on the barre. Drawing breath down to the back of my lungs, and my belly toward my lower back, I took in the sweet smell of ground rosin, wooden floorboards and leather: the unmistakable scent of a ballet class. It was an elixir for some deep pain I had long since learnt to live with. I would bottle that scent if I could.

Going Through the Motions Me had unwittingly discovered a portal that led to something crucial. Led back to something crucial. Something, or perhaps someone, she had almost wiped clean from existence, like a crime scene fingerprint. With two guilty hands resting ever so lightly on the barre, the feet belonging to Actual Me came out to dance.

Plié: A smooth and continuous bend of the knees. The stronger the plié, the better your elevation. Breathe. I slowly bent my knees, melting and stretching, growing taller as I lowered, then stretched to more than I had been before. *Plié, and up, plié, and up.*

Come with me, said the piano. *I will take you home. I can show you the way and we will go together. Listen, breathe. Listen, move. Something inside you knows what to do. Your muscles remember.*

Battement Tendu: to gradually stretch the working leg to the front, to the side, or the back, passing from flat through demi-pointe, to pointe with toes still touching the floor. A relatively simple-looking move, but the trick is to revel in, and even exaggerate, the friction between the ballet slipper and the floor. Like the pull-back feature of a toy car, the zoom promises to come later.

Quiet down now and listen, continued the piano. *Breathe. I am going to lead you. Let me. Let me hold you. My frame is strong and I know the way. I will contain you. You will not fly away. You are safe if you listen, if you stay inside my rhythms. I can hold you. I can lead you. My melodies will carry you. I will hold you and I will let you fly, but I will not let you fly away. Follow my lead; you will grow strong; you will find your shapes and hold them, delicate but unshakable, and I will carry you. I am going to take you home, where you have longed to be, where you belong. Listen, be quiet now. Let me lead.*

11

DAD HAD TAKEN early retirement and, while I was in my final year of university, he and Mum had moved a lifetime's worth of possessions out of the large flat, at the top of HKU's campus, and into a small house they had bought in Sai Kung. We crossed paths just as they arrived in Oxford for the summer and I set off back to Hong Kong, having completed my degree.

'We've been thinking about a name for the house,' Dad said before I left Oxford. 'I think we will call it The Jay's Nest, since all of you kids are Js and this is our new nest. For convenience we'll shorten it to The Nest.'

I went back to Hong Kong to live in The (empty) Nest. Mum had searched the length and breadth of Hong Kong, Kowloon and the New Territories in search of a home that would make sense for their retirement. The little white house was not a typical Hong Kong-style country house. Rather than the flat rooftop that most Hong Kong houses have, this house had a steep, sloping roof, overhanging the stone walls and a double-height glass front. It was a beautiful house overlooking a wild garden that had been cut from the side of the slope.

Hong Kong people are not famous for their love of nature, and people who move from the city to the country usually have their trees trimmed right back, if not removed completely, then slab over the ground in an effort to reduce the nuisance of mosquitoes. Not us. Our garden was dark, with a thick canopy of vines. The house backed onto a jungle slope, and a giant banyan tree protected the front. Just inside the gate there was a small, natural waterfall that burst its bank every time there was a red or black rainstorm. Thick moisture hung in the air, and the whole place crawled with life: huge insects mostly, with the odd snake, wild boar or occasional monkey.

Mum, addressing a lack that she alone perceived, had gathered dozens of tiny pots in which to plant fern trimmings she had taken from the garden. She arranged these three-inch ceramic pots in formation around the base of the giant banyan tree, and then on alternate steps leading from the front gate to the house. *Why?* was no longer a question I bothered to ask Mum. I accidentally kicked a couple of them over almost every time I passed by.

'We like it dark and wild, don't we?' she said, brimming with pride, not actually asking for a response. 'We like it to be an enchanted cottage in the woods, don't we? It's a perfect house for a witch and a warlock, hidden away from the world.'

Dad liked to launch into surprise history lessons, telling me about someone's first landing during one of Hong Kong's invasions, some monument, or some other historically significant fact related to Sai Kung. I have forgotten the details—not because I wasn't listening, but because of a self-fulfilling curse: whenever he sprung an informal history lesson on me, I worried I would not remember what he said. I wanted to internalise as much information as he could possibly transmit to me; so, whether it was directions to the airport, the best reasonably priced wine, or a piece of local history, I did mentally what I have done physically with almost every important thing ever entrusted to me—I carefully hid it somewhere extra safe, and immediately forgot where it was.

I expected to be alone in The Nest for the week until Cora, the new maid, returned from her holiday, but was pleased to find a pet waiting for me when I arrived. A huge, wrinkly, and very smelly dog greeted me in the garden. This gentle giant was a Sharpei and she had simply appeared one day and adopted my parents as her new owners. They named her Pulsinella and started putting food out for her. Each morning I played with the dog, and then set out from the jungle towards civilisation, to my ballet school in North Point, where I was enrolled in an intensive summer course.

. . .

TOM AND I were now 21. We were fresh graduates looking for our first jobs. All I wanted to do was dance and go to SNA. I had no professional aspirations at all; I didn't even dream of performing on stage, if I could have simply taken ballet class every day, I would have been content. I really didn't mind what I did, as long as I had my boyfriend to talk to at the end of each day and the weekends free for church. Saturdays needed to be kept totally open for SNA. This was non-negotiable. I was finally living in Hong Kong with no outbound ticket, and I felt there was lost time at SNA that needed making up.

The problem was that SNA, like everything else Hong Kong-related, had changed in my absence. The leadership team had all but completely turned over, and we, the kids, had all grown a little too old to qualify as SNA's target group. The perceived threat of 20-something guys dating under-aged girls was so pressing that the church had decided it was time to make some changes. A new group called One Eighty was established to cater to the 'young professionals', as we were now being called, and SNA would be restricted to those between the ages of 13 and 18 years. Before I'd had time to weigh up the ramifications of this, Tom and I were called into the church office for a meeting with the church elders.

'We would like you to consider staying on at SNA instead of moving up to One Eighty,' they said. 'With your experience and commitment to the vision of the youth ministry, we feel you could become part of the new leadership team.'

Tom and I couldn't believe our luck, and we agreed straight away.

I found myself a morning job as a children's creative movement teacher, got bored of it quickly, and three months later traded it for a trainee fitness instructor role at a large gym in Central. However, the commute from Sai Kung was too much for me to handle, so a couple of weeks after I started at the gym, I set out to look for a new home for myself.

I rented a little flat at the top of Old Bailey Street, Soho—or, to be more precise, I had Mum rent me a little flat. I had done the house-hunting, though. This consisted of stopping at a one-lady operation on the side of the road and telling her, in the Cantonese of a five-year-old, that I wanted to live by myself somewhere near here. She said that a foreigner had just moved out of a nice little flat up the road, and would I like to see it? I went to have a look, made a phone call to Mum, and then signed the lease.

I arrived at the flat after a short morning shift at work and jumped straight into the joyous task of setting up my independent new life. Neither Mum nor I had really stopped to consider how this newfound independence would actually work. My monthly salary was eight thousand dollars, rent was six thousand, and unlimited ballet lessons were almost two thousand. Never mind.

While out exploring my new neighbourhood, I stumbled upon a small animal adoption centre. I brought home a Chihuahua named Fatty, and called my parents to share the joyous news.

'Well, well, well, Beeps. It didn't take you very long to get yourself a pet, did it?' Dad humoured me as I expounded on the loveliness of the animal.

'I'm sure he is very lovely, Beeps,' he continued. 'At least he has a very lovely new owner. I'm not so sure about his name, though. You could come up with something more sensible. If he were a she, you could have called her Fatima, after the saint—and, of course, your Chinese kindergarten.'

Dad's knack for naming people, animals and inanimate objects had a flip side—an intolerance of silly names. Names were something that deserved a great deal of thought. The rationale behind Pulsinella's christening was 'it's a beautiful-sounding ugly name.'

I hung up the phone and experimented with calling the dog Fatimo, then ended up just calling him Puppy, despite the fact it was no improvement and he was definitely an adult. I toted the dog around under my arm in a bag for a few weeks, and then had to admit that it needed more attention than I was able to provide it with. I asked my parents if they would like to look after him for a bit, to help them with the empty nest feelings that I had convinced myself they were battling.

'Daddy's not very happy about it, Loulie,' said Mum, passing the buck. 'You know he bit Daddy the last time we dog sat.'

'It's not forever, Mum,' I lied. 'Just for a little while.'

The next time I visited my parents in Sai Kung, I found the dog snuggled on Dad's lap as he watched TV. His name had been changed to Don Filippé.

12

2000

TOWARD THE END of our graduation year, Tom found himself a job as a web designer with a dotcom dealing with women's beauty products. He was happy enough working in multimedia, maintaining the website. He Photoshopped facial hair off pictures of models without complaint. At the end of his first month he secretly spent his entire pay cheque on an engagement ring for me. He took me out for dinner and a walk around the Peak, then got down on one knee.

On hearing our announcement, Tom's mum, Dru, leapt into the air and shook her fist with a joyous whoop. It was the most un-British thing I would ever see her do. Tony, Tom's dad, appeared seconds later out of the kitchen with a bottle of champagne. We sat in their living room for an hour and then borrowed Tony's car to drive out to Sai Kung.

'Oh, but they're just babies!' Mum was lying on the sofa with the back of her hand pressed melodramatically across her forehead when we arrived at The Nest. 'My baby!'

'Mum, this is a good thing,' said Jus, who was home for the

holidays, and was always ready to speak sense. 'Tom's a good guy, and he's going to look after Cinta. It's a good thing, Mum.'

Tom was not fazed by Mum's performance. He knew she had her quirks, and he knew she would be fine.

'I am so sorry,' he said sheepishly to Dad. 'I was so wrapped up in buying the ring and proposing, that I forgot to call you first to ask your permission.'

'Well, you not only have my permission,' Dad said, 'you have my blessing. This is wonderful news.'

Tom had proposed on Christmas Eve, and on Boxing Day his boss called to say he no longer had a job to come back to after the holidays—the dotcom bubble had burst. No matter, he had put a diamond ring on my finger, and nothing was going to rain on our parade.

'We'd be happy living in a cardboard box as long as we have each other, right?' I said.

'Right.'

. . .

It was a joyous time. Wedding planning was the primary focus for our year-long engagement. We were only 21 and didn't need to hurry. It all felt too good to be true, but the ring on my finger was tangible proof that I had become someone worthy of love, and a lifetime commitment. I worried I would screw things up before the wedding day, but life was flowing along at such a fast rate that I figured, if I sat tight, we might just make it.

The only other big event that year was a Read family holiday to Australia. Tom asked if I would like to go along, and I said yes straight away, because the thought of us ever being apart was never a welcome one. But it was a conflicted yes; memories of my time in Australia were equally unwelcome. I felt uncomfortable about most of the time I had spent there. Tom unfolded the plan for the two-week holiday, and my enthusiasm dwindled further still. We were going to attend a huge conference for Christians in Sydney. I had never heard of the hosting church, but Tom named some of the songs they had produced and I had to admit to liking many of them.

We arrived at a Courtyard Marriott somewhere in Sydney and I was assigned a shared room with Tom's little sister, Carmen. She was going to be spending the week with the conference's youth group. Tom and I needed to choose between the youth leadership stream and the worship and creative arts stream. I had circled all the dance ministry sessions in the conference planner, slightly miffed that such a deeply personal part of my own life was common enough to warrant an entire conference stream. What the hell was 'dance ministry', anyway? Not knowing what to expect, we all set out for the first night's rally.

The conference was held at Sydney's Olympic Park. Hordes of people streamed in and I gawked, bemused and wondering how everyone would get in and out of the place safely. Mum had planted in me a strong wariness of crowds. Back in Hong Kong, on New Year's Eve in 1992, there had been a stampede in Lan Kwai Fong when the annual race around the block had gone wrong. Too many drunken people pushed and shoved their way through too slippery a small space, and the result was twenty deaths and many more injuries. Hong Kong reacted by imposing strict crowd-control measures on all major holidays and big events, and from that moment on Mum rarely ever let me out of her sight without warning me to beware of crowds, on top of the usual mention of holes in the ground I could accidentally fall into. She would not have liked the look of the Sydney Super Dome that night. I sure didn't.

The Reads and I shuffled into the throng of thousands of conference delegates filing into the massive stadium in a jovial, but orderly, fashion. It was winter in Australia and the air was cool, the stadium alight with anticipation for the night ahead. A Mexican wave broke out and was soon followed by the same thing again, this time in slow motion. I'd never seen anything like it. As possibly the only international child from Hong Kong never to have been taken to the world-famous Rugby Sevens, I'd never even been in a crowded sports stadium. I watched like an observer from another world. I took in the edgy Australian fashion; the smiling volunteer usher as she checked how many spaces were unoccupied in her section; the various signs with crosses painted on them and banners declaring things like, 'We love Jesus, yes we do!'

A three-man comedy warm-up act took to the stage. They spoke with heavy Australian accents as they bantered and played practical jokes on one another and selected members of the audience. As I chuckled, my guard began to slip. Feelings about my time in Australia jostled like the bag of mixed lollies being passed along the row in front. I had sworn to myself that, once secondary school was over, I would never come back. I'd tried to communicate my misgivings to Tom when he first told me about the trip, but he quoted catchy song lyrics before I was able to put a solid finger on what, exactly, my misgivings were.

The excitement rose as the comedians left the stage and the stadium went dark. We were summoned to our feet and suddenly flashing lights, smoke machines and loud rock music blasted from the huge stage. A long line of vocalists appeared in front of a large band and an even larger choir. The party had well and truly started, and I began to wish I hadn't come.

The crowd sang and clapped along with the singers whose faces beamed from the jumbotron. They moved in the spotlights and I froze in place, feeling utterly exposed and self-conscious. I tried to focus on reading the lyrics below the performers' angelic smiling projections, hoping and praying that the noise would soon stop. I was too uncomfortable even to look at Tom, but honestly hoped he was hating it as much as I was. We were far too alternative in our musical preferences to go for something this obviously mainstream. But what if he liked it? What if he started flapping his arms and laughing hysterically, like the people at the youth camp back in Perth?

Just when I thought I knew Tom well enough to marry him, I found myself questioning whether I really knew him at all. What was my problem? I could not believe I had come back to Australia and found myself, once again, in a meeting of what I could only imagine was the world's biggest cult. That is what this had to be. I was a defenceless child who had stumbled upon the witches' convention of a Roald Dahl story. They all had a look of giddy joy, and it seemed like every single person in the arena was in on a secret that I wanted no part in. Any moment now, the façade would peel back, and I would be turned into a mouse.

Sitting as still as possible, I listened to a dynamic preacher motivate the crowd to audible cheers of 'Amen' and 'Hallelujah', and I wanted to bolt. *God, I hate this,* I thought. *Please God, please make this all go away,* I prayed. *I just want us to be home in Hong Kong again. Why does everything have to go wrong? I don't want to be in a cult.*

When the first evening rally was over, I mustered up the courage to ask Tom what he thought of it, everything within me hoping he hated it. I was terrified. On another level, I was highly unimpressed. This big event did not comply with our previously agreed definitions of cool. It was mainstream and, according to everything we hitherto stood for, nothing mainstream could be good.

Tom had worked the popular crowd back in his time at school, but he chose to leave that, and that is how and why we had bonded. It was the post-popular-crowd Tom I loved; I hadn't signed up for this. It looked to me like he was faltering and in danger of renewing his membership with a club I wouldn't be able to get into. The mainstream had never worked for me. I lacked the social skills needed to balance on bandwagons, even the ones I secretly wanted in on. If this many people were excited about something, then it was almost certainly going to go wrong for me.

Tom loved it and had zero regard for my indie-sentiments. He told me to get over myself. He was sick of my thinly disguised snobbery and was drawing a line in the sand. A decision needed to be made, and it did not take me long. If there was a line, I needed to be on the same side of it as Tom. We were going to get married. I was going to spend the rest of my life with him; I was not going to spend the rest of my life alone.

I stayed quiet the next day. I had a whole week ahead of me.

There was baggage from the past that I needed to unpack, but the conference schedule did not permit. The days only got fuller.

On day three, I quit the dance sessions. They had taken something profoundly personal that I hadn't yet found the words for and diluted it to suit the palette of the masses. I was incensed. I stopped going and joined Tom and his brother, Ed, for their worship leading and musician sessions instead. I preferred the way the musicians talked, but more than that, I liked having two friends to sit with. With them by my side, I would manage. Then something unexpected happened.

I began to find myself strangely taken by some aspects of the conference. The women on stage were impeccably groomed. They smiled and carried themselves with a confidence that was rather irresistible—standing in high heels, endearingly dwarfed under their own massive projected images, saying things like, *Don't look at me and think I'm any different from you, we are sisters, princesses united under the love of one awesome king.* I wanted to know where they bought their lip gloss.

They were mainstream for sure, that went without saying, but maybe I did need to get over myself. I had felt utterly clueless for as long as I could remember, and here was an entire conference full of people who seemed absolutely certain that they were in the know, asking me to fall in line. For the smallest stretches of time, I challenged myself to suspend prejudices and experiment with the idea of not dismissing everything about them. If I squinted my eyes, I could see vague apparitions of something I could, perhaps, one day become, if I tried hard enough.

I lifted a metaphorical fork load of green eggs and ham to my matte lips and found that I did so like them, Sam I Am. These ladies looked sincere enough in their devotion to the God I loved. As far as I could tell, no one was saying anything overtly wrong, and I could test that all later. If Christ was all that we needed to have in common, then maybe there was a small chance that I could join the club after all.

. . .

And then there was Tom. Something inside him sparked alive that week, and I could see that he was preparing to enter uncharted territory. I had a choice as to whether or not I would go with him. I could make a run for it, shedding the diamond solitaire as I went, and be alone in life again, or I could stand faithfully by his side, donning a cute skirt suit and pillbox hat as he was sworn in for a term of 'worship music ministry'.

That was what I wanted to do—I wanted to be by his side, no matter what, and here was a stadium full of good-looking, happy Christians offering me an invitation to be that better person. It could have been worse. Perhaps it was time for me to eat some humble pie, to try doing life differently. *Let go and let God,* said the conference collectively. Perhaps it was time to give myself the chance to fall in line with the crowd. It certainly seemed the path of least resistance at that point.

The conference became an annual expedition spanning the next eight years. Memories of the first few years of our marriage are now eclipsed by our passion for church. The only year I missed the conference was 2002 when, just six months into married life, I was also a few months into running my first business.

I had grown bored of working at the local gym and Mum was

all too ready to back my first sign of entrepreneurialism. She helped me register a company, open a business banking account, put money into it, and sign the lease on a prime location. So, just a few short weeks after our wedding, I opened The Point, a dance studio of my very own, and was in the throes of discovering the ramifications of business ownership for the underprepared. The business would eventually fail, not for lack of demand, but for lack of skill and forward planning on my part. There were enough ballet schools in Hong Kong; the students that came to me wanted to learn the moves they saw on music videos. I needed to be relevant. So, I choreographed fresh material for each one-hour class and added new classes to the schedule whenever one or two people expressed interest. I saw no merit in paying a cleaner when I could do it myself, and I didn't know how to go about finding one, anyway. I did not know how to keep accounts, nor how to hire someone who did. I kept it up for as long as I could.

Tom, his parents, and a small group of friends went to the conference without me that year, and then came back on a mission to make our little church glorious. I enjoyed the album Tom brought home to me as a souvenir, and so far, I was enjoying my upgraded devotion to living the Christian life. The freshly invigorated enthusiasm of our church family was reaching tipping point. It was contagious and, before I knew it, the idea of making our church the most wonderful place in all the world had become a personal goal. It was certainly more appealing than running a business.

I organised my work schedule so I could return to Sydney with Tom again the following year. This time, since we were both so keen, we turned it into a reconnaissance trip, the plan being to bring several teenagers from SNA with us the following year.

. . .

IT WAS 2003, my second conference, Tom's third. We were there making plans to show the 'kids' around. I was going to chaperone them in this foreign land, to help them to navigate a place that, to me, had once felt so alien. I assumed an air of big-sisterly confidence, walking those same carpeted corridors, this time as an insider, too delighted by the sights and sounds to remember the hesitations of my past.

I continued to accompany Tom to the music sessions because I preferred to have someone to sit with. I continued to wince at the dance ministry's contributions that spilled into the main rallies, their idea of dance being so different to mine. By now, however, I had come to the conclusion that this huge conference and church probably knew better than I in most things, including dance.

At the end of the week, they announced the line-up for the next year's conference. I pricked up my ears so I could relay the programme to the SNAers. Someone called Joyce Meyer would be a guest at next year's conference. The crowd went berserk, roaring its approval, and I clapped loudly and shouted, 'Woo! Awesome!'

I laughed along with the joyous outburst of the throng, then turned to Tom and whispered, 'Who's Joyce Meyer?'

13

ONCE I GOT home from the conference, I delved headlong into Joyce's literature. I was going to be just like her. She was my role model of the moment. She advocated hard work in the name of being a better version of one's self. Her words were like fuel to my engine, yet I cannot blame her for what was about to happen in my life. I had bought several of her books and audio CDs on my way out of the conference, and I'd spend the year working my way through her entire catalogue, regularly visiting Christian bookstores to make sure I was abreast of the latest releases. I planned to be well and truly in the loop by the time the next conference rolled around.

Joyce was one sassy woman. She communicated with expert clarity, sharing her flaws as well as her triumphs. She pitched reason after reason for me to raise my bar in the name of the Lord. And this was what I genuinely thought I was doing. She convinced me that she battled her inner beast and, by the grace of God, was winning. I had an inner beast too, so I was sold. I wanted to refer to my struggles in the past tense. I wanted Joyce's confidence. I wanted to rid myself of doubt and misgivings and no longer be the person I once was.

Out with the old said New Creation Me. Surely Joyce would agree. Though I once was lost, now I was found. I needed to start 'enjoying everyday life', right now. In a matter of weeks, we were on a first-name basis, Joyce and I, albeit in an entirely one-sided relationship that existed exclusively inside my head. That's how it is, sometimes. The dividing lines between Joyce and I began to blur.

Joyce's God-given calling in life was to have a large and successful preaching and teaching ministry. She loved the Bible. Studying her from afar, I found she stood on solid ground. She wasn't perfect—she told me so herself—and I loved her all the more for it. She tossed out her nuggets of hard-earned wisdom like lifesavers to the drowning. As I tread water, I was inspired, and began tearing my floatation device into little pieces to throw out to others. I swallowed a decent amount of saltwater in the process, but I didn't mind.

'You are just so wise, Jacinta,' my friend, Dawn said to me, after I encouraged her with a line I had lifted straight out of Joyce's latest book.

This would be my life for the best part of a year, and a few months later I would find myself in the ER. I was so busy investing my capital-A-All into becoming someone I was not, I didn't notice that somewhere along the way my grip on reality had begun to slip.

. . .

TOM AND I were considered quite young for a married couple in Hong Kong. We got married at the age of 22 and were now leading very busy lives: he with his job at the church, me with my failing business. Now in our mid-twenties, about to celebrate our third wedding anniversary, we were beginning to think we knew what we were doing in life.

We were very comfortable living in a flat that Tom's parents had bought during the SARS epidemic. The entire population of Hong Kong was wearing surgical face masks because of the deadly outbreak of a highly contagious atypical influenza. The streets and shopping malls were empty because people were at home washing everything, on the hour, with a bleach solution. Shui Fai Terrace was a great location for us—it was in a quiet area, but just one flight of stairs up from the action of the city.

Hong Kong is a small and vertical city where people live in flats, not houses—there simply isn't the space. Every inch of usable land is occupied by a building, usually a very tall one. Looking back at the island from the perspective of the harbour, even the buildings look like they are stacked on top of each other, from the waterfront all the way up to the top of Victoria Peak. Historically, the higher up the hill you lived, the richer you were; but times were changing, and Hong Kong was all too quickly becoming a city in which none but the extremely rich could own anything at all.

This hadn't mattered too much to the expatriate community we grew up with. No one really planned to be there for much longer than the duration agreed upon in whichever employment contract had brought them out in the first place. However, since the handover in 1997, it had become clear that several *gweilos* (foreigners) did, in fact, want to stay. Tom's parents were among them. They lived in a large, rented duplex in Mid-levels, but made the wise decision to buy something of their own as soon as they saw the opportunity.

Shui Fai Terrace is known amongst locals as an undesirable place to live. It overlooks a large cemetery, and this is bad feng shui—

but it's great news to anyone who either isn't superstitious or who wholeheartedly believes that Jesus trumps feng shui. Prices are lower than average, even before you consider the economic dip that coincided with SARS. Once the sale completed, they offered Tom and I the chance to live in their new flat until they needed it.

Tom enjoyed his work at the church, and I was happy enough. At least, that's what I told myself. Somehow, I fumbled through a couple of years like this. But I was eventually exhausted, and so was my love of dance. The hip-hop dance style that my students wanted to learn was a far cry from the ballet I'd once loved. I began to dread each day and sought solace in drawing up plans to sublet the studio, then perused the newspapers for another job to use as an escape route. Eventually, I figured out a way to sublet my dance studio to other teachers, then found myself a job as a nanny. However, that didn't last long. I was fired within a few months.

The full effects of my sacking didn't hit immediately. I was focused on other things and had been for months. The two things at the forefront of my mind then were Jesus and pushing myself to be a better person. These goals had become entwined, and this had led me to miss several appointments while nannying: the 5-year-old never made it to the dentist, despite my rescheduling twice; the 9-year-old missed his check-up at the doctor's, and the 13-year-old walked himself home alone after football.

My head wasn't in the game, and my heart was not in the job. And I was fired. But I never saw it coming. The day I was let go I left in a state of utter shock. Tom and I had a dinner party to attend that evening. I faked smiles and drank until the smiles were less fake. I drifted in and out of conversations before the attention could turn to me. When we got home, I cried as I told Tom what had happened, thinking he was going to be furious.

'Easy come, easy go, hey? The money was good while it lasted,' he said. It seemed I was mistaken. 'Maybe you could try and find work that somehow lets you travel with me—I think there will be some more trips coming up soon.'

We had recently returned from Boracay, in the Philippines, on an eight-day, all-expenses-paid trip. It was the annual staff retreat for a Christian NGO. They had invited one minister and one worship leader to facilitate the daily meetings, and spouses were usually welcome in these settings. Each morning, the group of about twenty staff and full-time volunteers sang a few worship songs and then the minister taught a lesson out of the Bible. Feeling a need to earn my place, I sang harmonies as Tom led the songs. Afterwards, I would get changed into my swimsuit and spend the rest of the day on the powder-soft sand.

It was clear that Tom was a gifted musician. The tone of his singing voice was one of the things I loved most about him. Invitations from various people started appearing; things were on the up and up for Tom. We were both happy to focus on his career.

My days fell into a rhythm. Mum's educational charity was about to launch a project with a children's publisher, so she invited me to do some extra work with the team.

'Are you sure you can manage this on top of the studio?' Dad asked, when I told him I was planning to get involved in the project.

'Of course she can, Hob,' Mum answered on my behalf. 'Our Itch is a superwoman.'

I hated when she said things like this, but I was happy that she never questioned my capacity to take on new things. I could count on her being on-side most of the time, but she also had a habit of bringing up the one thing I did not want to deal with.

'I do keep forgetting to say, you need to collect up all your receipts. Have you got them all? We need to send them off to the accountant for the audit.'

My work at the dance studio was down to minimal levels, but the pressure didn't let up. Official-looking letters from the government continued to arrive in the post and, though I did my best to deal with them and toss them back, hot-potato style, there was one that I simply couldn't handle. It was a tax return that needed an audit, and I'd ignored it for too long before asking Mum for help.

'Oh Mum, can we talk about that another time?'

'Yes, darling, I know, I don't like dealing with these things, either. We'll do it next time.'

Perhaps, eventually, it would all just go away. Surely Mum would deal with it all before things got serious.

. . .

In my effort to become the best possible version of myself, I took up running. I liked the Bible verse about running and not growing weary. It all began in innocent curiosity—I wanted to see how many times I could run around Happy Valley's outer track, having been there almost weekly during secondary school. It was a hive of sporting activity, sitting comfortably inside the parameter of the Hong Kong Jockey Club's racetrack. The hockey and football pitches were where most English schools did their after-school sports. The

Hong Kong Football Club clubhouse is there as well; it's a significant landmark in expat history. Dad claimed it was he, having just arrived from Kenya, who had taught the bartender there to make a gunner back in the sixties.

I'd once tried going for a run a few years ago, back at university, and felt very naughty about it. Running was something my childhood ballet teachers frowned upon—bad for the knees, apparently. My first attempt at running had lasted about ten minutes and nearly killed me. But now, approaching my mid-twenties, and having read *The Beginner's Guide to Running*, I was armed with knowledge and ready to flip the bird at my old ballet teachers. On the third day, I looked up from my Mizunos, finally comfortable enough to take a peek at my fellow runners.

First, I noticed the group of men I dubbed the Horses. They were tall Europeans with long legs and short shorts. They trotted around and around, nonchalant and chatting in pairs as they overlapped me, again and again. Smug bastards. Same to the Firemen: the incredibly fit, deeply tanned Chinese men who seem to run all over Hong Kong all day long, wearing nothing but dark blue shorts. I was sure they were firemen because I saw them playing volleyball in those same shorts every time I rode a bus past the fire station on Garden Road.

The Welder *Tai Tais* were middleclass Chinese housewives who wore huge sun visors folded down over their faces, much in the fashion of a steelworker; a true Tai Tai values a pale complexion. For exercise, the Tai Tai is dressed in designer-label velour sweatpants, a fitted polo shirt and a fanny pack. In one hand, she might hold a folded face towel with which to dab at the first sign of perspiration, and, in the other, the mobile phone on which she will talk for the duration of her singular lap.

Then there was Mars Attacks, an odd-looking woman of indiscriminate age who walked her laps at an eerily slow pace, with a disconcerting smirk, swaying her arms in the slow, robotic motion of an alien squid. Finally, there were the Hopefuls. They were a mixed bag of novices, who huffed and puffed around the course with a sincerity that softened the heart. I considered them my comrades.

Each day, I gave a cordial nod to the overweight Sikh man running in his turban, to the ancient veteran I was sure had once been a champion (though, of what sport, I couldn't tell), and to Chubby Limping Girl with the red face and elastic knee supports on both legs.

My problems began the day I overtook an annoyingly slow Welder. She was an obstacle. I enjoyed the feeling of leaving someone in my dust and accelerated toward Limping Girl to repeat the experience. It soon became an obsession. I chose an unsuspecting victim and raced them quietly, either overtaking them as many times as possible, or else committing to stay running on the track for at least fifteen minutes after they had puffed out and gone home.

A typical weekday started at 6 am. I sprung out of bed, landed soft-footedly, got changed, gathered my iPod, earphones and a spare sock, then snuck out of the house without waking Tom or Diesel. Diesel was the pug who had a strong sense of entitlement when it came to morning walks.

The morning security guard made me feel uncomfortable—there was no clear reason for this, other than perhaps his clubfoot, goofy smile and lazy eye. His face was also unnaturally round, and it reminded me of the picture of a smiling oatmeal raisin cookie I had recently drawn. Tom was amused by my lack of political correctness, and named the guard Smiley so that he could tease me whenever he felt so inclined. Smiley was constantly limping toward me, trying to tell me which parking spaces my parents were not allowed to use when they visited, which one of our air-conditioners was dripping and how much we were at risk of being fined, or when the next owners' committee meeting was scheduled and why it mattered so much that I attend.

Every morning, I stuffed my earphones into my head and made haste beyond the building's boundaries, pretending not to hear Smiley's calls, pretending not to see him frantically waving in my periphery. But, once around the corner, my mind's eye taunted me with visions of Smiley now with a bite taken from his baked head, sprouting legs, gathering speed and breaking into chase. The notion sent shivers down my spine and I took deep breaths, trying to regain composure to switch my thoughts to the day ahead.

On alternate days I visited The Point Studio. It was down to me to wipe the smears off the mirrors and mop the wooden floor, even though I no longer taught there. It was still mine. Still my problem; one of my many problems. My dance studio was beautiful, though. I'd had a clear vision of what I wanted it to look like and, thanks to my investor, the vision had come to pass: floor-to-ceiling mirrors, fixed barres, wall-to-wall sprung wooden flooring. Unfortunately, I had no idea how to run a business. It was a good place to work out in private though, and at that moment in my life I preferred exercise to dealing with anything else. I balanced kneeling, leaning or standing on fit balls to engage my core as I lifted dumbbells. The sweat made it difficult to balance on the balls, but I devised the solution of stripping off my top layer to use as a grip to kneel or stand on. This also allowed for a long, honest look in the mirror. For the first time in my life, I didn't wince at what I saw.

Once every major muscle group had been sufficiently challenged, I cleared away the equipment, put my top back on, and ran the length of Queens Road East to get to Happy Valley. The Happy Valley racetrack always welcomed me. It was the site of my tentative first paces as a beginner; it had witnessed my swift advancement as a runner, and begged the question, *what have you got for me today?*

Some days, the run was set to a playlist of upbeat worship music on the first-generation iPod I carried in a sock wrapped around my wrist to prevent it from slipping out of my grip. This worked well enough, but I wondered about the physiological repercussions of the weight of the device and the subtle imbalance of the whole arrangement. The issue niggled to the point where, eventually, the iPod had to go. Music was a distraction, anyway, so it was replaced with a new soundtrack: the rhythmic thumping of footfall on concrete, and the percussive breath of a woman on a mission.

. . .

I HAD BEEN A Christian for about a decade and decided it was time to take my faith to the next level. An imaginary panel of Christian celebrities had moved into my head, and I would turn to them periodically throughout the day to check how I was measuring up. Up until then, I had lived the standard assortment of awful/average/good days, but now—armed with nothing but good intentions—I drew a line of connection between the amount of attention I paid to faith-related things and the general quality of my day. This is the biblical law of 'sowing and reaping'.

The thought occurred to me: *What if I really gave my all to God, every single day of my life?* Surely my potential of having a good life would increase. And, if it didn't, at least I wouldn't be to blame, since I had done literally all I could. No one could accuse me of being lazy. I was in control of my own work schedule, so the two-hour runs were to precede two hours of what some Christians call 'quiet time', or devotions, during which I read and colour-coded the long-winded Amplified version of the Holy Bible with highlighter pencils. I wrote out long passages of scripture by hand, listened to teaching tapes, and prepared sermons that I might or might not ever get the chance to preach. I put it all in God's hands.

Every one of my morning showers needed earning, and somewhere along the line I had set a standard of what I felt constituted an acceptable level of effort. I had it on good authority that Happy Valley's outer ring measured a distance of 1.2 km. I was never any good in maths at school, but while working in a coffee shop in my first real job I had surprised myself by mastering the skill of calculating change.

New Creation Me pontificated to Crap Old Me on the virtues of perseverance and tenacity as we counted laps around the racetrack. As each lap flew past, I turned the numbers into Tetris pieces, stacking them around each other in my mind. A run of 10 km became the minimum acceptable distance. This demanded nine complete laps, because stopping mid-lap was not an option, and there was something satisfying about finishing the laps and leaving a tip of 0.8 km.

Generosity was also a virtue. The problem here was that it meant an uneven number of clockwise vs. counter-clockwise loops. And changing direction was an important part of the morning ritual: imagined threats of one visibly dominant leg demanded it. Always keep limbs even—metaphorically and literally. Ten times round the track would be the best solution to the various difficulties I faced: five times in each direction. The order and frequency in which the laps alternated was subject to daily creative inspiration, as was the pattern of *en dedan/en dehors* (outward vs. inward) turns used to execute the change of direction. No need to be rigid about things.

Once the run was finished, I would head back up the hill toward home, scuttle past Smiley with forced nonchalance, drink one pint of water, shower, dress, eat half an Ikea rice-bowl's worth of granola-topped plain yogurt, make a cup of herbal tea and then settle at the dining table with the Bible.

The specific details of quiet times differ from person to person. For me, a typical quiet time involved reading a selection of passages, each taken from one of the following categories: Psalms, Old Testament, New Testament and Proverbs. The Proverbs were always saved, best for last. I wrote my thoughts and prayers into a plain paper journal, and sometimes wrote out Bible verses longhand. I also took notes on questions or points relating to some sample of Christian literature by some inspirational personality, and then regurgitated everything into bullet points to be sautéed into a snappy and relevant message to preach at the youth group.

I busied myself with quiet-time activities until noon, when it was time to walk Diesel, eat a lunch of one Ikea rice-bowl's worth of tuna fish and cucumbers, and then work on some sketches or writing before heading down to Queens Road East to catch a bus to church.

As the bus drove past the dance studio one day, I breathed a sigh of relief—though the accountant had complained about the lateness of my tax return, it had finally all been submitted. I was in the clear for now and wondered if there was any way to break out of my lease early, to avoid having to fill out any more of those forms.

My routine repeated until Saturday—time to run Revolve's dance practice, spend time with any of the youth group girls who wanted to hang out, and then head to SNA where, if it was a good week, it would be my turn to preach. I wondered if our little congregation realised just how dedicated a leader they had. I knew they loved me and appreciated having an older female to talk to, much in the same way I had appreciated Priscilla and the whole leadership team that ran SNA a decade earlier. The kids freely chose to spend every weekend with the youth group, so I went ahead and took this to mean I was doing something right.

'Jacinta is so cool,' one girl said to another.

'I know, she totally chose to give her whole life to God. It's the coolest thing anyone could ever really do.'

'Yah, and she's so amazing at preaching, too.'

'And she's married, and she has tattoos, and she is such a great dancer ... I wish I was like her.'

These were the voices that lined my thoughts and drove me to push myself up the hill toward my goal. I would be the best I could be. Soon, people would notice, and start saying the things I longed to hear on the outside of my imagination.

. . .

I pushed myself hard toward what I believed to be very positive goals. I kept a logbook of my running times and distances. I bought a heart rate monitor to ensure I was training at the right intensity. The word 'aerobic' became candy in my mind. I rolled it around my tongue and swallowed it in place of food. I ran, breathing rhythmically, picturing little cartoon O_2s getting sucked into my core, burning their way through every fat cell they encountered.

The miles clocked up and, before I knew what was happening, it was marathon-or-bust. My daily training sessions began to average two hours of running—after an hour of free weights and fit balls.

One day, at the height of summer, I went running later than usual and ended up with heatstroke. I lay on the bed after my shower, in a daze, shivering and crying, but I enjoyed the sensations in a strange sort of way. Somehow, unreasonably, running in dangerously high temperatures meant more, and eventually I rearranged the schedule to allow for running just after midday.

Tom never actually saw the frenzy. He was at work. He was simply pleased that his wife had finally stopped asking if she looked fat. Suddenly, she enjoyed going out with friends. The flat was immaculately clean—everything in its place. His T-shirts, even his boxers, were ironed, folded and put away, organised by colour. Hearty meals were ready on his arrival home from work, and there were always plenty of leftovers for a packed lunch the next day. Tom's wife had an endless supply of energy, and she seemed to be putting it all to good use.

The shape of my body was changing dramatically. I woke in the morning feeling full of energy. That old sense of shame I had harboured from early years spent in ballet class, being grouped with the big girls, now slinked away, taking with it the memories of feeling like an elephant in a leotard, apologetic for the audacity of her existence. The self-loathing receded from its former turf at the front of my mind, and left space wide open for delusions of grandeur. I had always wondered if skinny people woke up *feeling* skinny, and found that yes, yes they did. I savoured the feeling and swore to myself never to go back to how I used to be.

The daily need to run, either faster or longer, metastasised. The recommended day of rest, as well as sheepish mentions of cross-training, were like personal insults directed at me by the entire field of sports science. All I wanted to do was run. There were enough endorphins cruising through my veins to convince me that I would, at any moment, take to the skies.

'Doesn't it hurt?' Tom asked as I returned, shoeless, from a run. I had lied to him about it being my only run that day, the reason for the second run was that I felt too conspicuous running barefoot—my latest fad—in the daylight. So now there was a morning run with shoes, then a shorter one, barefoot under the cover of nightfall.

I found space to embellish the barefoot running theory with my own ideas: God's original design was perfect. God had provided me with the exact equipment I needed in order to do what he had put in my heart to do. My heart wanted to run: he had given me bare feet. His provision was sufficient for me and so I would run, run towards God and away from anything that I found less appealing.

'I can't believe it doesn't it hurt,' Tom said again as I headed for the door the next evening. 'Oh, and I forgot—call your mum when you get back, something about the accountant.'

I rolled my eyes and reminded myself not to worry, since the last round of forms had already been sent off. I exited the flat with a spring in my step, feeling smug at the thought of the fat cells I was about to incinerate.

If only I could also burn the pile of mail I'd passed on my way out the door. Official-looking letters from various government offices arrived in the post, asking me to renew licenses, file profits, salaries, employment records and more. Reminders that told me, officially, I was a grown-up now. I left them in a pile and pretended they did not exist.

Thoughts of those letters woke me in the night, until eventually I was forced to summon the courage to open them, sweaty-palmed. More often than not I found that, with a little presence of mind, I could fill out the forms and send them back (with a late fine, usually). Meanwhile, I would focus my energy on running.

. . .

When I ran, I was not really running: my spirit was flying higher than any substance had ever taken me. I was frolicking on the tarmac around the Happy Valley outer track. High on life. Abundant life. I leapt, like a gazelle. I stepped sure-footed, as a mountain goat. I was not running: I swam, athletic, through the humid and polluted city air, the front-crawler in a relay race, and after my own sprint I could volunteer to be the second, third and fourth swimmer, too. I was a fireball blazing through the darkness. I was no runner: I was a prophet in motion, stirring up the spirit of God, fanning the flames of supernatural passion. The result held mysterious and infinite potential, and spiritual significance beyond what human minds could fathom. God's ways are not our ways.

It was all invisible to those in the natural world. They could go about their day, marching to the rhythm of pile drivers and milk-frothing espresso machines. They could amble in the shade of the metropolis, and I would run circles under the shadow of the Almighty. This was a special time, just God and me. God knew where I was and what I was doing. Forget the pain. He'd have given me feet with thick, spongy, rubber soles had he felt I needed them, but he hadn't. He had equipped me with regular feet. Running shoes, therefore, must have been a result of the assumptions of man: a manipulative marketing ploy of the consumerist, fallen world in which we lived. I chose to run barefoot as a gesture to God. I believed his provision was sufficient for me.

But my feet did hurt. Large and deep blisters formed, and then burst. Fillets of skin peeled back, and I began to feel each step more than God could possibly have intended. After running, I retrieved the flip-flops I had hidden in a bush at the side of the racetrack, slipped them on and hobbled home to shower. I repositioned the skin flaps and bound it all in place with surgical tape. My Chinese ancestors had bound feet. I thought of them every time I got the tape out: my foot pain was nothing compared to what they had endured.

Finally, however, I decided perhaps a running shoe with the thinnest possible sole was a sensible option after all: good stewardship of the earthly vessel I had on loan. God gave me soft feet, but he also gave me a brain, so perhaps this was the best course of action, after all.

One morning run, my flight of fantasy was rudely disrupted by a sudden and non-negotiable need to get to the toilet. Happy Valley's outer ring had two exit points, and I passed the first one, reluctant to quit half-lap, confident that I was in control of the situation. I sped toward the next exit, to the changing rooms located in the middle of the ring. As I did so, the level of urgency escalated to apocalyptic proportions. As I broke into a cold sweat, I clenched every relevant muscle and speed-walked in disbelief, no longer able to assume control of anything, fighting an intense and downright primal desire to squat right there and empty out the entire contents of my digestive system. How dare my body do this to me? How was it possible for a 25-year-old to be in danger of shitting herself?

I made it into the empty ladies' changing room, but only just. A clean-up operation and partial shower later, I emerged and completed the rest of my run commando, undies left in the bin. No one had borne witness to what happened to me that day, but I was thoroughly embarrassed, disgusted even, by my inability to control my own bodily functions. Another brick in the great wall that divided me: me against me. We would never be one. No amount of trying would ever change things.

It was not an isolated incident, but I put in place an early warning system, and all future urges were treated with due seriousness. I continued to train during the quietest moments of the day, when I could hide from the rest of the world, and I would now run in the midday heat partly as punishment for bringing such shame upon myself. It would be a couple more months before I discovered the term 'runner's trots'.

Conveniently, I would soon learn about the practice of religious fasting. I was instantly taken by the notion. If you wanted to take your spirituality to the highest possible level, you had to say no to food. I remembered the book about Prince Siddhartha achieving enlightenment that Mum had read to me as a child and was delighted to find that the Bible agreed on the discipline. Fasting was all the things I liked at that point. It was extreme, self-denial, a hotline to God, another way to set myself apart from the crowd, and a great way to avoid needing the toilet whilst running. I was sold, and somehow was also under the impression that fasting and marathon training were not in the least bit incompatible. Aspiring to Jesus' 40-day fast, I began to skip meals, working up to full days without food.

14

I FOCUSED ON THE fact that teenagers need role models, and I locked target on my little flock of English-speaking teens at SNA. They didn't know what had hit them. When the youth group was in session, we all sang songs to Jesus and then sat attentively as one of the leaders gave a short sermon or led a time of discussion. I loved to preach and made the fact known to anyone who would listen, because *to she who knocked, the door would be opened.* I volunteered to manage the speakers' roster and, as a result, found myself prepping sermons most weeks. Sometimes, even if someone else was booked to speak, I prepared anyway, sort of like an understudy.

I was invited to visit one of Hong Kong's international secondary schools, to speak at a drug education class, to tell my story to a roomful of some of Hong Kong's most privileged teenagers. I snapped up the opportunity. Jump first, think later. This is faith.

'I didn't grow up in a Christian family.' As I delivered my opening line with an air of I'm-just-like-you-only-quite-a-lot-better-and-let-me-tell-you-why, it struck me that the kids in the room were not conference delegates. They were obligated to sit and listen to me, a stranger, who was brought in to tell them, essentially, to 'just say no'. Why had I begun with my family's religious background? Why was I invited to talk about drugs? Is that who I was? The former-drugs-girl? I hadn't even applied my lip gloss. My entire sense of identity wanted to unravel, but it was not the right time. I had no choice but to go on with the talk.

'I wasn't very good at school,' I continued, 'but I was pretty brave when it came to trying drugs. Eventually I moved country, away from the party scene, and couldn't get hold of any drugs…' Then I found myself talking about the night in Perth, when I saw the shooting star. They needed to know that it wasn't just the absence of a drug dealer that caused me to change. I felt I needed to prove that I was not ashamed of the gospel.

Standing in front of the class, it dawned on me that I had never told anyone my story before. How was it going to end? I had no idea. I was not Joyce Meyer: I had not recovered from an abusive childhood, could not cite a lifetime of overcoming self-centredness, did not have a functional family spanning four generations at which to point as evidence of God's redemptive love. I was still alive and far too young to really say anything of any substance, despite every ounce of my being wanting to spin something along the lines of 'it's all great now and I am living happily ever after.' I was not even sure if I was happy. I wanted to be but hadn't actually checked for some time—I'd been too busy doing church and trying to make something of myself.

I told the class that, on the night I'd seen the shooting star, I'd been confronted with the choice between doing things the way I'd always done them, which was not working well at all, or else trying life God's way, like everyone seemed to be telling me to do. I borrowed a line or two from the book of Deuteronomy, or was it the movie, *Trainspotting*—something about choosing life—and then closed with 'We'll see how it goes.'

The room was receptive—I saw one girl in the front row dab her eye. I was invited back again a couple of days later, and then a few weeks after that, and so on until speaking at this school seemed almost a regular part of my life. I was happy to oblige. I had a divine calling to preach and I needed the experience of working with teenagers. Should any of them be sufficiently moved by anything I said in the class, I could invite them to come along to SNA. One stone, many birds. This was God's economy. According to the world's economy, however, I needed to work, but life was getting too busy for that.

. . .

Our church was growing. More and more young married couples were in attendance. A decent crowd was forming. We hosted a small, mid-week group in our flat, which involved about ten 20-somethings sitting in our small living room, chatting, eating, discussing the Bible and praying together. Our social life started to change rapidly.

The group that met in our home consisted of married couples and singles from Australia, New Zealand, the UK and Hong Kong. We were all in the same stage of life and, as the hosts and international-locals, Tom and I found ourselves at the centre of this new scene. Totally unfazed by the stereotypes at play, the guys bantered about sports and computers, and the girls nattered about recipes, shopping and home decorating. It was all taking place in my own home, but I was the one who felt welcomed and drawn in by the other girls. They helped me to finally understand the stories Mum had told of her own Australian school friends. They were good, solid people. And so, for as long as I could, I did my best to hide a growing feeling that I was not really who they thought I was.

They had confused me for one of their own—a regular, normal married girl in her twenties. I had never, in all of my life, felt normal, or enjoyed what I perceived as the luxurious privilege of fitting nicely into any established category, where I could enjoy the company of others just like me. In the past, I had wanted this more than anything, but it was too late now. I was resigned to the fact that I would never belong in a genuine sort of way, so I planned simply to ride this new wave of friendships, enjoying any benefits it brought with it for as long as I could. Which was, until the inevitable would happen: the wind would blow the wrong way and my cover would flap, like a humiliated bald man's toupee. I told them about my time in Australia, the man on the street who had told me to go home.

'I am so sorry that happened to you,' each one of them said with complete sincerity. They extended to me a warm, generous friendship that began to soothe an ache I had failed to properly recognise was there.

I sat and chatted, all the while suppressing the tension mounting inside. But there was no escaping the feeling that my time was coming to an end. Once they got to know me a little better, they would not like me anymore.

And then another fear presented itself, this one worse than the first: if I continued to set myself within the context of this group of friends, Tom would eventually start to compare me to them. He had liked me for being different back when we were teenagers, but the novelty had long since worn off, I was sure of it. He was quick and perceptive, and he would see much sooner than everyone else just how badly I failed to match up. The worse I looked, the better everyone else would seem. In fact, the other girls were already looking much better in my own eyes, and one in particular: Peta.

. . .

PETA WAS EVERYTHING I was not. She was quiet and never spoke up in a group, so never drew attention to herself—a quality both Tom and I admired and, despite genuine efforts, one I was never able to imitate. She was easy-going and did not get uptight when her husband drank too much beer—something I was famously uncool about. She had big, blue eyes and brown hair, and looked like a beautiful porcelain doll. I admired her. I admired her for not being me, and could not believe that Tom did not feel the same way.

Tom increasingly became the centre of attention. As the worship leader at church, his talent was an acceptable topic of conversation. Our new friends soon became his biggest fans, and this soon became a threat to me. I had always been his number one fan and I did not know how to share the title. I did not know how to react to what was happening. These people were meeting my husband's need for moral support. Surely that was my job. I was in danger of being side-lined. I would be replaced because my normal husband needed his needs met by his normal friends. They were in a far better position to give him what he needed. I was doomed. I was a fraud, and nothing would change that. This problem pressed me beyond my ability to cope. I needed another explanation for my lack of peace.

I found my scapegoat in Peta. She seemed especially enamoured with Tom's music. As a girl of few words, when she spoke, people tended to listen. I spouted too much hot air, so my words had lost their impact. I was convinced that I could see how much Peta loved Tom, and I could not see how loving someone's music was any different from wanting to break up my marriage. I had to save my marriage.

Over the following months, I excused myself from more and more social gatherings so that people would have less opportunity to notice me. My danger of losing this game, and losing everything God had given me since joining SNA, was so real, I had no choice but to remove myself from the playing field. I turned inward, into a world of my own. I ran faster and farther. I prayed longer and harder. In fleeting moments of clarity, I watched myself become more and more like the injured bird I'd put in a shoebox as a child: defiant, desperate and totally beyond hope. I hid inside myself and panicked.

'So, Peta's nice ....' I needed to assess how Tom felt about her.

'Yah, I really like them both. Matt's hilarious.'

'She's got such blue eyes,' I said. 'I've never seen anything like it. I actually think they look a bit like brother and sister—it's a bit weird, don't you think?'

Nothing.

'I just mean, they've got an interesting look.'

He had lost interest in the conversation and was trying to steer us into safer waters.

'We should try and go on holiday this year,' he said. 'It's been a long time, and I'm sure we can find a cheap deal somewhere.'

I knew it! The next thing he was going to try to do was sell me on the idea of going on holiday with them.

'I knew it!'

'What?'

'You think she's pretty, don't you?'

'What?'

'Nothing. Forget it.' I hadn't meant to blow my cool.

'I don't know what your problem is, Jacinta. Why are you being insecure? I hate it when you're like this ... I am not going to let you do this. We aren't teenagers anymore, we are married. You need to grow up ... I can't believe how crap you are being—what the hell is going on with you?'

. . .

I retreated and turned my thoughts to church the next day. That is what I lived for. My function in life was to bring glory to my God by building his church. It was a time for me to walk tall and busy myself with good things instead of stewing in suspicion. It was Saturday. Weekends were for the SNA 'kids'. I felt mature and superior calling them that.

Our friend Mark was in the other room. Someone usually slept in our spare room on a Saturday night. SNA meetings could run quite late, and with church the next morning only five minutes away in Causeway Bay, there was often someone who wanted to make use of our guest room.

That particular Sunday morning I woke, feeling skinny, and resenting the fact it was technically a rest-from-running day. I headed straight to the shower to get ready for church. Tom snoozed as I worked shampoo into my scalp, scrubbing away the row from the night before, unaware that something out of the ordinary was about to happen.

Our bathtub had tall, sliding doors instead of a shower curtain. The doors were clear at the very top, then had stripes etched into the perspex at about shoulder height before graduating down to opaque. I was rinsing my hair and turned my face to the spray to wash away the lather that was sliding down my forehead.

Look at him! said an inside voice that was not mine.

Just as my eyes squinted shut in the water, I caught a glimpse of a small leprechaun standing perfectly still and happy, sink-height, just to the right of the toilet. Not a kitsch garden gnome, but a real, live leprechaun. Time slowed. I was looking at something that really should not have been there. I needed to rinse my eyes to get a better look, but was reluctant to see him again. What the hell was this little person doing standing in the bathroom, watching me shower?

From the pit of my belly I screamed, wiped my eyes, and looked again. He was gone. I knew he would be. But where was he now? When would he be back?

Tom pulled open the bathroom door.

'What the hell? Are you okay? What's wrong? What happened?'

I burst into tears and then laughed, and told him I thought I had seen something but I was wrong. My eyes were playing tricks on me.

A knock came at our bedroom door—Mark had heard my scream from the spare room. 'Is everything alright in there, guys?'

'Yes, sorry about that,' I called back as Tom threw me a towel, looking at me inquiringly.

'Yes, don't worry,' he called. 'Jacinta just spooked herself.'

The three of us chuckled about my blood-curdling scream as we sat in the taxi on the way to church. I had spooked myself, and there wasn't much more to it. We were all scheduled on the worship team that morning and preferred to discuss the set list. I preferred to stay busy.

. . .

No matter how hard I trained, or prayed, Tom and I fought increasingly often about my suspicions about Peta. A day could not go by without my insecurity surfacing, and my insecurity could not surface without causing major problems.

'If you will just admit it, then I will forgive you.'

'I am not going to admit anything, because there is nothing to admit!'

'Just tell me the truth and then we can work it out.'

There had to be a reason for the tangible unease that had taken up residence within me, and I needed that reason to not originate with me.

'You don't think I see the way you two look at each other?' I said. 'The way you talk to each other?'

'I look at her, and I talk to her like I'm looking at and talking to a friend, Jacinta! Because she *is* a friend! You need to grow up! You need to get a grip!'

'You are so horrible to me, but you are the sweetest, nicest guy alive, to her. You love her! Why can't you just be honest so I can move on with my life?'

Tom clenches his teeth when he is angry. 'The reason I am

horrible to you is because you are accusing me of something really serious. I can't stand the way you are acting. You are totally pushing me away from you, if that's what you mean by being horrible ... How the hell am I supposed to react to you?'

'Aha! I see, I get it now!' I shouted. 'You want to paint me as the bad guy so that, when you leave me, it will look like I'm the one who made this happen. Well, you and I both know the truth, Tom. Just remember that. One day, when I'm not in your life anymore, you can just think about that. You're the one who twisted this.'

'I'm not talking to you about this anymore,' replied Tom exasperated. 'Leave me alone.'

'And by the way, you should tell her to give me back my colander.'

'What?'

'It's gone. She's stolen it, right out of the kitchen.'

'The thing you wash vegetables in?' Tom stared at me totally discomposed. Then he said aloud, for the first time, the words I'd known all along were coming to me.

'You are crazy.'

He should have known better. This was the low blow he knew had the power to take me out. With a family history of mental illness, I had confided in him my deepest fear that one day my time would come.

'That's exactly what you both want me think, isn't it?' I said bitterly. 'You would look so innocent if I was the crazy one, so you and her can just go off and be together while everyone thinks I'm the crazy one! You want me locked away, don't you? In a mental hospital! I never knew you could be this evil, Tom. This is manipulation on the worst possible level. You know I am defenceless! To let some random person come along and play mind games with me just to get to you. Well done. It's over for us now. When I prove she took the colander, you will both be sorry. You think it just disappeared all by itself? I will make everyone sorry.'

The argument felt terminal, the sort that would send most people packing, and yet my husband had other ways of dealing with me. He bunkered down. He stopped responding to my allegations and my temper tantrums. He was not going to let me ruffle any more of his feathers.

He got up each morning and went to work, and came home every evening, ate dinner, watched TV, then went to bed. If I pushed hard enough, we could repeat the argument, and this I would do, sometimes daily. However, when my rage was spent, the silence endured.

I would go into another room and rummage through the stationery drawer. At the age of 25, I had been a cutter for only a couple of years. I don't remember what started it specifically; it was just a new attempt to release that bad feeling that had been with me all along. A few small slices of physical pain helped me to cope with the confusion inside. Bringing something out from within was a strange type of relief, but it wasn't enough.

I started vomiting again. I needed to expel more of the dark feeling inside. I needed to save my marriage. If I could run, and fast, and vomit up any food accidentally eaten in moments of weakness, then I would be very slim. It was unlikely that Peta had as sophisticated a plan as mine, so this meant I would soon be smaller than her. I needed to find an edge. Smaller is better. Bigger is the same as fatter. Fat is weak. Skinny is beautiful and strong. Skinny wins. This was the plan.

As the plan unfolded, I became a tight rubber ball, pinging between sadistic exercise, food deprivation veiled as spiritual discipline, binge eating and worshipping at the foot of the toilet. This cycle could not last long. The approach of Christmas broke it up. As it had done throughout history, the birth of Christ interrupted all the plans.

15

EARLY IN THE morning on 26 December 2004, we woke up to news of the Asian Tsunami. I was not there, and I did not personally know anyone who was. But something jolted me.

I had been out walking Diesel that morning, still feeling disgusted at the food I had eaten the day before. Tom had vetoed my attempt to fast over the holidays, and coaxed me into suspending our problems for a day. On the way home, I overheard the security guards talking about something happening in Thailand. I got home to find Tom channel surfing, soon landing on the news. As we took in the images of chaos and devastation, we racked our brains for anyone we knew who might be there. Thankfully, there was no one, yet we left the television on during that Boxing Day. Watching was the least we could do.

I cleared the Christmas debris of tinsel and wrapping paper from the carpet on my living room floor. One moment oblivious, the next drowning in the guilt of being alive. I still hadn't found any sense of resolution after 9/11, and here was another catastrophe, which I would inevitably have to wait until I got to heaven to ask God to explain. I wondered if the world was coming to an end. Perhaps that would explain why everything else in my life also felt so messed up.

I phoned my parents to check whether they had heard the news. Despite living in their Sai Kung house for eight years, they still hadn't hooked up to the local TV channels. Whatever the case, Dad would have something intelligent to say.

'Oh dear,' he said. 'Of course, the worst is yet to come. There will be problems of hygiene and risk of infection until they get things cleared up.'

The days ticked by and the death count rose. Bizarre sea creatures were washed up on shores. I started my fast again and focused on praying for all things tsunami. I wanted to help. I wanted to get my hands dirty binding up wounds.

At one point in my life, I had thought I wanted to be a doctor—my grades did not permit it though, but here was an opportunity to redeem my existence. I did not want to be a pathetic failure anymore. I wanted to do something so heroic that every other part of me could be forgotten. I wondered if I could volunteer to go and help. There was no reason not to try. The idea continued to germinate. It began to feel like a clear call from God. When an announcement was made at church that a team from Hong Kong was being assembled to go, I took to my journal to process my thoughts and to make a record of what was surely a pivotal moment in my life. I was of course, at the time unaware that those pages would forever more contain evidence of the ramblings of a madwoman.

. . .

10 January 2005

Last night, I prayed again that God would confirm whether or not I am to go on this aid trip to Indonesia. The response was not what I expected. I feel that I have heard God tell me that, not only will I go, but that I will not come back.

I'm writing this now with thanksgiving in my heart because God has shared his plans with me. This is not intended to be a glory diary; rather, it's a testimony. Solid proof, first of God's reality and communication, and second, of his goodness and mercy. I've often wondered about the best way to die. Now I know the answer, God has revealed it to me: it's doing his will in love (1 John 3:16). Not only that, but knowing God's plan, being informed about the future (or lack of it) here on Earth, and being given the opportunity to prepare for it. That's what I'm doing now. I'm leaving my message.

This is coming from that magical place of wisdom and insight and revelation that people on their deathbeds often get. Here it is. Not only do I get the privilege of writing this, I also get to enjoy my final days in the company of my loved ones—my biological family and my church family. They don't know about all this. God has informed me that he has shut their understanding on this matter. I was rather surprised that Tom hadn't displayed any anxiety about me going on this trip. But God says that it's not that he doesn't care—not at all—it's that God himself does not want anyone to distract me from this calling.

So many times I've sung songs and prayed prayers—the dangerous kind, about giving up my life for God. He heard me. He loves it when his children are available for his use—no matter what it is—leading worship, cleaning toilets, missions, staying home, living, dying ... It's all useful to God. Many times I've checked myself on the words I utter before God (Ecclesiastes 5:2). The truth is, I'm not kidding. I am prepared to give my life to God, for his use, no matter what it is.

I don't actually know what it is, exactly. All I can do is confirm in my heart that I'm willing, and try to communicate to anyone who wants to know, that God is real and he is good. My hope is that I will die making a stand for Jesus (I have a feeling guns will be involved). I pray that someone's life might be saved as mine is taken (I see a vision of a child, or a girl ...). Not only that, I pray that many will come to believe in, know and love God because of what I'm writing now, linked with whatever is going to happen next week. Especially my family. God has promised me.

This morning, I woke up beside my beautiful husband and asked God if there could be another way to go about all this. The response was John 12:24—'Unless a grain of wheat falls to the ground and dies, it can bear no fruit.' I must follow the example Jesus set, in life and in death. As I've gone about my day today, I have been flipping between tears of sorrow from the thought of leaving those I love behind, and thoughts that my mind might be playing tricks on me. Perhaps I have not heard correctly? Perhaps I should plead with God for my life?

Maybe I shouldn't go on this trip. No. I should go. I will go unless God says otherwise. I will prepare as if I am hearing correctly. Only time will tell.

I love the life I've lived so far, but, as it says at the end of Mark 9, if I love my fleshly life, I will lose the eternal one. Right now, I have no option but to choose eternity over my desire to live out my days on Earth.

Am I afraid to die? Absolutely not—I never have been. I'm sad to leave people behind, but the truth is, I know God will take care of them. Perhaps it's a good thing that Tom is enjoying other things and other people these days. If my leaving is the only way to get them to call out to God, then fine. I have no fear of physical pain. What can a mere man do to me? Rape? Mutilation? Torture? It will only last a moment. I will be with God in no time. Jesus will be there with me.

This is not for my glory. I do not want to be celebrated as anything other than someone who truly loved God. I hope I don't sound like a complete idiot. I only want people to hear my story in order for God's fame to increase. I always have wanted to do something great for the kingdom. Here it is! It's not what I expected, but God's like that. His plans are bigger and better than ours (Isaiah 55:8).

Later

Here I am again, hearing the sounds of the TV show that Tom was watching in the living room. Is this real? Is my time really coming to an end? Is God going to do a last-minute switch, like he did for Abraham and Isaac? I just can't know for sure. But I can declare this in writing: I don't care either way. I love God and I trust him. How trite and cliché that must sound ... along with most of the other prayers I pray ... unless, I can put my life where my mouth is. That's what I have to do.

Even if I don't die heroically while saving someone else's life, I want everyone to know that I'm giving my life in order to get God some attention. Don't feel bad. Don't wish there could have been another way—just stop wasting time with the temporary things of this world, and give yourself to following God. Please stop wasting time. There is more to life. God is real. There is work to be done. No, that doesn't mean that everyone has to run off to become missionaries; I just ask that, if you don't know whether or not you are going to heaven, you make the decision to believe in Jesus. He will take you on a wonderful journey. You will be glad that you went, I promise you. And if you already believe in him—keep it up! Sell out to your faith. Don't be lukewarm.

I'm rattling on a bit now. I should stop and get some sleep. No doubt I'll have another message from beyond the grave for you tomorrow. Sorry if this is weird ... It's got your attention, at least! God is real! What are you going to do about it? God is good. His peace doesn't make sense. His plans are not what we would have come up with, but he is God, and he is smart. I'm going to give him the benefit of the doubt.

11 January 2005

Time is moving very slowly. Should I even go to this meeting tonight? Maybe we can't afford for me to go. Maybe it's not God's will for us to be in debt. I shouldn't make matters worse by spending money we don't have.

I want to make it clear right now that I am no hero. I am full of good intentions and I know what the right attitude is. I know the power of positive thinking and speaking truth and pulling things from the substance of faith into reality ... I know all that, but I am still me. Pretty crap, really. This isn't false humility; there's no time for that. It's time to show my hand.

I've been fasting: 'cultivating a hunger for God', 'taking my relationship with him to a deeper level', 'learning the blessings of obedience', 'doing a spiritual overhaul', 'committing this year to him'. I don't mean to sound sarcastic; I'm feeling tense. I've cried out to God: 'Take all of me! Let your will be done in and through me! I'm available! Speak to me!' But I am SO not happy with what he's said. I thought I meant it; now I'm not so sure. You mean you're going to wipe me out, God? Are you serious? Following you is going to cost me something that actually costs me something? Oh dear. Perhaps. I don't know. Probably not. God's better than that. I don't know.

Fasting doesn't earn me anything more from God. That would be 'works'. But faith without works is dead. All that fasting does is tune me into God's voice more and allows God more access to me. I believe in God's goodness and redemptive power, so much so that I was confessing my sin as I was stuffing warm, buttery bread into my mouth. I keep breaking my fast. I can't do anything right. I am hoping, more and more, that this will all get called off, though. I wonder if there's some kind of deal I can strike. I just can't know for sure. I really can't know anything at all until I go to the meeting tonight.

I don't remember the last time Tom and I really talked. I can't tell him what's going on inside me right now. I just know in my gut that I mustn't. No one else can understand the personal things God does in someone else's life. Is all this from God? Is it biblical? Is it from the enemy, trying to waste my time and inject me with fear? I'm not fearful. If anything, only good can come of this—surely it is God? Either I am right, and I have been hearing correctly, and by the time anyone reads this I will be dead, and then my whole family will be saved and this testimony will fly around the internet or something—all to the glory of God ... OR I'm hearing it wrong, and maybe I am a little crazy.

That doesn't mean that I'm afraid. It just means that if, IF this whole thing is about God wanting my attention, then he's got it.

So, on the off-chance that I do come back from this trip alive, I know that my life cannot be the same. I will work with more purpose, love with more action, praise God with more effort. I will spread the gospel with no shame. I will live a life without compromise (or, at least, without falsity—I am not about to set myself up for failure by saying I'll never break a fast again). I will not waste any more time. I will invest in people. I will not fill my life with meaningless pursuits. But again, this is IF I come back.

12 January 2005

I'm not going. No saving Indonesians from tsunami destruction for me. No certain death for now, either. I was only at the meeting for five minutes. The guy in charge got up and said, 'Thanks for coming ....' Something about being encouraged by the turnout, but spaces on the trip were limited and now reserved only for medical professionals.

As soon as they announced this, Tom and I left the meeting so Tom could get some dinner (I'm still fasting). I was a mess, half disappointed and half relieved. Mostly relieved, but then also feeling guilty for feeling relieved. I broke down and started to tell Tom a bit of what I have been going through. His reaction came as a bit of a shock. Not only did he not share my relief, but he doesn't think I was hearing from God at all, and he actually got mad at me! He

> *was upset that I hadn't said anything to him. He says he's worried about me. And so he should have been! I guess he will never be able to understand why God tells me he wants things a certain way. I cannot expect someone who hasn't been fasting to understand me while I'm in the middle of a fast. I meant well. I just wanted to get my hands dirty by helping.*

. . .

And this is the point in the story when I did get some blood on my hands. The blood, however, was not directly tsunami-related, it was my own. I was the one in need of help, and I would soon be on my way to the emergency room to have my wrist sewn up, and to begin the long process of piecing myself back together again.

. . .

I HAD BEEN NAPPING on the sofa, a habit I had fallen into. Serious runners need plenty of rest, and this was even more the case for a serious runner attempting a 40-day fast. I slept in fits, waking to the conclusion that Tom was undeniably in love with Peta, and plotting to leave me, and by now he would have tipped her off about the colander and she would have disposed of it so I would have no evidence. Something had just not felt right for a long time, and I had finally put my finger on what it was. I had never been more certain of anything in my whole life.

Although I had stated my suspicions multiple times, I was never met with the assurance I wanted. If they were innocent, then he should have simply assured me; peace would have returned, and we could have all moved on. It had to be a guilty conscience stopping him. It was his cry for help. Every attempt had ended in a rip-roaring argument.

My nap ended sooner than I would have liked and, in a groggy state, I upgraded suspicion to all-out accusation. We argued again. Tom's calm but appalled demeanour did not fit the seriousness of the crime he hid. This sent me hurtling into a rage. I summoned every ounce of white-hot power from the beast that lived inside me. I commanded him to rise and either make my husband give me peace or grant me licence to burst.

Tom, however, was not in the mood. Before I had even fully woken up, I found myself storming down the hall spouting obscenities and then locking myself into the study. I rummaged through my drawer.

DO IT! ordered every fibre within.

My eyes squeezed shut and I pulled. In the flash of a second, I split from myself.

Time split. There was a scream, followed only by the awareness that the scream had been filled with more terror than I expected. The pull of the blade had happened faster and more forcefully than I had intended. The scream summoned Tom at an unprecedented speed. Not normally one to be hurried, he was now pounding on the door, demanding I unlock it.

'Right now or I'll kick it down!'

His tone made it clear that whatever game we had been playing was over. The concern I had wanted from Tom, and had accused him of withholding, was finally there. Mixed in with some fear. But that concern that I had yearned for, I suddenly no longer wanted: buyer's remorse to the extreme. Like a child wishing she hadn't thrown her sister's bangles off the balcony, wishing the stolen dresses weren't hanging in her bedroom, wishing she hadn't snooped in her brother's CD collection. I frantically searched for some way to undo it all.

Tom's stern voice commanded that I rise. However, as I reached out to unlock the door, my attention snagged on the warm stream flowing, silent and steady, from my left wrist, and the bright red puddle forming on the floor. Fighting the urge to faint, I turned the doorknob.

'Let me see it,' said Tom.

I clutched my wrist in a pathetic effort to hide what I had done.

'Show me!'

I released my grip slightly and more blood poured out. Tom's eyes trailed the stream out to the sea on the floor. He rushed out of the room and returned with a towel.

'We've got to go. Now.' He held me tightly by the shoulders, and in silence we hurried out of the flat and straight into a taxi that had just been vacated by a passenger. Fortunately, Shui Fai Terrace was just minutes from the nearest hospital.

'*Yi yuen* (hospital),' I said to the taxi driver, '*jun fai* (fast as you can).'

'Ho fai, mm goi!' Tom repeated. He wanted us there fast.

The driver looked over his shoulder and caught a glimpse of the blood-soaked towel. He told me I needed to be more careful when chopping food.

'Yes, I am very clumsy.'

We did not speak in the taxi. We entered the ER and approached the registration desk, where a male nurse told me to sit.

‘What is the matter?’ he asked.

I lifted my arm above desk level and unwrapped the towel, just enough to reveal the shameful cut within.

‘Are you feeling sad?’ the questioning continued. ‘Did you want to end your life?’

‘No,’ Tom and I said in unison.

‘I was angry,’ I came clean. ‘It was a mistake.’

‘Yes, okay,’ agreed the nurse. ‘Go with her for stitching.’ He motioned to another nurse.

I was led into a private room and told to lie down. The nurse cradled my left arm as she administered a tetanus shot, followed by the stitches. Finally, a hospital warden came, handed me a letter, and then led me back out to the main waiting area to meet Tom.

‘We are going to have to tell someone,’ he said. ‘We cannot keep this to ourselves this time.’

16

IN THE TAXI I cried as quietly as I could and turned my face toward the window—partly to avoid the glances of yet another concerned taxi driver, but mostly to avoid having to look my husband in the eye.

Tom had seen me throw a fair few tantrums in our time. We had been together since we were 17 and we had done a lot of growing up together. Arguments ranged from heated to verbally and emotionally abusive. We had both done our share of forgiving and forgetting of what other people might deem inexcusable behaviour. A different sort of couple would have long since split, but it seemed Tom and I loved each other more than we loved our own dignity. We always made up and tore up scorecards in the name of commitment, and on the Christian grounds that love covers a multitude of sins. But, somewhere in our minds lay the unspoken understanding that she who lands herself in the emergency room has crossed a line.

'I'm going to have to tell the senior pastors,' said Tom. Working for a church involves a great deal of personal accountability to your bosses. 'We can't deal with this by ourselves. Maybe I'll call James, he does some counselling now.'

'Do what you want.' In the slash of a blade I had relinquished my rights.

'Okay, I am going to call Daughin and Priscilla,' Tom said. 'We need someone to help us.'

The taxi delivered us to our building and we went up to our flat. As Tom unlocked the door, I told him not to follow me. I grabbed a couple of cheap workout towels and went into the room where it had all happened, closing the door behind me. Tom didn't need to see it all again.

. . .

I had set up a beautiful art studio for myself. There were tall bookshelves loaded with art books, sketchbooks and art supplies. There was a drawing table in front of a window for optimum lighting, and sketches were pinned up on the walls to make me feel like a real illustrator.

On the floor lay my Stanley knife beside two puddles of blood, one larger than the other. I remembered it feeling warm as it spilled out of me; but as I wiped it up, I noticed that the winter air had turned it cold. It wasn't nearly as difficult to clean up as they make out in the movies. I did not bother to rinse out the towels before I stuffed them in a plastic bag, knotted it, took it out to the stairwell and put it in the bin. I had never liked those towels, anyway. They represented just another failure in a growing list.

I had been so full of ambition when I set up the dance studio, choosing paint colours for the walls and quality paper for my stationery. It was a beautiful studio. I had bought those towels to keep on the shelf for my sweaty students to use. Every detail of the setup for my studio had been considered, but the same could not be said for the details needed for actually operating a viable business.

When The Point began to fail, I started to bring bits and pieces home with me, simply to avoid feeling like the capital spent had gone to waste. Those cheap towels served as a daily reminder of my failure in business, and the sight of them soaked in my blood was enough to warrant the trip to the bin. Once the clean-up was done, I returned to the sofa to sleep and to try to imagine none of it had ever happened.

. . .

DAUGHIN AND PRISCILLA knocked softly before letting themselves in. They had heard the desperation in Tom's voice over the phone, and understood the severity of the situation. They had dropped everything to come straight over. They approached gently, full of concern.

'What's going on, you guys?' Daughin pulled up a seat opposite me, and Tom sat down on my left, holding the fingers at the end of my injured arm. Priscilla sat down on my right and placed her hand on my shoulder. Tom drew in a deep breath.

'Well, Jacinta has been struggling a bit lately ... Today, things got out of hand ... she got upset and cut herself quite badly.'

I cried big, heavy tears, unable to speak, as I listened to the witness testify. As Tom finished his account of the events, we both hung our heads. Then Daughin began his response.

'Okay, you are both in shock. It's like your whole building has collapsed and you are just sitting here in the rubble, trying to figure out what's happened. You need to slow down. You can't do anything today. Just rest and pray and wait for the shock to wear off. This is a really big deal and there is going to be a lot of work to do, but not today. Today, we just need to pray. Everything will be okay, but you will both need to do some hard work. Tom, what Jacinta needs to hear right now is that you are committed to her and you are going to stay by her side while she works though this. Are you?'

Both Tom and I always felt a little silly when Daughin would ask us questions like this in front of each other. It was something he did a lot, but in all honesty, it was exactly what we needed. The questions were always followed by instructions to look into each other's eyes and tell each other things, and this time was no different. Tom did as Daughin told him to do: he turned to face me, and told me he forgave me for my actions and was committed to working things out. This must have happened after I had been told to look into his eyes and tell him I was sorry. We then sat still, as Daughin and Priscilla prayed that we would have a good rest and take things one step at a time. They stayed with us for hours, totally calm on the surface, only years later sharing with me that they had felt a need to be sure we would make it through the night with no further drama before they left.

As our time together drew to a close, Daughin moved over to the dining table.

'What's this?' He had found the letter the hospital had given to me. It was a single piece of A4 paper folded in half and stapled closed. The nurse had told me to take it to a different hospital the next day for specialist care. I had wanted to know what it said but didn't know if I was allowed to open it. It was stapled.

'I want to know what it says, but it's stapled.' I told Daughin, and then watched in awe as he popped it open for me, unfazed by the staple.

'I don't want you to worry about this.' He put the letter back on the table where Tom and I could see it.

Attempted suicide. Patient requires psychiatric follow-up.

The world crashed around me for the second time that day. There it was, printed in black ink. The words had been typed into a computer and onto a record that would bear my name forevermore. This had really happened.

'I'm going to be a mental patient,' I said. 'I have to see a psychiatrist.'

'You can see me.' Daughin had left SNA leadership in order to study and was now a fully qualified counsellor, offering me his help, repeating the words, 'Do not worry.' He and Priscilla put on their shoes, gave us hugs and then left, closing the front door quietly. They were no longer employed by the church, but would continue to care for us in a pastoral way for years to come.

I turned to my husband with a fresh pool of tears.

'Tom, I'm going to be a mental patient.' I knew Tom understood my fear. With mental illness in my family, he knew the graveness I felt as he held me again.

'You are going to be okay,' he said. 'We will get through this. I want you to go to your follow-up appointment tomorrow. You can see Daughin as well, but you need to do what the hospital told you to do. We are going to deal with this properly.

'I'm so sorry.'

. . .

THE MINIBUS CLIMBED a steep hill, up the driveway and into the bus terminus. The passengers filed off and dispersed, each with their own reason for being at the Pamela Youde Hospital that day. I wasn't thinking about them, though. I made my way to the directory board and then toward the lift that would take me up to the psychiatric unit. I had never been good with directions, but today felt like the homecoming I had always dreaded; the long-awaited arrival at the place I truly belonged. Like an outlaw tired of being on the run, I was finally ready to turn myself in.

The metallic walls of the lift were judging me on the way up. They had seen it all before and had no interest in hearing my side of the story. We stopped on the floor before mine, and I stepped back to make room for an orderly as he manoeuvred an elderly man in a wheelchair into the front section of the deep and narrow lift. The patient slumped to one side of his seat, heavily medicated. His eyes were focused steadily on something in another dimension. Drool hung from his chin and as he said, 'Ngah ngah ngah ngah ngah ....'

He was either saying *teeth teeth teeth teeth teeth* in Cantonese, or he was just making crazy sounds, it made no difference. He belonged here.

The lift doors opened again as we reached the psychiatric floor. It seemed to be empty. The wheelchair was pulled out and turned right, and I turned left to the nurse's station. The lighting was dim—it might have been lunchtime or some other off-peak moment. I approached the desk with a trembling in my soul, and was greeted by a man in a white coat with too eager a smile and eyeglasses so thick that they magnified his eyes.

They will make a movie of my life. They will make a movie and I will remember this and tell them exactly how to do this scene. They won't believe me. They will think I am exaggerating.

The man read my letter. He looked up at me, still smiling.

'How do you feel?'

'I'm okay.'

'Are you in immediate danger of hurting yourself?'

'No.'

'Okay, then I will give you an appointment slip. You need to come back to see the doctor on this date. If you don't want to wait, you can try one of these private doctors on the list—you can keep this list. If you are feeling unwell at home, you can come and stay here.'

'Thank you.' I took the pastel green sheet of paper that held the contact information for a selection of private psychiatrists. I took the appointment slip summoning me back to the Pamela Youde in three months' time. I turned and made my way back down the lift, and then through to the hospital minibus terminus.

We couldn't wait three months. My inner beast had not escaped, even though I had created a sizeable opening to let him out. Tom and I were fighting more than ever before. But Tom somehow always kept his head level; one of us had to. He entrusted me with the task of finding myself a doctor, so I chose one of a multiple Dr Chans from the list and made myself an appointment.

His waiting room was small and ugly, and his office was no better. He sat behind a large desk between several piles of papers and box folders. There were books shoved onto his bookcase in inappropriate ways, and a thick layer of dust covered the corners of the carpet and all of the places too inconvenient for a vacuum cleaner to reach.

He asked me to tell him why I was there. I told him I had been to the emergency room after hurting myself. He asked if I had struggled with mental illness throughout my life, if any family members had been diagnosed with mental illness, if I heard voices, or saw things that were not really there. He wanted to know if I felt I was very powerful, that I might save the world, or if I suspected someone or something was out to get me or to take something away from me. He wanted to know about my sleep, my appetite, my sex drive, my religious beliefs, my mood ....

I answered as thoroughly as I could, given the challenge of the environment. A cluttered desk is a reflection of a cluttered mind.

But, Jacinta, you are in no position to judge.

'I will explain to you what we are trying to ascertain here,' said the doctor, 'whether we are dealing with a hardware problem or a software problem. Some mental issues are to do with a chemical imbalance or with physical factors; others are more about thinking habits, attitudes and environment.'

'What do you think it is in my case?' I was sure he would say he didn't know because he would need to run tests—draw blood, do brain scans, things like that.

'You have bipolar disorder. I will give you some medicine to help you feel better. The first is an antidepressant—this will help with your low mood. The second is an anti-psychotic—this will help with your strange thoughts. The third is a mood stabiliser—this will help you feel more balanced. The fourth is anti-anxiety to keep you calm. The last one is to help you sleep better. Please make sure you are not pregnant before commencing these.'

'How long will I need to take this medicine?'

'Don't worry about that for now. Bipolar Disorder is an ongoing condition that will be lifelong. There is no cure. You are now about to enter a stabilisation phase that could last months, at least. Most people with your diagnosis are better off taking medicine for the long term. Come back and see me next week.'

I never went back. I didn't like his dusty, cluttered office, or his conclusions.

Shortly after I informed Tom I would not be returning to Dr Chan's office, I overheard him on the phone asking someone for an appointment.

'I'm worried about her,' I heard him say. 'Sometimes it's like she's possessed. I think she has some sort of split personality or something.'

I spent the next month visiting Jimmy, another former leader of SNA. Tom knew Jimmy and trusted him. Jimmy and his wife, Lynda, were in Hong Kong for the long run, now operating a prayer-counselling ministry in a small flat on one of Hong Kong's outlying islands. I was not altogether sure of what prayer counselling actually was, but Tom made it clear that, since I had dismissed Dr Chan, I was about to find out.

Jimmy asked me questions about my childhood, and then we asked the Holy Spirit to bring up whatever it was that needed bringing up. Then we went through all the details, every single one of them, asking for God to rewrite memories, and to reveal to my mind's eye a vision of Jesus in the picture, because the truth was that he had been there all along. It was an intensely thorough process of digging up the past, rubbing cleansing salts into wounds, crying and/or hyperventilating, and then collapsing in a heap of emotional and physical exhaustion.

Each session lasted hours. I would head home in a state of catharsis and utter bemusement over Jimmy and Lynda's ability to sit and care, with such sincerity, through so a vast a quantity of my crap. They were definitely saints.

Tom accompanied me to the first session, but opted out after that point. I didn't blame him. It was hard enough work for me to dredge up all of my own demons; I could only imagine how torturous it must have been for anyone else to have to sit through it all.

In each session, there was much talk of whether I had ever been abused. I didn't think I had, so I asked my parents. They didn't think I had, either, yet we all continued to ask God to reveal the source of my pain. It was clear that something was wrong with me; it was just a matter of figuring out what it was. I remembered that I had tried to sell my soul to the devil as a child, but the devil hadn't been interested. I had felt rejected by this. Jimmy, Lynda and I prayed and put a spiritual seal on it. I had watched every horror movie I could get my hands on as a child, so we prayed and sealed that up, too. I had renounced the horror movies a couple times before, once in Perth and again at a spiritual healing course in Oxford, but there was no harm in renouncing things more than just the once.

I wanted to know how long I would have to attend these sessions, though I didn't want to offend either Jimmy or Lynda. After four sessions I decided I simply could not bear to attend any more of what I had started to look upon as my own pity parties. I couldn't see how drumming up more problems was going to help me out of the current 'mental illness' related predicament.

Tom was not pleased—I had quit again. The bottom line was that I had to get some professional help. The prayer stuff was optional, but he was adamant about my seeing a real psychiatrist. The ideal would be to find a Christian psychiatrist, so I went on a hunt.

. . .

I phoned the numbers listed on several ads in the classified section of some city magazines. They all promised help, but none could refer me to an English-speaking Christian psychiatrist. They simply did not seem to exist in Hong Kong at that time. Perhaps this was due to the belief some Christians held that faith was a sufficient antidote to mental illness. Perhaps mental health was not meant to be a problem for serious Christians. Whatever the case, I was struggling to find professional help, and did not know how to go about asking for what I needed. Eventually, a sympathetic life coach from church called Jaime offered me the number of a psychiatrist that one of her clients had recommended—not a Christian, but English-speaking and just about affordable.

Dr Lee's office was pleasantly uncluttered and dust-free. He asked very similar questions to those that Dr Chan had asked, but the major difference was that he wore a light blue tie with small bumblebees embroidered on it, and this I liked very much. At the end of our 30-minute appointment, I was diagnosed, once more, with bipolar disorder. I made no mention of Dr Chan or the prescription I had given up on after a week. However, Dr Lee gave me the same number of drugs, this time with slightly different names, but with the exact same descriptions. I politely declined the further offer of Xanax because I did not consider myself a sufferer of panic attacks and had no plans to become one.

Tom held me as I cried that night. I fought flashbacks of myself as a sarcastic teenager who, when wanting to draw attention to someone's moodiness, used the phrase, 'Did you forget to take your medication this morning?' I was now officially someone who needed to remember to take her medication each morning—and after lunch, and at night before bed. Poetic justice.

But I could see the relief on Tom's face. He had known something was not right with me for a long time, and having things verified by a professional brought him a tangible sense of peace.

Remembering which pills needed taking and when was to be my next job. I bought myself several different little pillboxes to try. I decided on a favourite—a rectangular clamshell design made of semi-transparent plastic. When unclasped and opened, one half was divided into eight small compartments, each with their own flip-up lid. I liked that there were eight. I could fill up for a week and a day, so I would always be prepared and ahead of myself. The other half had one full flip-up lid and no compartments. I would keep my contraceptive pills in there—they were part of the regime. Babies had not been on our radar anyway, but now that I was officially in the stabilisation stage of a bipolar diagnosis, they were entirely out of the question: the doctor said meds and foetuses did not mix. When all the little lids in my box were closed and the main clasp shut, everything inside was very secure. There was no risk of anything falling out into my bag.

I used a white-out pen to write the days of the week on the mini-compartments, but then used a plastic ruler to scratch it all off again. I needed more than one compartment per day. There were too many pills and it was all getting confusing. In the end, I settled on using the box for four days at a time: I drew a sun for each of the four AMs and moons for the PMs. These would be my lunch and night-time doses. I had to move the breakfast pills into one of the other pill organisers—this one was a cylindrical, clear plastic stack of little round pillboxes, each screwed onto the bottom of the next. There was only a screw-top lid for the very top compartment, and the thought of losing this lid brought a mildly sick feeling that sat in my stomach for the entire duration of my medicated days. The round box would live at home. The cloudy, rectangle clamshell box would live in my handbag, its presence my albatross. It was what it was.

Once the pill logistics were all taken care of, a small wave of calm lapped over my toes. Perhaps I could manage this.

17

TOM ARRANGED A meeting with our church's leadership so that we could tell them what had happened. We didn't know what to expect. However, as a staff member Tom wanted to be upfront about his personal life, and since I was a leader at the youth group, we felt it would have been wrong to stay quiet. We wondered if I would be told to resign, or if Tom might even lose his job.

At the time I did not know how to describe my church in terms of style, theology or even culture, but I had seen American missionaries blush when offered wine at our newcomers' evenings, and so I would deduce that we were of a liberal bent. And, from time spent in the church office, I knew that, as a religious organisation, we were not especially organised. But I assumed that, written down somewhere, there was a minimum standard of got-it-togetherness required of a leader.

I racked my brain for our church's criteria, but came up with none. The truth was, much of our church involved sincere people making things up as we went along. Therefore, when it came to the disclosure of my 'attempted suicide', Tom and I weren't sure how to prepare ourselves. The church was inter-denominational—no one was ordained in an official way; no one was *technically* qualified. I believed that my leaders were people who were worth following, people who were worth my respect. This worthiness was what I had worked so hard to emit to the youth group. The logical flip side of this was the fact that, if someone were to lose their leadership-worthiness, then they should also lose their position as a leader. Now I had lost everything, and had nothing to offer anyone.

John and Tony, the two senior pastors, listened quietly as Tom talked them through what had happened and explained that I was now regularly seeing a psychiatrist who had recommended long-term medication. Tom held my hand as he spoke, and when he had said all there was to say, we waited for what felt like an eternity.

Finally, I could take it no longer.

'I'm so sorry for all the trouble,' I blurted out. 'I know I need to stop being a leader.' This got things moving.

'What we really need you to know,' replied one of the pastors, 'is that any break you take from any areas of church that you're involved in, whether it be in youth group, dance, worship team, or all of them, is going to be because you feel you need to rest. We are not saying you have to stop. It is important that you know you are not disqualified. You'll probably be feeling that way, and that would be understandable, but it's wrong. That is not how it works. None of us is perfect. If you want to rest, we will support you in that, and want you to know you will have a rest with our blessing. But you are not disqualified.'

What a relief. Yes, a rest is what I wanted. My head hurt, and I just wanted some peace and quiet. I wanted to be rid of every obligation, every duty, every responsibility. I didn't want to be a role model anymore. The church had just offered my freedom on a plate. I willingly accepted.

The only thing that stood between me and some tranquillity was The Point. My studio: it was my dream, my initiative, my undertaking. I had tried to walk away from it, and was honestly a little surprised that, in my doing so, it hadn't simply disappeared. There it sat, gathering dust, not going anywhere. It was my problem, and I needed it to go away.

. . .

I called Mum, fully expecting her to *Roger that*, wave her magic wand and make my business disappear. Her witchcraft did prove useful occasionally. But she did not know what I had been going through and, true to form, Mum did not respond to me in the way I had hoped she would.

'Absolutely not, my darling.'

'What?'

'I'm saying no.'

'What? Did you hear me? I'm saying I can't do it anymore.'

'Yes, I hear what you are saying, but Daddy and I have been talking and have decided that we've been too easy on you. We've let you quit too many of your things, and this time we think the best thing for you to do is to stick at it. You need discipline to be a dancer, and you need even more of it to run a dance studio. I think this is a good time for you to buckle down and commit to what you are doing and stop looking for a way out.'

She had tried this tactic a couple of times before in my life—I was flaky and we all knew it. I also knew from experience that, if I just pushed my case harder, she would acquiesce. But this time I lacked the emotional reserve to force Mum's hand. I realised that, as an adult, and as the sole name on the lease, I was not in need of her permission. It was simply that I had hoped she would take the problem off my hands to save me the trouble. But she wasn't going to do that without a fight, and I didn't have the fight in me. I would have to shut it down without her.

I gave the landlord notice. I closed down my classes. Day by day, I shuttled more bits and pieces home. I asked friends to come and help themselves to yoga mats and dumbbells. I donated stationery and office furniture to the church. Finally, it was time to hand over the keys.

I walked away from my first business venture, relieved to have dealt with a sizeable problem—I had plugged a huge hole in my bucket. The studio had been a constant drain on my energy, and I needed that energy to deal with my mental health. A sensible decision on all counts, surely?

Yes and no. In shutting down the studio, I had inadvertently unearthed a new problem, this one more formidable than my inability to run the business. In putting a stop to the dance studio, I had also put a stop to the thing that I had long considered my 'calling from God'.

. . .

BALLET HAD ALWAYS been a source of joy and comfort to me, and after becoming a Christian I had happily received appreciative comments about dance being a gift given from above. I never felt so right as when I was in a ballet class. I found my peace on rosin-scented wooden sprung floors, wherever in the world I happened to be. This is what had led me to take class seven days a week whilst at university, to put a barre in my room and to practise for an extra hour each day. This motivated my unwavering commitment to daily cardio exercise on a stationary bike, and to never find myself in front of a TV unless I sat in splits.

At the time I had known I was obsessed, and was self-conscious about it. But I had reasoned that faith was something we were encouraged to be extreme about, and that, if I linked dance to God, the unease softened. As I studied fine art and dance, I thought about the idea of God delighting in beauty and found comfort in it all. I built much of my faith on it. I had lurched at the opportunity to lead the church's dance team and had hurtled, headfirst, into running my own studio.

My family whole-heartedly supported each member's endeavours. Mum was fast to endorse my love of dance, and invested heavily in the studio. She attended Pilates classes every week, and did everything an ambitious daughter could ask of her. I doubt she ever entertained the possibility that I could fail. Maybe she loved too much. Add to that, the unwavering support of my church family, and there was a sure recipe for disaster.

I walked away from it all feeling defeated. I had let everyone down. I wanted nothing more to do with dance. What Mum didn't seem to understand was that there was a wealth of consideration behind my decision. I was not acting on impulse this time. I had committed a premeditated crime, a murder. I had killed a God-given dream. I didn't want anyone to try to revive it. What I wanted was someone to grab a shovel and help me bury the evidence. Instead, I buried it alone and ran home to cry, to wash up, and to garner the strength to feign innocence.

But dance—the dream, the calling—would not go gently. It came back to me in the form of well-meaning comments from church members. It was on the faces of a forlorn dance team abandoned by their leader ... The little sister-in-law who had followed in my footsteps ... The bags full of ballet shoes and leotards I could not bring myself to discard ... The mere mention of The Nutcracker each and every Christmas.

The dance dream morphed into a fat ugly frog, the one that had retrieved my golden ball from the depths of a murky pond. The frog who was now rattat-tatting the castle door, asking me to make good on all my harried promises. *But Jacinta, you did promise I could sleep on your silken pillow ... and you did promise you would worship the Lord in dance forevermore.*

I turned my back on the frog and focused instead on Mum. Look where her influence had left me! Why had I been audacious enough to think that I could run a business with no experience or training? Why hadn't I recognised any of the warning signs? How, at the age of 22, had I been allowed to set myself up for such a huge fall? Who did I think I was? Some kind of superwoman? A magical-extraordinary-genius-witch who could do anything she wanted, just as long as she wanted it enough?

'You can do anything you set your mind to.' That was her line. Her motto.

I lacked the courage to point my finger at her directly, so I attacked her philosophies instead. Her *anything is possible* attitude to life was a lie with legs for tripping me up.

Everything is possible, but not everything is beneficial! countered the Bible. Wise, and slightly smug. How I wish I had listened to the Bible instead of Mum. She was so wrong—so wrong on the most fundamental level. Being able to do anything I set my mind to was not a good thing at all; it was a curse. I had clearly demonstrated that this approach to life was flawed according to every detail of reality. All I had ever wanted was a mother who would call me home to safety, not one who double-dog-dared me to try my hand at absolutely everything under the sun. If she had caught me standing at an open window with a set of paper wings, she would have handed me a glue stick.

. . .

I **CRASHED HARD, AND** I did my time in recovery. Months and years would unroll. Eventually I would go to therapy, and only months into that would I tell, tell on her. I held out, out of a mix of filial loyalty and guilt. The psychologist and I explored every angle of my feelings of being not-normal, both of us fully aware that I was withholding vital information. Eventually, however, I cracked. I flung wide the floodgates. I rattled off a list of Mum's offences, so vast it was visible from space.

And then, when I was finished and she was successfully painted as the villain of my life, I stopped to catch my breath. Severed from the burden of keeping secrets, I collected myself, straightened out my top and looked around at my life.

. . .

THERE, ON THE last pile of mail brought home from the studio, lay an ominous envelope from the government's Inland Revenue Department. I still dreaded those envelopes and needed to give myself a good pep talk before I could open them. According to past findings, the content of these envelopes was never as bad as feared, but official-looking letters like this always filled me with trepidation: the authorities were onto me for something.

I did not know how to keep my business accounts straight, or how to file returns or records of paid employees. Whenever one of these letters asked more of me than I could give, I simply handed it to Mum—who, in turn, handed it to someone else and it always seemed to be taken care of. But not this time.

We were late filing the studio's tax return, and I had been summoned to court.

'Oh, I'm sorry about that, my darling,' said Mum, over the phone. She had been busy and had not managed to get this one thing done before the deadline—or the second deadline extension, as it were.

'I know it sounds a bit scary,' she continued, 'but I've checked and the accountant says it's just a formality. You just need to appear before the judge and say you are very sorry for being late, and then we will pay a small fine or something like that. I'll come with you. It'll be a learning experience.'

I felt myself going light-headed. *Stand before a judge?* This was a problem Mum couldn't make go away even if she wanted to. One thing I did know, though—if she could have stood beside me before the judge, she would have. She had coached me into this mess, and she was going to coach me out of it again.

'If what you've hoped for doesn't work out,' she said, 'you just have to let it go. Learn what you can, and say, *what's next?*'

She accompanied me to the courthouse when the appointed day came. Her job was to repeat the mantra of the day: 'This is just an administrative formality.'

But I was petrified, dry in the throat and only just managing cognisance. This had to be the last real thing I could force myself to do before surrendering completely to the fog that my medication was lulling me into.

I had grown to accept that, due to whatever it was that was wrong inside me, I was capable of terrible things. My scarred wrist bore testament to that. If I could do that to myself on a whim, what else was possible? Anything. Anything, really, was possible. And this was the most terrifying idea in the world, because now I was unsure of my ability to control the underlying badness that I had known to be there all along. This sense of being a threat to myself and others, this pre-empted verdict of guilt, was the reason I found myself trembling before all forms of authority—at letters from the government, at policemen passing by on the street, at the prospect of standing before a judge. It was just a matter of time before I would be found out; and once that happened, who knew?

Mum had a stake in the proceedings because she was a director of the company and its only investor. She held my sweaty hand as we sat in the courtroom waiting for my name to be called because she was my mother. When it was my turn, I stood to go forward, and glanced back to catch the reassuring kiss I knew she would blow to me. I was taking one for the team. It was my business, yes, but it had taken the two of us to get us where we were that day. The charge was read; I was asked how I would plea.

'Guilty, Your Honour.'

There it was. I had finally said it.

And then it was over.

It was the judge's job to decide what I had to do to make things right (a small fine and a completed set of forms to be handed in on time). I needn't have worried. I thanked the judge and turned to make my way off the stand, not expecting an epiphany.

. . .

The verdict had brought with it immediate relief. Fear of the thing was worse than the thing itself. And, what was more, I alone was able to take the stand for my actions, my choices, and my failures. It was down to me. I had needed to plea because I needed a verdict. I was the guilty party. I was not the judge, and Mum was not on trial. No one had asked for my verdict, and there was no sentence for me to issue. She was not a criminal. She was an unconventional mother loving her child the best way she knew how.

She was not a normal woman—and she was, indeed, the answer to the majority of the *what the fuck* questions that formed the wadding to my life. But maybe, just maybe, 'normal' was overrated. Maybe it was time I took responsibility for myself instead of blaming her. I had missed out on having a regular mother; but on that day, I began to suspect that I might have gained in areas that most other people don't even know exist.

I stepped down from the stand, knowing she would be there,

ready to take my hand again.

'You looked beautiful,' she said. 'And now we know what pleading guilty feels like, don't we? I think we should celebrate. Shall we go for high tea at the Mandarin?'

18

2005-2006

WITH THE DANCE studio well and truly out of my life, I was finally able to focus on my mental health. Tom took all of my art blades away. He did not want to leave me at home alone, so he dragged me to work at the church office with him and left me in an unoccupied room, where I could work quietly on my illustrations and lie on a sofa if I needed to rest. I always needed to rest. My eyelids grew heavy after just an hour at the office, so I lay down and fell asleep, only to be woken by Tom when it was time to head home. I don't know if people asked questions. I was tired and unable to function above the most basic level, and this is how I spent my medicated years.

Two friends from our Bible study group were getting married. They had asked Tom if he would lead the songs at the ceremony, and if I would sing with him. We did this gladly, but the day was stressful. My body wanted sleep during the day, and before the ceremony began, I was already exhausted from the war that raged on inside. Everyone looks good at weddings, and I knew Peta would be there looking beautiful, and Tom would see her and notice in contrast how ugly I had become in every possible way. I was ragged from weeks and months of eyeballing Tom's every move. Tom was smart, though, and at the end of the morning ceremony he took me home to rest before the reception dinner.

I raged and cried and screamed and surrendered, but stubbornly fought my need for sleep. This scene had become commonplace and, depending on Tom's emotional reserves, it could last anywhere between one and five hours. That day, Tom held me close and said a prayer.

'Please God, please help her to know that I love her. Please help her.'

I slowed my breathing and wished things could always be this tender. I wished he wouldn't speak again unless it was to say that we could skip the reception dinner.

'You can't do this every time you see her, Jacinta. This isn't how you want to be. It's not you.'

I looked at him through sore, red eyes.

'What if it is me? Have you even considered that? What if the other one isn't me, and this is me now? What if I really am crazy now? What if I've been faking all along without even knowing it? You can't tell me I don't know what I know. I do. I know exactly what I know and you can't change that.' No matter how tired my body felt, the rage was always stronger.

'You aren't making sense anymore,' Tom replied. 'You can't really believe what you're saying. I need you to listen to me. I need you to trust me.'

'Do you have any idea what you're asking me?' I said. 'You can't just ask another human being to not listen to her own instinct and listen to yours instead. *That* is crazy. That's how people end up in cults. Maybe you're the crazy one. Either you are asking me to listen to you and trust you, so you can get away with anything you want, or else you like the idea of being married to a brainless, stupid person who's happy to think whatever you tell me to, instead of following my gut. You're asking me to stop listening to my gut!'

'If you don't trust me, we're in trouble,' he said, still keeping his voice low. 'If you do trust me, we can get through anything—but not if you're second-guessing me every step of the way. Do you honestly think your instincts are in a healthy place right now?' He was asking me to turn away from myself. I was the only one I had, and if I turned on myself then I had no idea what would be left. But that day, he pushed it further. 'Do you believe that I love you?'

I couldn't answer.

'Well, I do love you,' he said, 'and I'm committed to you for life, and I'm asking you to trust me. I have faith in us, and I need you to have faith, too.' This was an exchange that we would repeat dozens of times over the next few months.

But that day, he held me, and we cried together for some time. Then he reached for his guitar.

He played quietly while I lay on the sofa. It was a new melody—he hummed, and I listened. I stared through glazed eyes at a notepad on the floor, full pages curled and crumpled. It had skidded across the room after I'd flung it, enraged, less than an hour before—still visible were the scribblings of a mad woman. A document of desperation. Earlier in the week, I had remembered something Joyce had recommended I do. I had looked up *God's love* in the index of my Bible, and then written out, in longhand, every single Bible scripture referenced. This had taken half the day and was an exercise in self-preservation. I was beginning to think it impossible for God, let alone Tom or anyone else, to love me, and I needed the Bible to either confirm or refute my suspicions. In writing out these Bible verses, letter by letter, word for word, from the Amplified version, I rediscovered that this God I professed was, indeed, in the merciful business of dealing with messes like me.

Tom hummed and I listened, and the words got up from my notepad to dance.

'I'm writing this song,' Tom said, 'but I'm stuck on the words.'

I reached to the floor and pulled the notepad closer. I unclipped the pen from where it lived in the coil binding and began to put the words where they belonged.

This is Love

What can separate me
From your love, oh God?
You will not forsake me
There's nowhere you cannot go

Neither death nor life
No depths and no height
Could weaken your love, oh God
And there's nothing in this world
In all of creation
That could take your love away

This is how I know what love is
Though I'm a sinner
Christ laid down his life for me
And that's the greatest act of love in history
When my Jesus died for me

. . .

A few weeks later Tom said we needed to go and speak with Peta and Matt. They were fully aware of the fact that I was not functioning well, and that my weirdness was somehow related to them. I needed to tell them everything that was going on, and to tell them I was sorry. For an agonisingly humiliating couple of hours I sat in their lounge and laid myself bare.

'I'm sorry.' I said. 'I don't want you to leave the church because of me. I will leave, well, I probably can't leave, but I'll back off. You can just be friends with Tom; you won't have to see me anymore.'

'We don't do that.' Peta said. 'You are a set and we want to be friends with both of you.'

. . .

WEEKS AND MONTHS passed. We did things and went places and the medicated fog endured. I only know we did things and went places because I have photographs. People, events, life itself blurred into the haze, and only the most important moments were able to pull me into focus.

I was in Ikea, holding a blue and white floral sofa cushion, when my parents called to tell me Dad had cancer. They had just returned from Oxford and Dad had needed to go straight to the doctor. He hadn't moved his bowels in two weeks. After a number of tests, he was told he had colon cancer. A complete blockage caused by a tumour the size of an orange. He was on the way to the Canossa Hospital for an urgent operation.

As I walked into the ward, I found Dad in bed directing Mum as she arranged loose papers from the hanging file she had pulled from the cabinet at home. Every important piece of paper in our world was in that cabinet. She was surprisingly good at filing. They had been going over his will, and she was now putting it away. They were both calm.

Several hours later, he came through the surgery and broke a record in doing so. Fifteen pounds' worth of tumour, distended intestine and waste had been removed. His surgeon had never seen anything like it, and said it was a miracle Dad had survived as long as he had without his gut bursting and killing him with toxic poisoning. *We always knew you were full of shit!* read one of the get-well cards sent by his colleagues at the university.

Mum stayed by his side for the duration of his hospital stay. Jus and I visited daily. I brought my wooden box of colouring pencils and a sketchbook, and busied myself for hours, and then went and ate vegetarian fried noodles in the hospital canteen.

Dad's recovery and discharge from the Canossa coincided with the time for Tom and me to move out of our current flat in Shui Fai Terrace. We would move into my parents' house in Sai Kung. We were struggling to pay rent on top of my medication and appointments with the psychiatrist, and it worked out that my parents were glad to have extra people around during this hard time. Mum and Tom left the house to go to work every morning, while Dad and I stayed home together with Cora, the maid, and Achilles and Cassandra, the pair of Alsatian-cross mongrels my parents had recently, albeit reluctantly, adopted and renamed.

. . .

I WAS TASKED WITH being Dad's carer, not realising it was I who would benefit most from our time together. We looked after each other, enjoying leisurely lunches and running errands in Sai Kung town, visiting the public swimming pool and taking slow walks to the pier, across the road from the house. We could sit in silence most happily. Conversations started and stopped naturally without any stress or pressure.

I'm told that most people reach a point, while growing up, where they are faced with the reality that their parents do not know everything. This never happened to me. Dad would always be an encyclopaedic source of knowledge, his brain was like the Radcliffe camera, filled with more information than I would ever need—but he was never impatient in the way that some very clever people understandably are.

I found his voice extremely comforting. Sometimes, we went on long drives around the New Territories in the second-hand BMW convertible he had named Ella, the Black Beauty, after the Queen of Jazz herself. If I wanted to hear him talk, I needed only to choose my topic.

'Dad, can you tell me the history of China?'

He would chuckle and request that I specify whether I wanted to know about China's ancient or modern history.

'A bit of both please,' I would say, and he was off.

We watched movies on DVDs purchased in Sai Kung town. Sometimes, we watched quiz shows on BBC Entertainment. Dad loved general knowledge quizzes and revelled in exercising his brain, but couldn't stand Anne Robinson from The Weakest Link, to the point that he had to put the TV on mute at the end of each round. Twice a day, at the appointed times, Cora would appear from the kitchen with fruit covered in a mix of unsweetened yogurt and flax seed oil—we were all working hard at health.

But the cancer kept on, and soon chemotherapy appointments were added to our schedule. Jus, Mum and I combined efforts to ensure that never once would Hob attend chemotherapy unaccompanied. With time and energy directed at caring for Dad, I found myself regaining a sense of strength, wondering if the time had come for me to think about my own life again.

Yes, said every voice inside. *Yes, let's think about your own life again.*

You have abandoned your calling from God, said the panel of Christian celebrities in my head.

You have disobeyed the one thing you felt God had asked you to do. What makes you think you can do, or not do, whatever the hell you want, and then still expect all to go well with you? You don't feel like dancing anymore? Do you think you can just have a new calling? The callings of God are irrevocable.

I was in my mid-twenties. If I could just hold out for another couple of years, making excuses as to why I wasn't dancing, then I would soon be too old to go back to it. Once I had met the retirement age for dancers, then people would stop asking me why I had quit. I just needed to hold out a bit longer.

Yes, this was the plan. This would work. I just needed to hold my head up. What right did anybody have to question whether I danced or not? It was ridiculous. What was it to them? How dare they? I just needed to walk on. Walking had, however, become more difficult. My medication ensured I tripped over my own feet daily, and people's well-meaning questions about dance did not cease.

Okay, fine, I said to the panel. *What do you want from me? Dance? You want me to dance? That is so unreasonable, and so unfair. But I'm not going to spend the rest of my life living under a curse. Fine then. Fine. I will dance. You want me to dance? I'll bloody dance, then. Fuck you. What exactly do you want me to do? Study dance properly? Full time? How about a Master's degree in Dance? And then you and everyone else can just shut the hell up.*

. . .

The next day, I travelled into town to visit the Academy of Performing Arts in Hong Kong. I needed a brochure or an application form or something tangible to take home and look at. As I entered the lobby of the APA, I hovered by the wall of leaflets, not really knowing where to start. Then there was that voice again.

A man is about to walk in through the entrance on your right. He is headed to the lift lobby. Stop him. Ask him if he is the head of dance.

No time for internal dialogue; he was fast approaching. He smiled an approachable smile straight at me, instantly shattering all hope of my chickening out.

'Excuse me ….'

'Yes?'

'Are you the head of dance?'

'Why, yes.' He was still smiling, now looking a little perplexed. 'How did you know that?'

Shit. How did I know that?

'Um, I think I saw you in a performance at some point … Were you one of the cygnets in the parody Swan Lake?'

'Um, no, not that I remember ….'

'Oh, sorry, I have a terrible memory ….'

'No matter, no matter … can I help you with something?'

The lift was taking a long time to come. I mumbled for a bit longer, then waved the words away with my hand, hoping the gesture would wipe the slate clean. There was no way out of the situation. I asked if he had a moment to discuss the possibility of my studying at the Academy, even at the late age of 26.

He took me up to his office and said that, by all means, there would be no problem with me putting in an application. There was a student doing her PhD in Dance at the age of 35.

Shit.

After a quick chat, he gave me the forms and a handful of printed information and sent me on my way.

I filled out all the paperwork, banked in the application fee and even paid my old ballet school a visit for a reference letter. I sent in the application, then hoped and prayed it would get lost in the post.

However, a few short weeks later, I found myself back at the APA seated opposite an interview panel. I fumbled through questions fired by the dance faculty. At the end of the interview, one of the females said that she liked me and all that I needed to do next was pass an audition.

It is plain to see that dance is part of your destiny. I can see it written all over you. You simply must dance, and you must dance ballet! You certainly are too old, and completely the wrong build by traditional standards, but I have a feeling about you ... I can't quite put my finger on it. I think there is a story here and I believe that you will, indeed, overcome all of the obstacles the next few years will throw at you. Now go, go and buy yourself a large collection of leotards and sweats. Bless you for your courage and obedience to God's will for your life. This is what she did not say.

What she actually said was, 'If you are to study dance, then you will need to prove you can dance. I feel that, at your age, with your build and your lapses in training, ballet will be far too much of a challenge, in which case you will need to choose a different stream. What style would you like to focus on? Contemporary, Jazz, Chinese or Musical Theatre?'

I hadn't prepared myself for this question. What I needed to do was go away and weigh up the options.

'Jazz, please.' I had a grand total of one week's worth of classical jazz training from elective classes thrown into a ballet summer school many years ago.

'Very good. For your audition, we simply ask you to attend one of our regular lessons with our existing students. That will give us enough of an idea. Would you like to join a beginner, intermediate or advanced class?'

Don't say advanced.

'Advanced.'

'Perfect. See you next week.'

It did not occur to me to be concerned by the fact that I was out of my depth. All I really knew about classical jazz was that it was similar to ballet in some areas, only everything was turned in from the hips instead of out. If God had brought me thus far, surely he would have to get me through the rest of the ordeal?

. . .

It really was an ordeal. I showed up to my audition class without jazz sneakers. I hadn't thought about what I would need to wear. I hated jazz sneakers. They were black and very ugly compared to the aesthetic grandeur of a ballet shoe. No way did I ever want to own a pair of jazz sneakers. A generous third-year student, who also happened to be a distant church-related acquaintance, lent me her spare pair seconds before the class began.

I was placed in the front line. I kept up with the warm-up routine reasonably well, even though it seemed to drag on far longer than was necessary. I was flexible enough, but my reserves depleted quickly trying to follow nothing more than verbal instructions from the teacher and the other girls' reflections in the front mirror. The warm-up finally ended and it all went swiftly downhill from there. I blundered through to the end of the 90-minute lesson, entirely void of grace, ability, or the dignity-preserving wherewithal to simply stop. We stretched down and said thank you to the teacher.

He dismissed the others and then looked to me with a sympathetic chuckle.

'Well, that was fun. Thanks. Goodbye.' And he took his exit, fast.

The rejection letter arrived in the post three weeks later, and I breathed a big sigh of relief. That would be my final attempt to obey the dance calling.

. . .

After laying low in Sai Kung for several more weeks, I recovered from the embarrassment. I felt some strength return, and with it the desire to venture back to Hong Kong Island—to show my face at church, to walk the familiar streets of my city, and to look into the possibility that it was now time to move on with my life. But, every time I ventured away from The Nest, strange things happened.

The first instance was truly confusing to me, both when it happened, and to this day. I had gone to the hairdresser—Freddy, a mutual friend of a girl called Mabel from church whom everyone had adopted as their regular stylist. I had been lying back over the top of the basin, having my hair rinsed by one of the junior guys for what seemed an abnormally long time. Freddy came by and said something to the assistant that I couldn't make out over the sound of the showerhead, then they both laughed. Then I heard that voice, distinct and clear as day, but as internal as a thought of my own.

He is up to no good. He wants to ruin your hair.

I ignored it, but wondered what was taking so long. Finally, I was told to sit up and return to the salon chair. Freddy came over and started to comb through my long hair. Suddenly, he stopped short and, with a dramatic gasp, he held up a portion of hair close to my left ear: it was a six-inch dreadlock. It looked freshly back-combed.

'What is that?' I asked. I knew for certain that it had never been there before, and was bewildered as to why he had done it and was now pretending he hadn't.

'You have a very big knot!' he said, with an equal, but far less-convincing level of bewilderment. 'What happened here?'

'Your guy! You told him to do this!' I was sure of myself, and ready to make the accusation.

'What are you talking about?' said Freddy. 'Why would he do that? He doesn't even know you! I think maybe your hair got stuck in the drain and he just tried to pull it back out … It's very long … I don't know what you're saying, but just sit still and let me fix it … We might have to cut it off.'

'Don't touch me!' I shouted and felt ready to make a scene. 'Give me back my jacket. I'm leaving.'

I stormed out of the salon with hot cheeks, tears in my eyes and wet hair dripping down my back. I rushed back to the church office, where I told Tom what had happened. Tom called the salon and asked for an explanation. He was given the story about my long hair being caught in the drain. They begged him to send me back to the salon so the situation could be fixed.

Tom hung up the phone and turned to me. 'Why don't you just go back and let him fix it? He says he wants to do your hair for free.'

I was incredulous. 'I am never going back there again! He did this on purpose! I'll tell everyone. He's going to lose all his clients!'

'Jacinta, you need to calm down. Please, just tell me what possible reason he would have to do that on purpose—what could his motivation possibly be?'

I was unable to give him a reason, and this was the point at which I felt Tom was no longer on my side. We argued for a few minutes, but then I realised the significance of what was happening. Either I came up with a reasonable explanation for Freddy's unreasonable actions, or I was acting like a crazy woman.

I retreated to the church lounge downstairs, where I found Mabel. She received my report in horror and immediately got on the phone to give him a piece of her mind. After she hung up, she told me he had sent his sincere apologies, he had fired the assistant and again begged for me to go back to the salon so he could fix my hair.

Now things had gotten serious. I couldn't be 100% sure I wasn't crazy, but someone had lost his job over what had happened. I told her to call him back and say I would not return, but I didn't want the assistant sacked. I would let it go. I went home with my wet head hanging low.

You lost.

. . .

The second incident, coincidentally, also involved a drain. There was an American guy called Craig hanging out in the church lounge. I hadn't really spoken to him and had no real opinion about him, other than hoping he might make a good match for one of the many single girls in the church—single girls outnumber eligible bachelors in most churches. That day, however, after a brief 'hi/bye' encounter at the lift lobby, my opinion of him changed.

He's up to something.

I went about my business at the coffee bar and then decided to use the toilet before heading back upstairs in the lift. I pushed open the door of the ladies' room and immediately noticed a small, thin snake, about a foot long, flipping about in a puddle on the tiled floor of the cubical in front of me. I shut the door again as fast as I could, and rushed back to the lounge to find help.

'There's a snake in the toilets!' I screamed.

The only people in the centre that day were some girls practising a drama in the studio, and Craig, who was reading a magazine. He leapt into action, a little too readily if you asked me, and ran toward the girls' loo without hesitation. Then, with his bare hands, he heroically seized the snake and took it to the coffee bar in search of a biscuit tin to put it in, all the while ignoring my plea to call the SPCA so a professional could assess whether or not it was poisonous.

He denied owning the snake, or having anything to do with its being in the ladies' room. I asked him what on earth a snake was doing in a second floor lavatory of a building, in the middle of Hong Kong's central business district then. He reckoned it had come up through the drains. I walked away from the encounter confused and almost sure that he was, indeed, up to something, but I had no idea what it might have been.

. . .

IT WAS HARD to know if I was having these moments of craziness precisely *because* I had situated myself in a church—a church by nature, when functioning as it should, is, among other things, a haven for the broken, confused and downright crazy. By this measure, our church was functioning well—we had several colourful characters who had made it their place of worship. They were all welcome, of course, but staff were asked to respectfully monitor their behaviour.

One harmless, but unsound, gentleman wet every chair he sat on. He had been caught targeting newcomers, offering them small cakes, saying it was his birthday and asking for money. We were asked to gently remind him that the church would meet some of his financial needs on the condition that he stopped soliciting visitors. There was also a disturbed young lady who loitered in the lounge area on the second floor throughout opening hours, seven days a week. She scratched her head and muttered to herself. She occasionally cried and demanded attention, but more often just wanted to sit in on whatever was going on.

And, of course, there were a couple of the crazies that I always assumed it reasonable to find in a church. I called them the Angry Prophets, the ones who genuinely believed they had inside intel from God, and needed to enlighten the rest of us. These guys all operated independently of one another, but I developed a knack for spotting them, even before their behaviour got really strange. The clue was in the eyes, and if they changed when talking, or when they would ask a seemingly innocent question like, 'How are you today, Jacinta?' I would know straight away. It was a look that said they wanted you to know that they knew something, and they were, in fact, trying to look straight into your soul, but failing. They had opinions, usually negative, about every aspect of church life.

Tom was often on the stage at church, so he was an easy target for the Angry Prophets—who, in all fairness, were not always angry—more like disappointed on God's behalf.

'God was not happy with your worship today,' one of them said to Tom at the end of a Sunday service. This guy had stopped shaving some time ago, and had also grown his hair to shoulder length. It was only a matter of time before he showed up in sandals and a white robe.

Another severely volatile young man, who had once sworn his devotion to Tom's music, started sending emails containing nonsensical accusations, and even a death threat. But Tom was not too bothered by the mentally ill people he encountered at church. In my humble opinion, the death-threat guy had crossed a significant line, but who was I to judge? I had probably issued a similar threat or two to my husband along the way. Tom was equally even-keeled with us, every one.

Most congregations contain one or two from the whacky and obviously mentally ill categories, but then there are the closet weirdos to take into account, as well. These people make totally normal first impressions; they fit right into the scheme of things quite pleasingly, but somewhere down the line the weirdness starts to surface. These ones come in a variety of shapes and sizes, as follows:

The Premature Missionary: Many an excited young Christian has moved to Hong Kong, feeling called to China, hot on the heels of famous missionaries like Jackie Pullinger or Hudson Taylor. They vow never to leave, only later to discover that lofty claims made in one's early twenties can make a flimsy foundation for the long haul.

The Lovesicko: A young and single person who has fallen in love with someone at church. They get busy being a hyper-involved example to all, and then say things like, 'God says I'm going to marry you.' He or she struggles to handle the inevitable rejection, and then disappears from the scene altogether.

Or they might be people who find a safe place of consolation in God's house and start dealing with difficult events from their past. The process draws out character flaws. Some people get over-zealous about church things and then their self-esteem gets tangled up in their various roles at church, whether or not the pastor has noticed all their hard work. Or perhaps they get over-zealous about God things, and bypass gentle recommendations for theological grounding.

This is the stuff church is made of: flawed people in a broken world, drawn towards the hope of a remedy. I write what I know.

Brokenness is supposed to be the reason church exists. But some people are trickier than others; some personalities are just harder to deal with. The kindest code name I have heard given to these difficult people is EGR: Extra Grace Required.

I was now aware that I had become someone for whom Tom required extra grace. I had crossed the point of no return: a foregone conclusion. But I was unsure of just where on the spectrum I fell as far as the majority of the wider church was aware. Most people knew I had withdrawn, but few people knew why. Did the fact that I was able to keep my craziness in the closet mean that I was less troubled than the guy who clearly thought he was Jesus? Did the fact that I had enough self-awareness not to mutter to myself mean that I was fine?

Was the snake episode a case of Craig, a possible weirdo himself, wanting to act out a deranged need to solve a snake-related emergency? Or was my suspecting him just another case of Jacinta having a bipolar moment? Was Craig messing with me? Was the devil messing with Craig? Was the devil messing with Craig in order to mess with me? Did the snake just swim up through the toilet? Who knew?

'What if I'm not actually crazy at all?' I asked Tom.

'You aren't crazy, Jacinta,' said Tom. 'You have to stop saying that.'

'I'm not? What am I then? Am I fine? Normal?' I was a little annoyed that he had interrupted my getting to my point with semantics.

'You have bipolar disorder. It's an illness. You are currently suffering from a mental illness.'

'Yes, I am mentally ill. Let's call it crazy for short.' Tom rolled his eyes and I continued. 'Well, have you ever even considered this: what if I'm not crazy? What if I'm actually a genius, and it's all of you who don't understand me?'

Tom let me continue for a bit longer, even though his reply was ready to go. This was an easy one. I continued, nonetheless.

'If someone tells a joke and no one laughs, does that mean the joke wasn't funny, or the joke-teller has a crap sense of humour? Or, could it be possible, that her sense of humour is so far advanced that no one who happened to be in the room at that moment was able to appreciate it?'

'You have a mental illness right now, Jacinta,' Tom said. 'You sliced your arm open.'

19

TOM AND I moved out of Sai Kung into a large flat in Causeway Bay, on a grimy dead-end street called, ironically, Haven Street. Ours was the last building on the left. Our building was very old and had a lift with the traditional two-door system—one heavy metal door with a small, reinforced glass window that opened onto a sliding wooden grate, both needing to be opened manually.

It was here that I lost the next two years of my life. The days ticked over painfully slowly. I did not know exactly how many of them I would need to surrender in the name of recovery, and this in itself was a form of torture. I had packed my pillboxes and taken my place on the sidelines of the game of life, confined now to the spectator's stand.

People got married, changed jobs, moved flats, left Hong Kong, came back again, went out for drinks, threw dinner parties, celebrated birthdays, went to church, went on hikes, asked after me and said they wished I would join them. I didn't want to join them. I didn't have the strength to put up the appropriate front for most situations.

But I needed to go to church. Every shred screamed out from

within me, *'YOU NEED TO GO TO CHURCH!'* And I did. But I didn't want to deal with any of the people. With great precision, I would time my arrival just as the service leader began to greet the congregation, sparing me from any attempted contact. But I would arrive before the band began to play, so that I wouldn't miss the very thing I had come for: the music.

Tom had gathered a good team of musicians and singers, and the church was gaining a reputation for being particularly strong in the area of musical worship. Our church congregation loved to sing, and it seemed everyone was of one accord and totally unashamed to give it their all, physically and vocally, when it came to this first section of a church service.

The church founders had pioneered a way into contemporary music in church, by songwriting and free expression. They cleared a path for us to skip down, and skip down it we did. Plans were underway to collect and record songs written by members of the congregation, as a sort of musical snapshot of that moment in our church family's history. Excitement about the project was building, and it added to the collective participatory enthusiasm each week. For me, though, the music was something almost entirely personal. It was a lifeline.

For those forty or so minutes (that never felt long enough) peace came. The notes that Tom plucked on his guitar would fall like drops of rain, pitter-pattering over the keyboard's synthetic pad. I closed my eyes and raised my arms—it was an action I would force myself to make in a deliberate act of public surrender. It was as close as I would get to dancing in church again. I would raise my arms, and all at once the heavy swell churning within me stilled, just for those forty brief minutes.

Though no one ever questioned me, I was sure of the fact that, had I needed to, I could defend my right to sing in church. I could reach into my glove compartment and produce a licence to worship any day of the week. The God I sang to was the friend of sinners, and my qualification in that area was one thing I never doubted. I would sing, and listen, and pray, and cry. And then, when the music ended, I would sit and listen to the preacher's message.

Here, I struggled somewhat—over memories of my past pursuit of the pulpit; intellectual questions about what was being said; and what gave that preacher any right to say it so confidently. Worst of all, I struggled with a yearning that cried out for God to deliver me a prophetic message, right there on the spot, to tell me there had been a huge mix-up and that I was not crazy at all: that, in fact, I was wonderful and perfect and just plain misunderstood.

Although weekly I sat hopeful in the corner of the front row of the church, the prophesy didn't come, and I was left to get on with the daily grind of taking my medicine and trying to keep out of trouble. I visited the church centre daily, mostly just to have something to do. There were a couple of girlfriends at church who were a life stage or two ahead of me, who treated me like a little sister. I told them some of what I was going through and they immediately became my supporters. Jaime invited me to join a course she was running; I confided in her about my urges to self-harm and received nothing but reassurance and support in response. Heidi, Tamara and Karla shared personal stories of their own and sent me encouraging text messages, and in doing so helped me to feel less alien. They gave me one small but vital option to reach for before I would otherwise have reached for the stationery drawer.

Other people I encountered must have known something was up with me, but no one ever asked. I told myself they had heard about Dad's cancer battle and would probably connect that to my own change in comportment.

The Revolve girls, who I had led in the dance ministry, grew increasingly impatient with my reluctance to call a team meeting or resume training. I had told them I needed to take a break from leading the dance team and had given my blessing for them to elect a new leader and continue on without me. However, good practice in the culture of our church called for any leader who wanted to step down to first identify and train a successor, and this was yet another thing I was unable to do. I bore the guilt of killing a ministry as I walked through the church lounge, avoiding eye contact with the dancers.

. . .

REHEARSALS AND LOGISTICAL preparations were underway for the church's live album recording. Two sound engineers and a preacher were flown in from Sydney. The recording was to take place over two nights in order to maximise our chances of capturing the best quality sound possible for the album. We had rented a small auditorium in a government facility and, due to strict house rules, each seat had to be ticketed.

I was in two minds about whether or not to invite my parents. From a young age, I had always felt self-conscious about letting my family mix with the rest of my life. Not so much for reasons related to witchcraft or alcohol, or me worrying what my friends thought of my family. My reluctance to mix worlds was more about a worry of what my family would think of me. I never felt shy about them coming to dance performances, but they had never known me as a singer and I didn't want them to make a fuss.

It wasn't a big deal, really. I was one of two backing singers, in just two of the ten songs for the night. Maybe it would have been more effort than it was worth for them to come. On the other hand, Dad had cancer and maybe by coming to the event he would have an encounter with God and be healed. I gave them their tickets a few days in advance, and then tried not to worry about what would happen next.

I greeted them when they arrived, but they slipped away straight after I had sung my two songs. Three days later, I still hadn't asked for their feedback—I was trying to avoid any potential embarrassment about my singing. But, as it turned out, my mortification would not be related to the music at all.

When I finally called Dad, he sounded strangely distant. I plucked up the courage to ask him what he thought of the concert. He made a light-hearted comment about loving seeing me 'so happily singing on stage like a Ra Ra Girl'.

I felt a small pang of feminist offence, but pressed further because I sensed something wasn't right.

'Didn't Tom do well?' I asked. This was the first time Dad had seen Tom in his role as our church's worship leader.

'Yes, Beeps,' said Dad. 'Tom is a very good singer, and he's very clever if he wrote all of those songs and organised the whole thing.'

'Well, he did write on most of them ....'

'It's just ....'

'What?'

'Well, it's just ....'

'Dad?'

'Well, the man giving the talk ....'

I knew it. The talk had, in fact, given me goosebumps, and here we were, about to share in the memory of it all. It was a passionately delivered sermon. Life-changing, even. Dad was hesitating, but I was eager to hear him say how beautiful it all was, perhaps that he was so moved he wanted to receive Jesus as his personal Lord and Saviour. I knew he was an Anglican, but I didn't know if that involved being born again ... so I pushed it.

'What about the talk, Dad?'

'It was awful.'

'Huh?'

'Dreadful. Absolutely terrible! I mean, do you really, honestly, subscribe to all of this?'

I was blindsided. The visiting preacher was one of the most inspiring speakers I had ever heard in my life. Ever since I was a teenager, I had cried every time I'd heard him speak, and he had certainly delivered that night—and in the face of some major technical challenges, as well. He was dynamic and animated; he dressed stylishly, spoke from the heart...

'Huh?'

'Beeps, it was absolute twaddle! Awful! All hype and no substance whatsoever. Pandering to the lowest common denominator. Totally condescending and hammed up. Absolutely ridiculous. I am sorry to say that I think the whole talk was nothing short of emotional masturbation!'

His closing statement hung awkwardly over the silence as my face flushed hot and my eyes filled with tears. Dad had hated what I loved. Why was he being so aggressive? Why was he being such an intellectual snob about something as sincere, and potentially life-changing, as this sermon?

'I'm sorry, darling,' he went on. 'I don't want you to think I'm angry at you. I loved seeing you on stage and you looked so happy and beautiful—you always look beautiful—and Tom is a very good musician. It's just that ... if that sermon was any indication of the style of your church, I can't say that it's something I'd enjoy in the least.'

I made an excuse and got off the phone as fast as I could. I went to the ladies' room to cry. After I had composed myself, I went to tell Tom what had happened. It was the first time I had found myself in a situation where my husband and my dad would stand on opposing sides, and I would have to make a choice. Tom didn't see it as such a big deal. He wasn't devastated at all and said that it didn't matter if Dad didn't love our style. Tom hadn't expected him to like the message, anyway. It was probably too loud and 'youthie'.

'Even my mum thinks it's all too loud, and she's a pastor's wife!' said Tom. 'Try not to worry about it too much.'

Dad was an academic and, according to what I had heard preached from more than a couple of pulpits, intellectuals were some of the hardest nuts to crack. They let their brains get in the way of faith.

But I was embarrassed about enjoying what Dad had hated. He was the smartest person I knew, and one of the only people on Earth who had no possible ulterior motive for wanting the best for me. If he could see something wrong with it, then the chances were very high that, somewhere along the line, I had started kidding myself—or would, at least now, have to start. Was I the lowest common denominator? Was the whole thing a little hammed up? Well, yes, I suppose it was.

As I allowed myself a moment to ponder this possibility for the first time, I heard the clear sound of a crack forming deep in the foundations of my faith. The structural integrity of the metaphorical floor on which I stood, wearing my footwear of the gospel of peace, had been compromised.

20

THE CHURCH OFFERED me a part-time job. They promised it had nothing to do with the fact that we were not making ends meet, but insisted that the church had a strong vision for 'couples in ministry'. This job offer was a gesture in that direction, but at that point the job description could not allow for us to double up in any areas. So, for the time being, it was more a case of 'couples working in completely different areas of the same church'.

I spent time organising volunteers, copywriting, and just generally helping wherever I was needed. When I had done as much as I could manage on any given day, I clocked off and spent the rest of my day waiting around for Tom to finish so we could go home together. He was my life support, and my survival was pegged to being near him at all times.

We had come to accept that preparing evening meals was too big an ask for either of us, so we often ate out with anyone who was around after work. Or, if we felt like an evening in, we bought microwave meals from the tiny Circle K next to our bus stop.

Hong Kong is full of compact convenience stores, sometimes less than a hundred square feet—just big enough to house the minimal stock of snacks and sundries, newspapers and magazines, a freezer for ice creams, a microwave for heating packaged dumplings, hot water tank for instant coffees or cup noodles, and two seasonal items: a display of umbrellas that would appear from nowhere, prices inflated, whenever the sky turned grey, and a hot fridge for winter staples like warm soy milk and cans of Nescafé. The inner wall is always fitted with a fridge for drinks such as soda, box drinks, Taiwanese milk tea, and beer.

Once all the stock is accounted for, there is usually only space for about three adult-sized humans at any one time. No pleasantries are ever exchanged in these shops—you go in to get whatever you need, or to refill your Octopus travel card or pay a phone bill at the till, and then get out of the way as fast as you can.

Tom and I broke convention by loitering at the chilled food area long enough to discuss whether it was to be a Chinese-style spaghetti bolognese, Singapore fried noodles, chicken à la king, or beef stroganoff sort of evening.

Beside the Circle K sat a hole-in-the-wall boutique selling naff rhinestone-bejewelled fashion, and next to that was my fruit shop. Hong Kong fruit shops like these had featured heavily in my upbringing. Mangoes, tangerines, mandarins, pomelos, grapes, mangosteens, pears, apples, lychees and persimmons were on display, often individually cradled in a polystyrene nest and collectively presented on a bed of coloured tissue paper. They sat atop an assortment of stacked polystyrene or cardboard crates that cascaded unapologetically out of the storefront and onto the pavement. This display was invariably lit by large lightbulbs under bright red plastic light shades hanging from the entrance. Suspended in the corner, above all the excitement, was a small bucket on a weighted pulley that would serve as a till.

Every day, I insisted on buying and consuming an unreasonably large amount of whatever fruit looked good—this was mostly to deceive myself into forgetting the nutritional sin we were about to microwave for dinner. So, the fruit shop was always the last stop before heading home.

. . .

I always tried to go to bed at the same time as Tom, but most nights sleep alluded me. I was back on the broken record, laying awake in the dark, eyes forced shut, listening to Tom breathe as he drifted off, leaving me alone to contend with what I referred to as Phase Two of the night. As Tom's breathing relaxed into effortless depth, my eyelids would spring open at the realisation that I was alone, and my digits would start to party. The tips of my fingers and toes became restless and my brain wanted to dance. I would allow this but try not to disturb Tom.

It always started with a physical warm-up on a minute scale. There was nothing I could ever do to stop it. The knuckles of both thumbs would bend and flex, bend and flex. Next, the big toe and second toe of each foot would join in, flicking across each other, a foot's equivalent of quiet finger-clicking. These two sets of movements would soon need variation, so as the thumbs pointed up, the big toes pointed down. It would always take a couple of false starts to get this coordinated—something like rubbing your tummy whilst patting your head. I found immense satisfaction in getting the toes and thumbs right.

One of my earliest memories of a ballet class involved learning the concept of opposition: we were told to experiment walking with the same foot as the hand swinging together, to feel how unnatural a lack of opposition is. This simple lesson stuck with me, and continued to demand my attention more than that ballet teacher probably ever intended it to.

Brain party warm-up would follow a consistent sequence: Tom's breathing, thumbs up, toes down, repeat, switch, remember ballet class, attempt to add left-side/right-side variation, fail at that, start again, this time going for a bit longer. *I'm really good at this.* Then switch in accordance with my own inhale/exhale, trying to add gentle rhythmic grinding of molar teeth, keeping in mind the issue of left/right variations, thus trying to keep both sides of the jaw at equal tension (though this was not possible because of my imperfect bite, and I could not allow myself to dwell on this fact because it would be my demise). By the time I looked at the clock, Phase Two would have been in session for at least an hour.

Next, Phase Three: the dreaming of possibilities that would inevitably climax in visions of grandeur. I would imagine myself as a successful health supplement saleswoman, then as a motivational speaker, then as a singer, an Olympic athlete, a fashion designer, a children's illustrator, a toy maker, a puppeteer, an ender of world hunger ... The thoughts raced round and round, darting in for frenzied pit stops, back onto the track, eventually crashing into each other after another hour or two had elapsed.

Phase Four is what I dreaded most. If I hadn't fallen asleep by then, chances were high that tomorrow would be a total write-off. The illuminated digital clock would now become the focal point. I would watch and wait, probably drifting in and out of a light sleep, but waking each time with an urgent need to decipher what the glowing digits were trying to tell me.

It was starkly clear that the numbers were indeed trying to communicate, but the meaning of the message was the problem. 02:50 was a visually pleasing number on the digital clock—symmetrical and reminiscent of sections of the designs found on ceramic rice bowls the world over. 01:01 and 23:32 were quite good; 02:20 wasn't bad; 01:23 annoyingly sequential and far too cute; and 22:55 was rather glorious. I considered the option of spending 24 hours in a dark room with the clock in order to enjoy the best numbers, but became aware that this would be considered unusual behaviour.

These interesting-to-look-at numbers were starting to haunt me though, and I would fall into the unfortunate habit of looking at the clock only when the time was approaching a good one. I never seemed to check the time and find an arbitrary line-up of digits, and this realisation bothered me something awful. As my eyelids opened, I would will the numbers to be something random rather than meaningful, but they never complied. They were clearly trying to tell me something, I just couldn't figure out what. I would rationalise it as coincidence at first, then fight hard against the prospects of supernatural conspiracy and self-sabotaging mind games.

If I looked and the clock said 03:20, the fact of the matter was painfully clear: in precisely 12 hours and one minute's time, the digits would read 15:21. But then there was a strong possibility that 12:51 was actually a superior line-up, so ... then I would try to figure out where this had left me.

On some level, I was aware that things were getting out of hand, but because this would all happen when I was alone and physically exhausted, I was unable to ask anyone for help. Tom deserted me back at Phase Two. I would try to reason with myself, promising that, in the morning, I would go out and buy a notebook and draw out a list of every possible digital time combination, highlight the significant ones and then make an honest assessment of whether pure mathematical probability meant there was nothing noteworthy actually happening, or if (and I very much hoped not) it was something more sinister that demanded further exploration.

Yes, I thought to myself, *I really must write them all out. I should buy a book of graph paper.* At this point, I would check the clock again; it said 05:20 and that meant the night was lost.

. . .

The brain parties were morbidly entertaining at night, while they were happening, but I skulked through my daylight hours mentally hung over. Getting out of bed was the biggest challenge of the day—11am was the earliest I could seem to manage. The glance at the clock was always followed by thick lashings of disappointment because I hadn't even managed to hear Tom leave the flat, let alone been ready to leave with him. On a really bad day, I would only make it as far as the sofa before collapsing asleep again until about 3pm. On a slightly better day, I would faff around the flat for about an hour and then head to the office.

My days of running off boundless energy had been a small but significant part of my life that were now fading from living memory.

I walked around the flat looking ruefully at the bookcase full of art books, then at the trainers buried at the bottom of the shoe pile by the door. I felt no desire for the things I used to love, and I was sure it was the medication's doing. I was wearing a chemical straitjacket.

. . .

Sometimes, I dragged myself out of the flat in a feeble attempt to exercise, but the meds had laced my veins with the weight of lead, and my limbs would not cooperate.

The challenge of the week was, without fail, getting to my appointment with the psychologist. Robert had approached Tom at a church event, asking after me. He knew a girl in need when he saw one. Tom said he was the answer to our prayers—we had finally found a qualified, mental health professional who understood the world from whence we came.

Robert's office moved four times over the years I was seeing him. The first two offices were both less than a ten-minute walk from my home, and yet getting myself there was a sizeable ordeal. I always wanted a nap right when it was time to leave the house, or I thought it would be a good idea to try an alternative route to get there, or I allowed my mind to fill with questions of whether or not we had changed the regular appointment to some other day.

For what felt like months, I would sit awkwardly as Robert reminded me that it was fine if I didn't want to talk, that this was an hour in which I could sit and feel peaceful—a profound act of kindness. At the time silence was very challenging. Every week I wrote lists of ideas of things to discuss with Robert, for fear of that awkward hour of silence; but every week I forgot that I had made the list, and had to fumble through anyway.

Tom managed to get me to a band practice one Saturday morning. I stood in my usual spot during the sound check, but I soon found myself beginning to nod off. While still singing, mic in hand, I crawled off the front of the stage and sat on the ledge to rest my elbows on my knees, my head resting in one hand and the other hand wedging the mic in place under my lower lip. I had sung these songs so many times, I could literally sing them with my eyes closed. And my eyes really needed to close. They were dry and sore, and if I could just let their heavy lids have some relief for a minute or two the world would be a better place.

On a matter of principle, Tom and I had both tried to keep rehearsals sacred—as the leader, Tom had to set an example by showing up on time and arriving prepared. As a band member and a classically trained dancer, I had made it my business to give my all in every run-through at every practice. So I sung on.

I didn't skip a note, but my weary eyes stayed shut for longer than I had planned. My face had started to relax, too, and had I not been disturbed I probably would have started to drool. I woke with a snort because the song we were working on had ended, and I became aware of the giggles that had escaped from a couple of other musicians. I opened my eyes to see several of them in silent hysterics, pointing at the sorry sight I must have been.

'What is the matter with you, Jacinta?' they asked. They were thoroughly amused. I was not.

There wasn't really any way I could explain my attempt to sleep-sing through practice, so I slipped away to the ladies' room to splash some water on my face. I was dry inside and out. My skin itched, and broke out in a devastating throwback to adolescence. My eyes clicked when I blinked, and my tickly throat, constantly parched, made me sound like my voice box had detached and slipped down into my thigh, where it continued to try to make itself heard.

. . .

DESPITE THIS VOCAL challenge, however, I eagerly accepted an invitation to preach at One Eighty. I had been on a break from church leadership for too long, and I was desperate to end my time on the bench. The young adults were working their way through a teaching series based on the theme of worship songs, and Derek, their leader, wanted me to share the story behind *This is Love,* the song Tom and I had written together.

'What do you think you'll talk about?' asked Tom when I shared the joyous news.

It had been over two years since I'd last preached. I hadn't taken to the pulpit since just before the Incident. My ministry comeback was eminent; I could feel it. Through the mental fog came a vision of Joyce waving her support at me from the headquarters of Joyce Meyer Ministries in Fenton, Missouri.

'I'm going to tell the whole story, totally raw and honest,' I said. 'That's what people used to say they liked about me. I'm raw—whatever that means.'

'Really?' said Tom. 'Not sure that's a great idea, not yet. Maybe give it some more thought? It might not be in your best interests to reveal all ....'

'Why? I've got nothing to hide, and absolutely nothing to lose. There is no way I'm going to get on with my life pretending it didn't happen, because it did. And it's relevant to the theme, because it happened right before we wrote the song.'

'Look, I don't want to get into a fight over this,' said Tom. 'I'm supporting you. I know you'll get the right opportunity to tell your story one day, but I think it's just too soon right now.'

'You're ashamed of me, aren't you?'

'Please, will you just trust me? You said you were going to trust me with the big decisions for a while. This is a pretty big decision, since it doesn't only involve you. I have no problem with people knowing about our lives, but what about Peta? What about you? You're still on meds now, and maybe that's not the best thing to share just yet. I don't want people to judge you.'

Tom didn't understand my sense of urgency. I was quite certain that, if I delivered a deeply personal and confessional sort of talk, we could officially mark the end of my journey. I felt that, if I was talking about it, then I was looking back, with hindsight, from a different vantage point, removed, and that meant I wasn't there anymore. If I was no longer in the moment, that meant it was over. I wanted nothing more than to tell the world what I had been through. What I had now come through. I wanted to be through it, and telling the story was the only path that I could see that would get me there. It was all taking too long.

I had already tried speeding up my healing process. I had tried to harness the power of positive thinking and can-do statements in attempts to un-mental myself. Physical illnesses are easier to deal with in this respect—a blood test or some other official form of the all-clear tells sufferers their recovery is complete, and they can now return to the functioning world. Once someone who had a broken leg in a cast has that cast removed, everyone can see that they are now better.

When someone has a fractured mind, however, it is not so easy to know when, or if, the recovery is complete. I had thought I could swing this idea to my own advantage. If the problem with mental illness is that there aren't really any immediate or easily recognisable indicators that a sufferer can take as an official all-clear, then how would I, or anyone else, know that I hadn't already been cured? Maybe I was better already?

This was an attractive possibility. I took it upon myself, ignoring all sound advice, to experiment with cutting out my meds. I wanted to see if they really did make any difference. I had promised Tom I would comply with my prescriptions, but perhaps they were all placebos. I didn't want to overtly disobey my husband, so I tried 'accidentally' forgetting to take my morning dose now and then, and I also tried taking half-servings of everything. I felt so utterly doomed to a lifetime being a failure, that nothing I did really mattered.

No attempt yielded the desired results. I never knew whether I was having a bad reaction to the inconsistent dosages, or if my own guilty conscience was toying with me—days when I had messed with my meds always ended very badly. On one occasion, I got into a heated argument with the church's sound technician and ended up assaulting her with a running shove. Tom ran off to do as much damage control as he could. I had yelled at and pushed a person I very much considered a dear friend, and I was left in a state of shock and shame.

Alone at home I ransacked the flat for something sharp but found nothing but my phone. I sent a call for help to one of the few people who knew the full extent of my mental state: Peta. It was late in the evening but within quarter of an hour she arrived at my home and was talking me down, in her gentle and calm way. I sat, draped over the arm of the sofa, snotty and unable to hear, say or think much at all. Peta told me that she knew I was going to be okay. After a spell she said she was going to leave me to rest, but I was allowed to call her any time I needed to. She said a prayer and let herself out of the flat. She may have been gentle and calm, but there was nothing timid about her. She only spoke when there was something worth saying and that night, she left me in a new state of shock. Not catastrophic shock, but the quiet revelation that comes with allowing for the possibility, for the very first time ever, that despite how things looked, I was going to be okay. It would be quite a long time before I would see any tangible evidence of this, but from that night on I dared to leave my feelers out.

. . .

AFTER A HANDFUL of unsuccessful experiments in self-medicating, followed by confession, followed by a severe scolding from Tom, I vowed to follow doctor's orders evermore.

Dr Lee had made it plain to me that I would be taking medication for many years to come, despite the fact that I had been lying and telling him I had felt completely better for months. As a result, I knew he wasn't in a hurry to give me a clean bill of mental health. He had no interest in my desire to be chemical-free.

I was given regular pregnancy tests to confirm I was not pregnant before being issued with more drugs. The thing that confused me was that Dr Lee regularly said that, if Tom and I had any plans to start a family, I needed to tell him with plenty of notice so that he could taper me off my medicine for the lead up, duration and aftermath of the pregnancy. Medication and babies didn't mix.

I had no interest in making babies at that point in time—in fact, I felt that the one positive thing I could do for humanity was not reproduce myself. If I couldn't get myself out of bed in the morning, how was I supposed to produce a decent human being?

But, more pressing was the question *why on earth was pregnancy the only possible reason to have me drug-free?* If a pregnancy test had ever come back positive, I would have been taken off further medication immediately. What about the simple (and, in my opinion, legitimate) reason that I hated being on the drugs? That I was in a living hell? Why was that reason not sufficient? However, as Dr Lee gave me his usual family-planning precaution at the end of one appointment, a thought struck me like a ding-dong bell. *He will take me off my meds if I say I want to have a baby.*

So I did. I told my doctor I wanted to have a baby. And then I went home and told my husband that my doctor said he was going to taper me off my meds. Enough said. And here is where I began a six-month journey out of the rabbit hole. It would take no less than half a year to safely reduce my medication down to nothing.

. . .

I preached at One Eighty as requested, but I did not tell the full story.

I steered the talk toward the Bible verses that featured in the lyrics instead. It went reasonably well. The lasting memory of the night was my dry, dry throat. I choked and croaked my way through my notes. I was warmly received, but unable to engage with anyone at the end of the talk. On the way home, Tom chuckled and said, 'Daughin really liked your talk.'

'That's nice. He did tell me. We spoke briefly just before he left ….' I was always encouraged to see that our former leader still took the time to show up to these meetings.

Tom was still smiling about something when he said, 'Yah, he told me he spoke to you. He asked me if you were praying in tongues.'

'What?'

'He said that when he was talking, and you were listening, your lips were moving like you were praying in tongues or something.'

'Huh?' What was Tom talking about and why was it funny?

'Are you?' His smile grew.

'What? I'm really confused.'

'You don't know you're doing it, do you? You've been doing it for months. You look like you're muttering to yourself when other people are talking. Like this ….' And after an absurd impression that made me laugh, he continued. 'I just thought you were listening to them and pre-empting what they were saying, like a smartarse. It's pretty cute that Daughin assumed the most spiritual explanation. That guy.'

It turned out that my lips had been involuntarily twitching for months and I was totally unaware of it. Another possible side effect of the medication. It took too much energy for me to do anything about it, so I tried not to let it bother me. Just another reason to lay low as much as possible. Tom was right: I wasn't ready for my ministry comeback. I was feeling deflated.

'Don't worry, Loops, you'll be okay,' he said. 'One day you will be all better. You'll get to share your story and it will help lots of people.'

'Who is going to be helped by me and my mental story?' I was feeling sorry for myself.

'Mental people,' replied Tom. 'Seriously, there are a lot of people in the world who need help in this area.'

'Oh God, no. Please, no. I really, *really* don't want to specialise in mental people. Once I've crawled my way out of this hole, I don't want to have to climb back in to deal with all the other crazies, and we know there are plenty.'

'Why not? Isn't that what being a Christian is supposed to be about? You're supposed to want to help people. You could make a real difference ....'

'Yah, to mental people ... No thanks,' I said angrily. 'I've decided I don't really like people at all, any of them—all too complicated. I don't want to deal with any of them, not even the normal ones. Sounds mean, but whatever ... This is all easy for you to say, Tom. You get to have the cool music ministry—you don't even have to talk to people, or deal with any of their mentalness, if you don't want to.'

'Don't I?' He looked at me with smiling eyes.

'Okay, fine,' I said. 'Here's the deal. You and I will do it together, we can finally be a 'couple in ministry'. Yup, we'll call it Mental Ministries.'

21

BACK IN THE church office, I had been asked to write out some worship activity ideas to offer to the small group leaders, each of whom facilitated Bible studies and social gatherings for about a dozen people on a weekly basis.

Music and communal singing is the go-to option for dedicated times of worshipping God in a church service, and it has been for centuries, where numbers can range from anything from a handful to tens of thousands of attendees. Songs led by voice and an acoustic guitar work well in small groups, but the problem we were facing was the fact that, statistically, it would have been a challenge to have a guitar player in every small group, even though our church was considered well-endowed with musicians. Some groups chose to sing along to a CD, but everyone agreed that this was not ideal.

The mandate given to me was to think up some creative ideas for how to worship God without being dependent on worship music or communal singing. The finished product was a spiral-bound in-house publication called *Creative Worship* filled with exercises to utilise body, mind and spirit and involved coloured pencils, scrap paper, lemons, and imagination. It was something I was very proud of, so much so that I decided to mention it while on the phone with

Dad. We hadn't been in touch for some time.

'It sounds like a lovely book, Beeps,' he said. I wondered if his enthusiasm was an attempt to mend the damage done by his reaction to the night of the album recording.

'Thanks, Dad. Would you want to see it? Maybe proofread it?'

Part of me felt like I was asking for trouble, but the other part knew Dad loved me and had always approved of my writing. He had made me believe in my ability to write. But we both knew that my dyslexia left my work in sore need of proofreading, and I didn't think anyone in the church office had time to read the thing through before it had to go to the printer.

'I'd be honoured,' he said. 'I'll make my comments and send it back straight away. I'm looking forward to seeing it.'

His comments came back to me within the space of two hours. It was marked up and all I had to do was click a button to accept or decline his suggested changes. I accepted all of them. The comments and notes attached were full of encouragement and affirmation of not only my writing style, but the ideas themselves.

Tears of relief poured from my eyes as I read and clicked 'Accept'. When the time came to send the document to the printer, I knew everything was going to be alright.

. . .

TOM AND I were surviving, living month to month, with our bank balance hovering at, or just below, zero dollars. I signed up for a vitamin-selling pyramid scheme that Mum was interested in, in a futile attempt to contribute to society, and to our income.

Several of our friends bought in, but little came of my efforts, other than luminous yellow pee for all involved.

It had been months since I had last talked to Dr Lee about our money troubles, hoping he would recommend I stop coming to him. Instead, he agreed to reduce the length and frequency of our appointments, and said we could do fewer of the expensive blood tests as long as I purchased my own pregnancy tests from the pharmacy. It would not be safe to start trying for a baby for several months still.

Babies were not actually in our plans, anyway. Once in a while, I wondered if a baby could be the answer to all of my problems, but I aborted this notion before it had time to take hold. I could not allow myself to be so awful and selfish. Anyway, in my mind there was a very strong likelihood that I would be unable to conceive. Nothing so perfectly miraculous as a child would ever just happen to someone as utterly undeserving. There ended the dream, and I soon developed a bit of a fixation with buying and using home pregnancy tests as a precautionary measure.

Tom rolled his eyes every time I emerged from the bathroom with a negative test in hand. We had read that it would take up to six months for the contraceptive pill's chemicals to clear from my body, and between his busy schedule and my lack of self-esteem, there was not too much going on in the bedroom to worry about, anyway.

Money was a problem. Our salaries combined were just enough to cover rent, bimonthly half-hour visits to Dr Lee, our tithe to the church, a bit of food and some travel money to put on our Octopus cards. Once the Octopus money was blown, we resorted to scraping the coin jar for tram money to get us to and from work. Every now and then caring friends would appear with a gift of money. The people in our church really did put their money where their mouths were. Though we never asked for help of this kind, we probably would not have survived if it hadn't been for the generosity of our community.

We had become closer friends as a result of it, but the dynamic had changed. Tom had once been my teen sweetheart, trembling, down on one knee on top of Victoria Peak, asking me to spend the rest of my life with him. More recently he had morphed before my eyes into The Sucker Who Married a Crazy Person. His religious convictions and decision to marry young had screwed him over big time, and now he was stuck with me.

I didn't need to check with him about all this. I was convinced. I was certain that no up-and-coming Christian worship leader could be divorced—or, worse yet, be known to have abandoned a crazy woman in her time of need. So, Tom had no choice but to stick it through, to soldier on and attempt to manage me as best he could.

If we could just get me to the point where I could put on a normal façade for small stretches of time, perhaps not all was lost. I had behaved badly by being bipolar. I was the bad child, and he had been forced into the role of the angry grown-up. It wasn't fun for either of us, but it was all we could come up with at the time.

'You can't keep spending like this, Jacinta,' said Tom when I offered him a hot cup of lemon green tea.

'I know, I know,' I replied. 'I just thought it would be good to have some teabags at home. It's much cheaper than buying a latte, and I've really missed having a hot drink.'

'Whatever.'

He was in a huff, and I was offended that he had not even

acknowledged my kindness and subservience in offering him a cup of tea.

'What on earth is your problem, Tom?'

'Well, since it looks like you're going to push it, it is definitely not cheaper than buying the occasional coffee ... You're kidding yourself! I saw the receipt in the bin. You spent $700 on tea, Jacinta. Tea! I wish you'd just bought yourself a bloody latte—or better still, got one from the church. That's what it's there for!'

We had a very nice coffee bar in the church lounge, with a proper espresso machine that had been donated by a coffee-passionate member of the church.

'You know how I feel about that, Tom. It's dishonest—there's no integrity in drinking the church's coffee and not paying for it. It's stealing.'

Exchanges like these could go one of two ways. That day, things did not bode well for me. The vein on Tom's neck was showing.

'I didn't say "steal it"!' he shouted. 'Even the suggested donation is cheaper than Starbucks, *and* you get a staff discount ... All of that is a hell of a lot cheaper than 700 freaking dollars for crappy tea. I don't even like herbal tea! You're going to have to drink all of it by yourself! Every last bag! Did you stop to think that maybe you could buy something for me? Do you ever think of me? Do you ever stop to think anything through at all? We have NO money, Jacinta. What the hell are you doing?'

Tom was reaching his boiling point, and I could see that he needed help cooling down. Perhaps if he would just calm down enough to hear the facts, he would be able to understand.

'My books say it's a good idea to avoid stimulants,' I said calmly.

'I've stopped taking caffeine or sugar. I don't know if you've noticed. It was stopping me from sleeping.'

'Drink water, then! Don't talk to me anymore.'

I was not good at not talking to him anymore.

'I'm not using this as an excuse,' I continued, 'but my book says that people with bipolar disorder do tend to be a bit crap with budgeting.'

As soon as I got to the end of my sentence, I regretted starting it. There was steam coming out of Tom's ears and I could hear the faint sound of a kettle's whistle.

'First of all,' he said, 'if you keep using every symptom listed in your stupid books—which, by the way, I know you are also spending too much money on—as an excuse to be irresponsible, then you're going to have to stop reading them all the time. It's like you're looking for permission to do these things. Just because the book says you might gain weight or have trouble sleeping, it doesn't mean you have to pig out and stay up all night! When was the last time you did any exercise? Maybe if you went for a run instead of going shopping every day you would start sleeping better!'

The mention of anything remotely linked to my physical appearance was a high-risk manoeuvre on his part. A move to be made, as far as I could see, only for the express purpose of hurting my feelings.

I was in tears. My husband hated me and it was all because I was so fat. It had very little to do with the mess my head was in, or the fact we would struggle to pay the rent next month. He would be much more able to handle everything and support me more compassionately if I were slimmer. Nothing good would come my way until I had lost all this awful weight the meds had made me gain. That was why I needed the tea in the first place. If only he'd listen.

But he felt it was my turn to listen. 'Secondly, don't blame your inability to control your spending on your bipolar disorder. For as long as I've known you, you've been crap at saving money. I'm not saying I'm much better, but I don't spend on things for myself the way you do. I am saying that if we don't start pulling in the same direction with this, we're going to end up in serious trouble. You can't just have everything you want. I know this is news to you, Jacinta, but you just can't. Our parents aren't going to be around forever to keep bailing us out every time we get into debt. We can't live like this forever. We have to start saving money, and it's never going to work if you are doing this kind of thing.'

There it was. I was fat and Dad wasn't going to be with me forever. Tom had covered the two big ones. I retreated to my laptop. He would be getting a letter from me in the morning.

. . .

This was the new strategy for when things turned ugly, which they did at some hour most days: I headed to my laptop. I'd been a sporadic diarist from childhood, ever since seeing *Twin Peaks* at age 11, and I had recently decided it would be worth documenting my healing process. My mind was more a jumbled mess of questions and prayers than ever before, and the only way I could deal with it all was by writing it down.

The incident with the Stanley knife, at this point roughly two years behind me, had served as the detonator that led to an implosion of my world. While I had hoped for a quick clean-up operation in the form of a prayer or two to get me up and running again, in Jesus' name, the truth of the matter was that the ordeal was far from over. The dust from my self-inflicted demolition hung in the air, but when it finally began to settle, it became clear to me that the scale of destruction was beyond what I could manage.

Most of what was left recognisable was past the point of repair, and I had all but resigned myself to the conclusion that the best I could do was to clear out the debris, and try to fill the empty shell of my life with some modest and affordable flat-pack furniture. The idea of being a world-changing, inspirational Christian personality was off the table, and the thought of me being long-term mental did not appeal. Now, my only hope was to eke out an existence somewhere in between the extremes—uncharted territory for me thus far.

Yes, I would need to join the ranks of the unremarkable—those who did nothing of much interest, drawing no attention to themselves, just getting on with it, just showing up and playing their unremarkable part in the world. I would live out my unremarkable days, never forgetting I had only myself to blame for my sad state of affairs.

Days, weeks and months blended into each other. I was becoming a creature of the night, never fully present in the daylight hours, just biding my time until I could get to the computer. But as I typed, I found that the ramshackle ruins of my mind started to heal.

I gave myself permission to write, free flow, any and all thoughts, ideas and questions that needed dealing with. My head was a huge ball of tangled wires, and each new paragraph was a thread to unravel. For the first time in years, I stopped self-censoring and pre-judging—habits that had served me well in a church setting, but looked dull and insincere on the laptop screen, no matter what font I chose. What I needed was a space in which to express myself completely, free from worrying what effect I might have on anyone else. This was a reasonable need, but one I found hard even to admit to having. I finally dared myself to revisit my Before Christ inclination toward colourful language, *fucking* this and *fucking* that. This writing would become a defiant act of self-indulgence.

If I was feeling crazy, I wrote crazy. Sometimes, I typed 'in tongues'—an innocent, but mildly sacrilegious, practice that I think I invented, which involved rolling my eyes back in my head and letting the tap-tapping of my fingertips do the rest.

If I was aching, I wrote out the pain. I let it bleed into type, each word a cool blade to the skin until there was nothing left. It hurt, but it was better than actual cutting. If I was fantasising about making lemonade out of my acidic life, and getting rich off a career in selling vitamins, I drew up lists of specific, measurable, achievable, realistic and time-bound goals. If I was mad at someone, I ranted angry letters. And, when I felt I couldn't make it through another day, I drafted suicide notes.

I enjoyed the writing sessions that involved chuckling over gibberish and spontaneous sass much more than those involving Dear John letters and death threats. Eventually, therefore, the goal became to write myself out of my funks and into better moods. I never had to manipulate things, though. I found that I could begin anywhere. The starting point could involve confessions of doubt toward God's goodness, or irritation caused by some piece of unsolicited advice I'd been given, or outbursts of the rage I felt about my situation. I wrote and left no stone unturned. I prodded each issue from as many different angles as I could, and the purgative result cleared me some room to finally breathe.

. . .

One Sunday, the pastor talked about journalling, and said the problem was that those who practised Christian journalling often limited themselves to writing down their prayers to God, rather than writing down responses. So, he had the volunteers pass out paper and pens and then asked us to write a short letter to God. Five minutes later, he instructed us to write, by faith, God's response to our letter. This was something novel. Who was I to put words onto God's page?

How presumptuous, I thought. Nevertheless, I complied with the instructions and wrote out a rather glib attempt at sounding God-like—using phrases like 'Oh my child, my precious daughter' for God to address me with, before paraphrasing chunks of Bible promises I could recite by memory: 'For I have a good and perfect plan for you, my beloved ....'

I was underwhelmed by the exercise yet found myself experimenting with it at home in the privacy of my own MacBook. The God who wrote to me there was a little edgier than I had given him permission to be at church. I could usually get the ball rolling with accusations, followed by question upon question about why he hadn't healed Dad's cancer; whether he actually wanted Christians to be fundamentalists, or if it was honestly a bit unfair to confuse Christians who possess the gift of self-awareness with being lukewarm; when I could feel peace about stopping my medication; whether God would ever get over the fact that I had stopped dancing.

I was not sure if I was hearing from God correctly when his answer about the dancing came as *'I don't care as much as you think I do. Dance if you want to but don't do me any favours.'* Some nights, 'God' would give me in-depth theological expositions that involved directing me to evidence and citable references. Other times, he would cop out with something like, *'This is not the right time for you to know the answers to these problems ....'* Every once in a while, he would tell me to stop being silly and go to bed. The night I asked whether I should invest more of my time, money or effort into my vitamin business, he told me he was not a magic eight ball.

As the nightly word count grew, the cloud usually hanging over me during the day lifted, and along came an unexpected breeze of humour. The climate here was nothing related to holy, peaceful, refined joy. It was akin to hilarity. Lunacy, even. Some might have said it was a bipolar swing from depression to mania, but I was having too much fun to bother with that. Everything suddenly got very funny. Laughter was coming fast, and it came at the expense of my regular life. It was pure mockery of the sane world, and the absolute cherry on the cake of it all was that Tom had come along for the ride.

One evening, as we sat eating microwaved beef stroganoff in front of the television, the evening news cut to a story related to the government's health policy. The segment was being reported from outside the Pamela Youde Hospital, where I had seen my first psychiatrist. On hearing the location named, involuntary muscle memory caused me to raise my hands and shout, 'Woooo! That's my psych ward!'

We fell about laughing at the memory of the thousands of Christian conference delegates cheering as their country was called out from the stage, a memory juxtaposed against the absurdity of where our lives now hung in limbo.

It had been a tough couple of years for us. Tom and I relished the spell of comic relief. We lay in bed at night doing impressions of each other, and then of people we knew. We spent the days trying to come up with one-liners to unleash when we got home. We changed the lyrics of several worship songs, far past the point of irreverence, all in the name of cheap kicks. During meetings at work, we fought bouts of the giggles whenever a co-worker said anything too spiritual or kooky (something that tends to happen often in a church office). We wrote down a list of parody taglines for each of our church's ministries and cried in hysterics at our own genius, then promised never to tell anyone we'd done it.

This season was for us alone. Life had gotten too difficult and too serious in ways we hadn't yet found words to express. So, instead, we joked. These post-Jacinta-going-crazy jokes were location jokes (you had to be there) that we both would have preferred not to have been there for—but, since this was not an option, we were unanimously all in.

The funny phase was an important milestone in our marriage. It meant that we had both given up on taking ourselves so seriously. Where we used to disagree and argue daily, suddenly we were at the end of our strength. It was a drop-off, and we were going to plummet, hand in hand, like Thelma and Louise. We just couldn't be bothered to keep going round and round in circles, going over and over the same arguments. Instead, we would cut straight to the chase.

'You suck.'

'Up yours.'

'Butthead.'

'Douchebag.'

'Arse Munch McDowell.'

'Ballsack Jones.'

Typical rallies continued until insults were exhausted and then someone would say, 'I forgive you, even though you are so unworthy.' The other person would respond with, 'Your mercies are new every morning. Shall we watch *Seinfeld*?'

Things were just more manageable this way.

22

'REMEMBER WHEN I used to care about how I look?'

The sound waves carried my question over the living room to where Tom was sitting, and he looked up at me. This could be a trick. He would need to proceed with extreme caution. But he knew he couldn't hesitate for too long. He replied well.

'You are beautiful to me, no matter what, Loops.'

'Yah yah yah, right answer, but I'm not fishing right now. I am sick of looking as bad as I feel. I'm like the living dead, only puffier. I need to sort myself out.'

History had proven that no level of enthusiasm on Tom's part was acceptable when tackling this subject. He stayed silent and waited for me to continue.

'I don't even remember the last time I plucked my eyebrows. Look at my eyebrows! Why didn't you tell me?' A question meant that he needed to respond.

'I was wondering if maybe you'd lost your tweezers ... But I mean it, you are fine. I'd really rather you just focus on being mentally stable. Don't start thinking you're going to go on a fast or anything, okay?'

I looked and saw the fear behind my husband's plea. I had put him through so much. I wanted to do something nice for him. I wanted to give him the gift of a good wife. It had taken me a good long time to get myself into this mess, and I was smart enough now to know there was no quick fix. Or, perhaps the truth was, I had been forced to concede that there was no quick fix, after a tragic process of elimination. A small step in a better direction was all I would be able to manage.

I set myself the goal of having nice fingernails. I pulled out my nail polish collection and got to work. The smells wanted to take me back to my boarding house room in Perth, but I declined, and would need to do so for some time. Every day, for the next couple of weeks, I painted nail polish onto the tips of my fingers, all the while fighting the urge to then shove them down my own throat. Gradually, the urge lessened. It receded and allowed me to relax and take a moment to remember my time in Perth—so much had happened to me while I lived there, and so much more had happened since.

One Monday, I painted my nails a soft nude pink. What if I hadn't said the Sinner's Prayer? What if I had never left Hong Kong? What if Dad had never left Wales? What if Por Por and Gung Gung hadn't met in Chicago? It became clear that one small edit to any of the details of my history could have resulted in significant changes to where I now found myself. But, maybe that was the case with everything in life? Maybe there wasn't anything interesting about that, after all.

I thought about this again on Tuesday, after removing the pink and choosing the brightest of my reds. Had I been in an optimistic Christian mood, I would have concluded that life had conspired to get me to the place where God could make a personal introduction and become a real part of my life. But I wasn't in a very optimistic

Christian mood—where had that introduction gotten me?

The next day, I reached for a bottle of blue/grey varnish and shook it until I heard the little metal balls inside clink. Why would God have orchestrated things so I would believe in him so fully, and devote my life to him so entirely, only then to fade into the background and watch as I made such a spectacular cock-up of the whole thing? That didn't feel like the God I thought I'd known.

In the bookstore a few days earlier, I had paused to look at the cover of Richard Dawkin's *The God Delusion*. For a brief moment, I worried that reading the book could cause me to lose my faith. The absurdity of the thought hit only seconds later. *If I'm afraid of someone else's opinion, then my faith was never worth much in the first place.* My life had fallen apart, but that was all on me. I could not pin it on God or try to float the excuse of pretending I had doubts about his existence. For me to do so would just have been a different type of 'God delusion'. I knew I believed in God, but I began to wonder if I might have kidding myself in other areas. Who was this God I thought I knew? What did he want? I had made so many assumptions. I knew many people who did the same thing and would happily continue to do so. We were all sincere and doing what we honestly had thought was right. I wasn't out to place blame ... Maybe, just maybe, we had gotten some bits of it wrong?

I didn't bother to do my nails on Thursday, and by Friday they were chipped and needed repainting. By this point, I didn't want any more colour, just a coat of clear gloss. I had needed to isolate myself. Away from other people I finally allowed the questions to come, and found them to be surprisingly good company. I did not feel alone. The Bible said that, if I believed in God, he would never leave me, and this was an idea I had not given up on. I would have liked something more concrete, but it was becoming apparent that God was not on tap. He could not be conjured by the rub of a magic lamp, nor summoned by forces of sheer charisma. It had been a very long time since I felt sure about anything; but, for the first time since slashing my wrist, I wondered if this strange new lack of certainty might just put new emphasis on the idea of faith.

. . .

You have a God-shaped hole in your heart, said the clichés from memory's pulpits, and they were nearly right. There was definitely something hole-like in there. There was a pool, a deep cavity somewhere—my soul, maybe. It was murky, and beneath its surface lurked all sorts of trouble. It held within it invalidated feelings strong enough to wipe me out; questions so threatening I dared not set them in words; prayers too perfect to utter. They were all mixed in together—sometimes stagnant, sometimes agitated, always potentially eruptive. Somehow, that pool needed to be syphoned.

I could only sit and wait.

Be still, and know that I am God, said the Bible. So that is what I did. I would sit, wait, be still, and slowly find a way to go on, to know something—but not with my brain, not with my unreliable mind.

Every day, I painted my nails and then sat, very quietly.

. . .

TOM AND I had been invited to attend a musical theatre adaptation of *Chasing the Dragon*, Jackie Pullinger's memoir. It had been over a decade since I'd first heard of her, first saw her in action at Hang Fook Camp with my cousin, Amy. Most of our youth group leaders had come through her ministry, and several people I knew had spent time working with her. I had finally read her book and marvelled at her faith, at how she had discovered that prayer alone could help a heroin addict through the withdrawal process without pain.

The team from St Stephen's ministry performed a refreshingly light-hearted and beautiful show. I stayed awake and alert for the whole thing, despite having sat for two hours in a comfortable seat in a cool, dark theatre, still foggy with medication.

After the show, I went home to paint my nails. As I sat quietly, I thought about Jackie, wondering if the same prayers that got addicts through heroin withdrawals could help me through my own medication-tapering process. I then noticed, for the first time, that the breakthrough in Jackie's work came only after someone had advised her to spend fifteen minutes each day praying in tongues. I remembered that my aunty had asked me to pray in tongues every day, too, and so I wondered if it would do me any harm to try.

My rational voice, that, in recent times, had begun to sound more and more like my husband, cautioned me against hoping for a magic bullet, and I reasoned with him: no major harm could come from it. Perhaps Tom needn't even know. All I would do was mumble some incomprehensible prayers for a few minutes after painting my nails. Although Tom took no issue with the idea of tongues, I was self-conscious and embarrassed by the thought of him hearing me, so

I planned to pray early in the morning when I knew I would have some privacy.

Every morning, at 6am, I pulled myself out of bed and snuck into the living room to pray. I was only half awake, but by the end of the fifteen minutes I felt newly alert and ready to face the day. These morning rendezvous roused parts of my brain that had lain dormant for months. Suddenly, I found myself wanting to go to bed early so I could get up early to pray. I wanted to read the Bible, then write down my thoughts and prayers.

Looks like you're getting set for another round of religious frenzy, I said to myself at the end of my prayers one morning. I was right to worry; it was dangerous to feel this alive and excited again. It could take a nasty turn at any moment. I needed to put limits on myself: one page's worth of journalling per day, and only as much Bible reading as I could manage on top of the fifteen minutes of prayer, keeping the entire session to a maximum of thirty minutes.

You're kidding yourself, you know that, right?

I had read somewhere that you should talk back to the devil when he casts critical thoughts and doubts into your mind, to displace his lies with God's truth. I was no longer buying into this so much. It felt presumptuous, like a slightly sad form of self-bolstering that I couldn't afford.

What am I doing, God? I asked, five minutes into my fifteen minutes of prayer the next day. *Is this crazy?* I closed my eyes and continued to pray, taking deep breaths, filling my lungs and then exhaling, mumbling in an unknown language. I walked across my living room, opened the window, and stood praying for a moment longer. Then I flew out of the window, over the busy streets, over the racetrack and up the hill to Kennedy Road, where Por Por and Gung Gung used to live.

. . .

The flat was large. It was the penthouse of a building facing out to Victoria Harbour, offering one of the best views of the annual display of fireworks. There were a couple of large basins of soil on top of folding tables on the balcony—there was also a plastic colander and a pair of chopsticks ready for anyone wanting to have a poke around in the soil. This was Gung Gung's worm farm.

Inside the flat, dark wooden panelling covered every possible surface. Most of the furniture was built-in. There were cabinets, drawers, sliding doors and cubbyholes everywhere. Upon entering, we usually walked straight past the sliding door to the right, not needing to go into the old nurses' changing room or the kitchen behind it. The kitchen was mostly used for the mass production of *jiao zi*—Northern Chinese dumplings. Trays and trays of them would be piled up on each other, waiting to be frozen. There was always a rather strong smell of spring onions.

Just past the kitchen/changing room door stood a tall reception desk. This was the point past which Jus and I were never granted passage without the perfect execution of a *gok-gong* (bow of respect). The main room was partitioned by dark blue velvet curtains forming a large waiting area, an eye test area, an acupuncture area and some cabinets full of medical records. It could all be packed away and transformed into a dining room, or into a concert hall for the family orchestra.

A door to the right led into another world within a world. Met with clutter wedged onto every shelf and piled precariously on every surface, I was always unsure of where to settle my eyes. A framed inspirational quote on the wall reminded us that *All things are possible. Nothing is impossible.* There seemed no end to the sliding doors coming off every room in the flat. The number of drawers and cupboards were more than I could count with my eyes, and if I let my hands reach out, I found compartments within compartments. Upstairs, on the roof, was another whole apartment, complete with veranda, electric organ, and cupboards containing things like plastic flowers and boxes of ribbon samples. Imagine a bag lady with a prime harbour-facing property instead of a shopping trolley. Every time I visited, I felt both the need and the freedom to explore to my heart's content. I would dig around, feeling simultaneously comforted and overwhelmed.

I flew through the sky that day and landed on the balcony, my bare feet pressing down onto the cool white tiles and the sesame seeds scattered earlier for the sparrows. I stood at the door to Por Por's room, still quietly mumbling my prayers, looking in to see if the mess was still there. I was relieved to find that it was, exactly where my memory wanted it, even though I knew the flat had been sold off over a decade earlier.

Then there was movement. I watched as bags of clutter and boxes of random collections came to life and began to slide about the room. Cupboard doors opened and things set themselves on shelves; blankets folded up and placed themselves in drawers; furniture eased across the room, rearranging itself into calm, logical, tidy, and aesthetically agreeable, configurations.

I stopped praying and the room became inanimate. I started again and the tidying continued. I flew back to my living room, still praying. *So that's what you are doing.* Then I asked again. *But what am I doing, God?*

. . .

This time, I went inside, inside of me, down into my own pit, where I finally found my cavity, a lake so large it looked like a sea. I stood at the edge, peered in and saw only murky waters reflecting back my own frightened face. I knew that, in the darkness, lurked the beast; I wondered if the darkness was the beast.

I mumbled more prayers, and they spun out of my mouth like silk and spiralled into a tight coil, a long straw, a hospital tube. One end dipped into the pool, making contact with the inky black, like the mouth of a fountain pen's converter, ready to fill its reservoir. The other continued to extend upward, above my head. It stretched and drew itself higher and higher, up, into the atmosphere, out beyond what I could see or understand. Then, something in the skies took a long, slow sip of my darkness and I watched as the tide withdrew. I did not feel the need to question the practice again.

23

2008

SOON IT WAS April. I was turning 29 and we were having a joint birthday celebration at The Nest. Dad's birthday and my own fell just ten days apart. My parents were now complementing Dad's chemotherapy with a host of alternative treatments. Outside of her work, Mum spent most of her time and energy seeking out a miracle cure to put an end to Dad's cancer. This effort included eating the Budwig diet, heavy on flaxseed oil, and something called quark, that we couldn't get in Hong Kong so substituted with plain yogurt. Gentle exercise was undertaken to oxygenate the blood; numerous natural health supplements, including multivitamins, oils, spirulina and chitosan (a derivative of seashells that were meant to draw toxins from the body); acupressure; finger tapping on meridian points; and a general harnessing of the power of positive thinking. The diet was highly restrictive, allowing mainly for organic vegetables and oat groats. It was free from gluten, sugar, meat and anything processed. Therefore, to celebrate Dad's seventieth birthday, Mum lovingly embedded seventy wax candles into a mud pie. A mud pie.

I thought it would be a good idea to join my parents in their efforts toward health. It was a show of solidarity, as well as an attempt to better myself. By now, I was finally feeling ready to tackle the issue of my fitness, or lack thereof. I had joined a gym near work and signed on for a summer fitness challenge, so the lack of birthday cake was not a problem.

I took public transport to get to The Nest, and then Dad drove us to the Prince of Wales Hospital in Shatin. Chemo took up the best part of a day. The first two hours were spent seeing the oncologist and paying for the medicine; the last four hours were taken up by the chemo itself. I always went prepared with something to work on, but usually spent the time chatting and taking catnaps in the unexpectedly comfortable chairs provided. Whenever called upon, I enjoyed spending a day like this.

This particular visit to the hospital was going to be shorter than usual. It was Dad's last chance to see his doctor before leaving for his summer visit to Oxford, and he was getting the results from his last round of blood tests. The results were not good. The young oncologist, who had been on the receiving end of a great deal of impatience from this particular patient, remained calm and kind as he delivered the news.

'I do not recommend you pursue alternative treatments,' he said. 'And I do not recommend that you go to England this year, Dr Sweeting.'

Dad was equally composed. 'If further chemotherapy is purely palliative, then I have already made up my mind. I choose to decline it.'

'I understand,' said the doctor. 'If you do choose to go to England, please be on the lookout for any rashes or yellow colour on your skin.' He offered many more details and some advice, and then we thanked him and left. Staying in Hong Kong over the summer was not something my parents would consider.

At the time, I really did not understand what was happening. I had just witnessed Dad turn down all further treatment, which, according to the doctor, was a fatal decision. I had bought so much into the idea of finding an alternative cure that I hadn't really allowed for the possibility of death.

I drove us back to The Nest and we chatted. Achilles, my parents' big ferocious-looking mutt, had been behaving badly ever since Cassandra had died. Achilles howled for her at night. He had never been trained, and my parents thought he made a better guard dog that way. He was energetic and highly territorial, and therefore a great deterrent to anyone who approached our gate. In his excitement, he jumped up and locked his huge jaws around the nearest forearm. It was an overly enthusiastic, but friendly, gesture.

Dad wanted to tell me about the nosy neighbour. She had been getting out of her car ('which she has now taken it upon herself to park right in front of our gate!'), when she caught Achilles jumping up on a man from the gas company. The man left unscathed, but the neighbour urged him to lodge a complaint against us as irresponsible pet owners.

'Can you believe the audacity of the woman?' Dad had never liked her much. 'Achilles was inside our property, and the man entered without being invited, so I don't see what case anyone could build against us—he's a guard dog, for Christ's sake.'

'I know, I know,' I said. 'And his nip looks so much worse than it actually is.'

'If anyone is going to lodge a complaint, it should be us against her, for trespassing.' Dad loved to get in a huff about things every now and then.

'When did she trespass?' Occasionally I thought it was okay to indulge him.

'Did you not hear about this? It was over a year ago; she had the nerve to accuse us of growing marijuana in our back garden! The illegal drug, marijuana! She said she had paid us a visit to inspect our tree because she claims she was worried about falling branches. Can you imagine your mother or I growing illegal drugs? Well, your mother would be more likely to than I would, and I suppose she might have suspected it was for medical use ... Then we had to bear the extra cost of calling out a tree doctor to inspect the banyan. That busybody was saying she thought the whole tree needed to be removed—no respect for nature or other people's wishes at all. Thankfully, the tree doctor said the banyan was in perfect health. It didn't even need trimming–that shut her up.'

'Yes, but try not to get yourself worked up, okay, Dad? You'll be enjoying the peace and quiet of Oxford soon, at least.'

We parked the car, and I walked Dad up the garden steps and said goodbye.

. . .

I went back to Central and threw myself headlong into winning my fitness challenge. I was delighted to find that the new gym offered Capoeira classes. The Brazilian martial art was beautiful and something I had wanted to get into, even making (failed) visa applications for an instructor to work at The Point. I devoted myself to the group, and then got busy trying to learn the basics of the Portuguese language. I left the flat at six every morning, exercised for an hour and a half, showered and dressed, and then went to find a private spot on the building's outdoor podium where I could journal, pray and read my Bible for half an hour before heading to the office.

The pounds were falling off, and I felt mentally alert and at peace. There were similarities between my current behaviour and that immediately preceding The Incident, but I was doing all within my power to keep myself in check.

Tom and I were getting along well. And it was good that we were on the same team, because another upheaval was about to happen. We had been notified that our building on Haven Street was scheduled for demolition, so it was time to start house hunting again. There was no money to spend on a new rental deposit, or for a moving van for that matter, but we were hell-bent on not turning on each other. We had just spent our entire overdraft on flights. Summer was approaching, and after the regular journey to Sydney for the conference we would head to Oxford to spend a few quiet weeks at my parents' house. We decided to put all of our things in storage until after the summer, when we could look for a new home.

. . .

THE 2008 TRIP to Sydney came at rather an inconvenient time for me—I was trying to win the fitness challenge and did not want to miss a single workout. I found a chemist near the hotel and bought a detox kit, so I could rid my body of toxins as well as any extra weight. I also found a deal on budget pregnancy tests; there were more than enough of them to last me through the last stage of my medication taper. As long as I didn't eat anything too substantial, and was able to fit in a daily workout, it could still be a great week.

Instead of attending conference sessions, I snuck off to exercise. I found a small patch of asphalt tucked away from open view, and there I lost myself in the joy of callisthenics. I moved to the soundtrack of Capoeira songs in my head, complete with mental recordings of my teacher's voice shouting instructions over the top of the music.

'Are you going to be disappearing like that all week?' Tom asked when I finally returned.

'I'm one week away from my weigh-in, and I just have to win it.' I assumed that would be reason enough. It was the truth, and I was committed to being truthful now. I just really wanted to win.

'Please, can you just try to be a little more sociable?' continued Tom. 'I know you don't love it, but it means a lot to me and I think you could really enjoy the conference this year.'

'I'm only going to the main sessions this year,' I replied. 'It's just too tiring for me. I want to save some energy to work out. I do promise to come to the main sessions, though. I really like that "Healer" song—did you see the clips of the live recording?'

. . .

Every year, the hosting church released a new album at the conference. Delegates sang songs from the new release all day, every day. History had proven that, no matter how we felt about them at the beginning of the week, by the time the conference was over, the lyrics and melodies would be ingrained in our minds, intertwined with freshly acquired convictions inspired by what we heard from the stage. By the week's end, we were hooked and primed to purchase multiple copies of the album in an attempt to savour the life-changing experience, as well as share it with our loved ones. The album would invariably sustain us for about twelve months, until it was time for the next release. It was an excellent event, with excellent merchandise.

I liked the music. The fast songs were good exercise fuel. That year, I was particularly interested in the album, which featured a song called 'Healer', written and performed by a man fighting his own battle with a rare and aggressive cancer. The DVD of the live album recording contained a powerful performance that involved him leading a crowd of thousands whilst wearing tubes in his nose, hooked up to a machine to assist with his breathing.

I believe you're my healer / I believe you are all I need / I believe you're my portion / I believe you're more than enough for me / Jesus, you're all I need ... Nothing is impossible for you / You hold the world in your hands ....

It was a striking image that I caught snippets of on various flat screens around the venue all week. I found a clip of the performance online and sent it to my parents, hoping that God's healing power would work as an email attachment. Dad had taken a turn for the worse.

Another DVD clip that I kept catching was an interview with one of the female worship leaders, talking about her experience of God's sustaining grace after the loss of a baby. She played guitar and sang out, *All of my life / In every season / You are still God / I have a reason to sing / I have a reason to worship ....*

I was inspired. I wanted to sing these songs. Figuratively and literally. I had been practising my guitar, and was keen to make some musical progress after eleven years of singing backing vocals. God's message to me that year was clear: Christians could stand firm in faith amidst the toughest trials. He could sustain us as we faced our challenges. He cared for me, his suffering child, and in the company of his brave saints I was going to overcome my battles. I bought the DVD bundle.

We returned to Hong Kong exhausted from a full week of conference joy. Most of our earthly possessions were now in storage, and we had just what we would need for the summer.

I hit the ground running. I needed to go for my weigh-in and to get back to Capoeira class. Despite my best intentions, though, I left the class feeling flat. It was a long session and, try as I did to push myself, I just couldn't find the strength. I excused myself for a bathroom break, where I collapsed onto a changing bench and called Tom to tell him how tired I was feeling, trying to stall for as long as possible before returning to the studio to fake my way through the remainder of the class.

I had finally hit a wall, and this was not something I had ever experienced before. Apparently, I did have limits. This was a bitter pill for any superwoman to swallow. I went home to rest and vowed to do better at my next class.

I never made it back to class. That afternoon, I received a phone call from Jus, who was with our parents in Oxford. Dad was really sick. Tom and I were not due to join them for another week, but we changed our flights and stuffed our suitcases.

Before boarding the flight from Hong Kong, I called The Nest to check with Cora on how everything was. Neighbourly relations had deteriorated even further just before my parents left for England. The busybody had engaged Dad in an email battle about her right to park her new car in front of our gate, and Dad was increasingly annoyed by her accusations about Achilles.

'Yes ma'am, everything is fine with the house, ma'am,' said Cora. I felt horribly embarrassed about being called 'ma'am', but she had ignored my numerous requests for her to use my first name.

'And is Achilles behaving?' I sensed there was something she wasn't telling me.

'Ma'am ....' She sounded troubled.

'What is it, Cora?'

'Ma'am ... Achilles has not come home for two weeks.' She said that, the last time she had seen him, the neighbour was pointing him out to someone wearing a uniform.

I knew this was serious. But it was time to get on the plane.

. . .

'**JUST TO PREPARE** you, Dad has a slightly yellowish tinge to him,' Jus said, when he met us off the bus at St Clements.

We arrived at our home on Iffley Road and I ran to the living room to Dad—who had become a completely yellow man—sitting in his favourite armchair. He was himself, but frail, and very yellow. Spirits were low. He had seen the local GP, who had given an honest assessment of the situation.

'Final stage.' Dad said.

It still did not register. Dad had been in stage four—what I had understood to be the final stage of cancer—for two years now. We chatted and ate our dinner. Then, one by one, we went to bed.

I woke, jet-lagged, at 3am the next morning. Bored of lying awake in bed and in need of the toilet, I remembered the pregnancy tests still in my suitcase from Sydney. Morning pee was the best for test accuracy, and was it just me, or had it been a long time since I'd last done a test?

I wasn't going to wake Tom. I would spare him the effort by rolling my own eyes at myself. *How much more money would I waste on these stupid tests? We aren't actually trying, remember?* I peed and balanced the stick on its box on the back of the toilet, then went to examine my tired self in the mirror. I didn't let myself think about babies. I had already made peace with the idea of not pursuing motherhood, but still found myself a little sad every time I threw away a negative test.

I washed and dried my hands. Then, as I reached over the toilet to nudge the test and box into the bin, I realised that there were two little stripes staring up at me.

'Tom!' I said his name like a swear word.

'What?' came his groggy response from the bedroom.

'I think you had better come in here. I need to show you something.'

He stumbled into the bathroom, rubbing his eyes, and then let them settle on the thin strip in my hand.

'Seriously?'

As I nodded, my eyes filled with tears. We were both overjoyed. We had not been trying for a baby, but neither had we taken any preventative measures. However, having been married for seven years, a child suddenly felt completely appropriate. We got dressed and walked into town, and sat in the 24-hour McDonald's to wait for Boots to open.

'Just buy one more test,' said Tom. 'Don't go crazy, okay? They aren't cheap ... Do we even know how accurate these things are?'

'It's very difficult to get a false positive,' I said. I had already checked. I was nervous and twitching, holding my breath until I could see another result. Only then would I truly admit to myself how terribly much I did, in fact, want a baby.

Nothing had changed in regard to my feeling undeserving, and I didn't want to set myself up for disappointment in case the second test came back negative. But, try as I did to rein in my thoughts, I found myself swearing before my husband and my God that, if I were to become a mother, I would commit everything I had to be a good one. I'd give every ounce of strength I had in me to shield my child from any harm. I would claw my way, tooth and nail, in the opposite direction of the crazy places I had visited, just to have a shot at being some little person's mummy.

I could see that Tom was beginning to feel the full weight of what the future could hold. He looked very serious. I needed him to control the urge to give me the reality check I knew was coming.

'Please be happy, Tom,' I said.

'Of course I'm happy.' He sounded a little hurt by my doubt.

'I just mean, I really, *really* want this to be real, and I swear to you I am not going to screw this up. I promise you, I won't be mental anymore. I'm just not going to do it. I am going to be a really good mum. I'll learn. I'll read all the books and learn how to be a good mother.'

'Of course you'll be a great mother,' he replied. 'I know you will be, no matter whether this is real now or when it happens later on.'

'Do you really think that?' I said. 'You have to say that ... but I thought you thought it was better for us not to have children?'

'No, I never said that. I said we weren't ready before, because we weren't. But things are much better now, and I do actually feel like it might be the right time soon.'

We sat inside McDonald's at the window facing the street. I watched impatiently as the Boots staff shuffled around the inside of the locked shop opposite us and prepared for opening time. It was surreal.

24

TWO MORE TESTS confirmed I was, indeed, pregnant. We rushed home and tried to sit patiently, waiting for everyone to gather in the living room.

'So,' I began, 'it seems we could all do with some good news.' The hopelessness filling the house was palpable, but I had everyone's attention as I made my happy announcement.

The news lifted everyone's spirits, and we spent the rest of the morning talking about babies. Mum listened and chimed in now and then, but I knew by the absence of her usual squeals and giggles that she was not entirely present. Her heart was heavy with the burden of finding a cure for Dad. If only she could find the right thing.

'What are some nice Welsh names for a baby?' I asked Dad.

He was the best at this. Despite being so ill, he had named the summer rental car's GPS Henry the Navigator, and we all said that was a good name—but he had not supplied the history lesson that would usually have accompanied such a christening. He looked tired. He was trying his best to be upbeat, but he was weary from his battle. I was starting to wonder if Dad would last another nine months in order to get to hold his grandchild.

I hoped he would suggest something good and claim the honour of naming my first child. But my request was also an attempt to divert attention away from the other disturbing matter that was weighing on my mind—where was Achilles?

'I have always loved the name Myfanwy' *(Ma-van-way)*, Dad said, thoughtfully.

Jus, Tom and I erupted. We never hesitated to laugh at things Dad said, whether or not they were intended to be funny. He never had a problem with it, either. The ability to see the humour in oneself was a survival skill in our family, and the greatest lesson he ever taught me.

'Well, it's certainly Welsh,' said Tom. 'My mum would probably like it.'

'What kind of name is that?' I laughed. 'Is it even a real name? I've never heard it before ... I don't think we can call our child a name I can't spell, and one that no one in Hong Kong will be able to pronounce!'

For the next couple of days, we pulled together to keep our spirits in check. We talked, and I dodged questions about how things were back home. We ate British soul food and watched our favourite English TV shows. Every evening after Mum had said goodnight to Dad, she and I would go for a walk around the field near our house, sometimes trespassing onto university grounds to walk the rugby pitch. We talked and cried. Her tears were not of grief, but of frustration that she still hadn't found the miracle cure.

'If we could just find someone in this country to inject Hob with enough vitamin C ....'

'Mum, don't worry about the vitamin C anymore.' I spoke as gently as ever I could.

'I won't ever stop looking for a cure, my baby,' said Mum. 'I will never forgive myself if I don't do everything I can to help your daddy.' She was trying to explain things to me, and at the same time, I was trying to explain things to her.

'You've done so well already, Mum. Dad's done so well. But we have to let him rest now ... He can't swallow any more vitamins or drink any more juice. Let's just let him rest.'

'I know he's very sick, my baby,' said Mum. 'And I know he needs to go to heaven one day, but I don't think it's his time yet. He just can't go yet. I can't stand the thought of burying him in a wooden box with that awful velvet, and worms and bugs eating him up. It makes me want to scream.' She sobbed and said how good it was that we had the whole field to ourselves so we could cry as loudly as we wanted to.

. . .

The next afternoon, while I was sitting alone with Dad, he said to me, 'Beeps, was I a good father to you? Did you ever feel I was too distant? Did you ever feel unsure if I loved you?'

Tears filled his eyes and mine before I had a chance to respond. I sat on a stool beside his armchair and hugged his arm and cried. I looked up at him and assured him, the best I could, that I had no regrets about having him as my dad, that I knew he loved me. I held onto his arm and cried with him for a few minutes more, and then I felt it was the right time to broach a very difficult subject.

'Dad, I know Mum and I don't always get along very well, but I want you to know that Jus and I will look after her. I can't promise I will be perfect, because I won't be, but I will do my best.'

He was smiling through his tears. 'I know better than anyone how infuriating your lovely mother can be, and I do want you to be very good to her. You just do your very best, alright? Because she is very lovely—infuriating, but lovely. And you can be rather fierce yourself.'

'I know, Dad.' I was ashamed of a lifetime's worth of mouthing off to my parents and was regretting every harsh word I'd ever spoken to either of them.

'I don't think she understands that I can't swallow any more of those bloody pills,' he went on. 'There are just too many of them, and too many times a day. If it means so much to her, I'll force myself. But I'm finding it very unpleasant, even painful.'

'Don't worry, Dad,' I replied. 'We've talked to her about that and she says she won't ask you to take any more of them ... but there is one thing she's worrying about.'

'What's that?'

There really wasn't any way I could say it without just saying it. 'She doesn't want you to be buried in a coffin for worms to eat you up.'

He chuckled again. 'You tell her that I'll have a cremation, then. It really doesn't matter to me.'

We hugged and cried together. After that afternoon, he spent all of his time sleeping upstairs.

. . .

NURSES VISITED TWICE a day and showed us how to give him small sips of water with something that looked like a big cotton bud. In quieter moments, Jus and I took turns searching the internet for advice. None of us knew what to do. We found a list, *The 5 Things a Dying Person Needs to Know*. This was the most helpful discovery, and it became something solid for us to hold at a time when nothing in the world felt sure. Hob needed to hear that he would be missed, he would be remembered, he had been forgiven, that we would all be taken care of, and that he was released to go in peace.

I found the phone number for the Oxford Crematorium. A sympathetic voice answered, and I choked on a lump in my throat. I could just about handle the situation, but only if I did not have to say the words out loud. I hung up the phone.

On Dad's last day, the family gathered and sat on the floor at the end of his bed playing a board game, believing that, although he was no longer conscious, he would hear happy sounds and know we were there for him. The day turned to dusk, and Mum found the strength to give Dad her blessing to go.

A few hours later, we gathered around his bed, and one by one we said goodbye. As he released his last breath, we could see the hint of a smile on his eyelids.

Loud sobbing emerged from the depths of Mum, as if rising from another world. This would be the third time her tears shook me to the core. I had never seen her look so beautiful in all my life. As our tears came, the night nurse moved forward to cover Dad with a sheet and tell us what to do.

The doctor soon arrived to certify the death. It was a process we all wanted to watch very closely. We had each witnessed his passing, but it was very hard to believe the body on the bed was not going to change its mind and draw another breath. He looked surreal. It was him, our most beloved man, and yet the part of him we loved most had gone; only his shell remained. How could the passing of a few minutes change Dad, Mum's soulmate, into nothing more than a corpse?

Once the death was official, Mum, Jus and I went and stood on the balcony to look up at the stars.

'Goodbye, my Hob,' called Mum into the night sky.

An hour later, his body was driven away into a silent night, in the back of the undertaker's black van.

'Goodbye, Dad,' we whispered.

Mum and I slept in the guest room that night, because the master bedroom needed a break after the miracle it had just been through. Tom volunteered to sleep on the sofa and Jus went to his own room. Jus and Tom had suddenly become the men of the house, and they knew they needed to be brave. Mum and I had unexpectedly become a little scared of the idea of ghosts, and wrestled with the question of whether Dad had actually left or not.

'Don't you come back and haunt us now, Hob,' said Mum as we turned in. 'You just go on your way, now.'

The next morning, I threw out all the bedding. None of it was soiled, but I felt it was the right thing to do. Mum said it was a waste, but didn't press the matter. She went back upstairs and got into her side of the big bed, where she would spend the next five days. She existed on a steady supply of coffee that Jus's girlfriend brought up to her—none of us had ever seen her drink coffee before.

She typed fervently on her laptop. She had always been the most dedicated and entertaining communicator in her extended Chinese family network, scattered all over the globe, and now she simply needed to tell and retell, and retell, the events to everyone on her list. She spent the next several weeks typing out emails to personally explain things to everyone she knew. This was her way of coming to terms with what had happened.

I kept checking my emails, all but convinced I would soon receive a note from Hob, letting us know, in his normal wordy style, that he had arrived safely at his destination. The fact that no email came was much harder to accept than the arrival of the imagined email would have been.

An intimate funeral service was held a few days after his death. As we left the room, my brother played a recording of Ella Fitzgerald singing the song Dad had told him he would like at his funeral: 'Into Each Life Some Rain Must Fall'.

25

ONCE BACK IN Hong Kong, Tom and I were homeless, so we were immediately available to keep Mum company back in The Nest. When we arrived, I had no choice but to tell her about Achilles' abduction, and the neighbour's involvement. We knew that Dad, had he been there, would have blown his top over this. We also knew that, had he been there, Mum would have been the only one able to calm him down. What we did not know was how Mum would handle the information on her own.

'That evil bitch!' she shouted. 'I know she's at the bottom of this. I have no doubt! I am going to tell her exactly what I think of her. I am going to report her to the authorities—no, better yet, I am going to cast a spell on her, and she is going to be very sorry. How dare she tamper with an animal's life? Hob is not going to let her get away with this!'

Mum was going to take about twelve months to recover from the immediate shock of losing Dad. This came as no surprise to us: half of her soul had been torn away. She continued to work, and to exist more or less functionally. She had moments of disorientation, like forgetting how to sign for a credit card payment, or how to use her mobile phone, and these moments served us as reminders of just how much she had lost. She verbally processed her feelings to anyone who cared to listen, usually leaving them in tears. She cried freely with others, but would don her huge, bejewelled sunglasses when she walked through the crowded city streets if she wanted to cry alone.

'No man will ever come close to what your daddy was to me,' she said. 'He filled me in such a way that I will never, ever need the love of a man again. He was my world. He was a great wizard, and now his magic has entered all of us.'

That first night home, after we had arrived at The Nest, Tom and I lay in bed chatting through our jet lag.

'I can't believe she called her a bitch!' I mused. 'She's not usually much of a cusser.'

'It was pretty crazy,' said Tom. 'I've not seen her mad like that before ... It's so strange to be back in this house again, with your dad not upstairs on his computer.' Technology and sports were the two major common interests Tom and Dad had shared. 'I just can't believe he's gone. I keep thinking he'll just come down the stairs and turn the TV on or something.'

'I just want to see him again,' I said. 'I don't know how I'm ever going to get over this. It's the strangest thing. Where is he? Where is my dad?' I allowed a fresh stream of tears to flow. 'I can't wrap my head around the fact that I could spend the rest of my life searching the whole planet and never find him. I just want to know where he is.'

'I wish I knew, Loops. It's life's biggest mystery.'

'I feel like the whole world has changed, and we're the only ones who really know why.'

'Things are definitely going to be different now,' Tom said. 'It's good that he doesn't have to suffer anymore, and I promise I am going to look after you. Before he died, I told him I would help your mum with her computer, and he liked that. It's early days still, but I promise you will be okay. We've got a little baby to start thinking about, as well. I know you're going to be a very good mother.'

I tried to smile. 'I read in my book that my emotions can affect the baby's development. I'm going to have to wait till after it's born before I can mourn. I wish I could be depressed for a while, but I'm not going to let myself because I have to think of the baby. I'm going to try really hard to be positive, but I need you to know it's not because I'm not sad about my dad.'

'I don't think you need worry about that too much, okay?' he replied. 'Just try to get some rest and let things happen naturally. We're all sad about your dad, and happy about the baby. It's bittersweet. Don't worry about things, okay?'

Tom and I sat up in bed for hours, just marvelling at all that had happened, and speculating on what was to come. Eventually, I started to nod off. Tom was still wide awake, so he pulled out his laptop.

'Oh no,' he exhaled. I knew by his tone that something important had happened, and I gave a tired grunt so he would go on. 'The guy who wrote the song "Healer". He's ....'

'He's died?' I asked, realising immediately that it was too obvious a guess.

'Nope.'

The news had just broken. The songwriter had just confessed to lying about his illness. He had faked the whole thing. It was a bizarre hoax. He did not have cancer. He'd tricked everybody. He had lied to his wife, asking her to leave him at the hospital entrance for chemo sessions, telling her he needed to face his battle alone. He had lied to his church, and to the tens of thousands who had cried for him, prayed for him, bought his CD, and made donations toward his treatment. It was an interesting situation, some might have said scandalous, but in the moment, I found consolation in the fact that all over the world, even within what I had thought of as a perfect church, people were dealing with their own special problems. Who was I to judge? Another set of assumptions crumbled away. We lay awake for another hour trying to make sense of it.

'I feel like the whole world is falling apart,' I said.

'It is pretty crazy ....' said Tom. 'And in other news, there's a really big typhoon heading straight for Hong Kong. Could be a T9!'

'End of the world,' I said, and then rolled over and finally went to sleep.

. . .

TYPHOON NURI WAS an extremely rare T9 tropical cyclone that hit in the early hours of the morning. Our world truly was in turmoil. However, due to jet lag and emotional exhaustion, we all slept in. I woke again at about 10am, worrying about Achilles, who we would normally let into the kitchen during bad weather. At least I was relieved of the burden of ever having to tell Dad about the dog's disappearance. I crept out of the bedroom so as not to wake Tom, or Mum, who was still asleep upstairs.

My attempts at being quiet were dramatically thwarted by a

blinding flash of lightning, closely followed by an almighty crack of thunder, and then by an even bigger crash. The world was indeed coming to an end. I froze for a moment, half expecting the house to collapse on top of us.

I steadied myself and then rushed toward the glass front of the house, wondering if a tree branch had fallen onto the garden steps—the only pruning that ever took place in my parents' garden was done by Mother Nature herself. As I got closer to the glass, daylight smacked me in the face like never before.

The giant banyan tree, that had previously blocked most of the natural light from the front of our home, was gone. I crept closer to the window and saw that it had toppled, roots and all, out of our sloping front garden. It was enormous. Its trunk alone stretched beyond the width of our property. In the face of real dread, I stepped outside to check how much damage it had caused our front neighbours—the nice neighbours, the ones my parents liked. Their house sat directly in front of ours, and I knew that the force of the giant tree falling downhill from our property onto theirs would leave us liable for thousands, if not millions, of dollars in repairs.

It was raining hard, fat raindrops, and the air was full of falling leaves and tension. I peered down from the top of our slope and found, to my utter astonishment, that the enormous tree had somehow completely missed our neighbours' house. It was as if it had fallen around a corner, to the left, onto what would have been an empty footpath ... Had this footpath been empty, then the tree would not have caused a cent's worth of damage; the tree hadn't so much as dented our garden fence. But the footpath had not been empty for some months.

The neighbour to our right, the one Dad despised, and Mum was now calling an evil bitch, had taken to the idea of using the footpath as her parking space. She had bought herself a new luxury car, and argued that, since it was too precious to be left parked further down the path where everyone else parked their cars, she would instead use the space beside our fence as her own personal parking spot.

I stood for a moment longer in the rain and stormy weather, trying to make sense of what I was looking at. Bright daylight in my eyes, an empty space where the giant banyan had once stood, the enormity of the tree now magnified as it lay on its side—and, finally, the crushed luxury car, only just visible beneath it. The car was a complete write-off. For a split second I smiled at the thought that justice had been served from heaven, but I quickly tutted to myself, knowing it was not a very Christian thought. Dad would have gently pointed that out to me had he been there. But he wasn't.

I allowed myself to ponder, if, perhaps, Dad's ghost had pushed the tree. It had fallen at a very strange angle, and there was no visible damage to the tree itself. It was as if the roots had simply released their grip on a whim. I surveyed the surrounding area and noticed the arrangement of the tiny ceramic pots containing Mum's most recent batch of fern clippings. There they stood, in perfect formation where the base of the banyan had been, each one of them sitting perfectly at ease in its designated spot around the base of the tree, and on alternate steps leading down to the garden gate.

Dad knows about Achilles, and he pushed the tree over and left the little pots standing to prove it.

In her state of utter grief, Mum proclaimed that Hob, my great wizard of a father, would be taking care of us from heaven—another heavenly father—and that we need not ever worry. Unsure of just how many theological fallacies were at play, I decided to just agree with her—God would forgive me, anyway.

It had been some time since I had last prayed. I had been giving God the silent treatment. If life and death were in his hands, then Dad's death was his responsibility—God had let Dad die. I wasn't mad; my own belief system didn't really allow for that. His ways were higher than mine, and he loved me, and he loved Dad, more than I could possibly know. So, with all that in mind, we were left with only a new and awkward kind of silence. What was there to say?

Why did you take my daddy away from me, God? I finally allowed my heart to whisper the question as I walked through a shopping mall a week or so later.

I am sorry for your loss, came the God-voice response from the depths of my aching soul. *I cannot change that I had to take him from you. But forgive me, and let me try to make it up to you.*

None of us ever spoke to our busybody neighbour again. Mum did speak with the nice neighbour in front, though. On the trust of a handshake, she sold The Nest to her exactly one week before Lehman Brothers brought the world's economy crashing down. We were going to sell high and buy low. The old had gone and it was time for a new season. Property prices fell, and our family was ready to move.

Tom and I went for an ultrasound scan and were told to expect a healthy baby girl. Mum presented me with a contraption that made thumping sounds, to strap to my growing belly for one hour, twice a day. This, she explained, would stimulate the growth of the foetus's brain.

'Our new baby will be a little prodigy,' she said. 'A tiny little superwoman Itch, like her mummy!'

Mum was still in the depths of mourning, but I took her interest in my pregnancy as a good sign—she would eventually be herself again.

'There is no point playing classical music to the baby,' she added. 'Some people do, but there's no point because the baby is in liquid. The sounds would be too murky. These rhythms are much more effective, very good for infant intelligence ....'

I rolled my eyes at her and complied. There was no harm to be done by it, anyway. The only question I could foresee would be just how much credit to give the thumping device when my daughter's genius would, in years to come, be officially declared.

I endured the thumper's rhythms at varying tempos as the weeks and months ticked by.

. . .

One week before the baby's due date, the church band was given the opportunity to be the supporting band at a Delirious concert, one of the biggest names on the Christian music scene. Delirious had taken contemporary Christian music to a new level and provided the soundtrack to the formative years of faith for many of us. After ten years on the road, they were going to retire—this was their final world tour, and a once in a lifetime chance for Tom to share the stage with his heroes.

'Keep your legs crossed!' Tom said as he left our flat to head to the venue for the soundcheck on the day of the event.

I pottered around our new home, cleaning and setting up the nursery while I waited until it was time for me to leave. The night was a huge success, and an incredibly special milestone for our band. Tom and I fell into our freshly made bed at three in the morning.

'I am so happy, I could just die now,' Tom said and then fell asleep.

At 8am the contractions started. By noon, we were on our way to the hospital. At about four in the afternoon, the pain was so intense I felt sure that God was testing my faith and wanted me to pray out loud before he would take the pain away.

'Jesus, please!' I groaned. 'I love you, God, please help me, in Jesus' name! I'll even pray in tongues out loud if you want me to!'

The pain grew worse and my prayers evolved into loud profanity. The nurses looked at each other knowingly and muffled their smirks, while the rest of the maternity ward just got on with breathing through their contractions quietly, clearly not experiencing anything close to the pain that I was in. When the anaesthesiologist had finished his tortuously long list of epidural-related disclaimers, he held out a form for me to sign. I was writhing in pain and could hardly see the A4 sheet he held in front of me.

'Don't worry if you can't make a whole signature, just make a mark,' he said.

I stabbed the pen through the paper into his hand so hard he squeaked and retreated as fast as he could.

Just before midnight, our baby girl was born. We named her Layla Belle, the beauty of the night. A perfect thing that came out of a dark time. I sent birth announcement cards to the Three Js in England and they replied quickly with congratulations and gifts.

. . .

THE GOOD NEWS kept on coming. Jus proposed to his girlfriend, Meg, and a year later we all sat as a family on the other side of the world, in a field with lush green grass somewhere in Philadelphia, where the wedding was held. We watched in awe as Layla took her first tentative steps. We remembered Dad and marvelled at how far we all had come. Cancer, death, pregnancy, life, marriage, travel, property, realising dreams, and giving birth to new ones. We marvelled at how full life was, and how full it was likely to continue to be.

'Your father was a great wizard,' said Mum, as she was in the habit of saying every now and then.

None of us felt any need to confirm or challenge her statements. Mum, I was finally coming to accept, would never be straightforward by any standard. I reserved the right to dismiss her magical thinking—a lot of it did sound crazy—but I was now beginning to suspect that, to do so, could be to my own detriment. I pulled at the grass and pressed my fingertips into the cool, damp earth. There was solid ground within the mystery, firm reality recognisable only through magic.

And besides, as Tom often reminded me, *no one is actually normal.*

'How could he have missed all this?' Mum started to cry.

'He hasn't missed it, Mum,' Jus said. 'His spirit is with us. He's here.'

'Yes, he's here, my darlings. He is in heaven and he is also here,' she said and pulled us to her. 'He looks after us. He's given us each other. He's given us everything we need.'

I leant forward to reach out a hand for my perfectly wobbly daughter. She took it and steadied herself, unaware of how little her mother really knew of life. She released her grip and toddled on again. For that moment, I had done what I needed to do. *Perhaps that's all I'll ever be able to do, just what's needed in the moment.* This is what I told myself, and this would have to do. Not the words I would have chosen, but there you go. This seems to be how it works. The only thing I'm certain of is that this is not the end.

ACKNOWLEDGEMENTS

Thank you to every single one of my Kickstarter backers.

Thank you to my writing teachers for guiding me through this process.

Thank you, Pam. I am so glad we did this.

To my long-suffering support network, you know who you are. Thank you. I will try not to let this become a habit.

Jacinta Read is a writer and illustrator who was born and raised in Hong Kong, and also spent time in Australia and England. She holds a PhD in creative writing from Goldsmiths, University of London, and an MFA from City University of Hong Kong. She lives in Oxford, England with her husband and two children.

Patchwork Someone is her first memoir.

www.ingramcontent.com/pod-product-compliance
Ingram Content Group UK Ltd.
Pitfield, Milton Keynes, MK11 3LW, UK
UKHW041631190726
13854UKWH00006B/2434

9 781838 190934